CLARIDGE'S

THE COOKBOOK

MARTYN NAIL & MEREDITH ERICKSON

WITH PHOTOGRAPHY BY JOHN CAREY

MITCHELL BEAZLEY

Contents

Foreword
by René Redzepi

I grew up between a 60-square-metre apartment in Copenhagen and a farmhouse in Macedonia where we slept door-to-door with our cows, sheep and chickens. Several generations lived together, crammed and hot. The number of times I woke up with somebody's foot in my face are countless. Growing up and moving out of my family home, I thought to myself that would never happen again. Until, of course, I started having children and then you realize it all comes full circle. Those were my formative years, where I grew up with very little in terms of fancy décor or the comfort of space, but surrounded by people and feeling the safety of having family and friends around me.

Being asked to write a foreword for this book made me revisit some of these childhood memories. I tried to distil what it is that I like so much about Claridge's and why it feels like home to me, because it is very much the opposite of what I grew up with: luxury in its fullest, an extra-sized king bed and people everywhere to help carry your luggage.

There is even the tiniest of sofas in the tiniest of elevators just in case you feel the burden of travelling two floors up to be so overwhelming that you need to sit down.

It really boils down to the culture of Claridge's – that thing that only happens when a group of people work together every day in a profound way. The more I think of it, the more it becomes clear that what makes Claridge's special is the people there. So many places have the latest designer, or a bed that is an inch bigger than that of the guys next door, but at Claridge's it is the staff who make the difference.

They are simply the most professional people I have witnessed working, and we saw that during our two-week Noma pop-up at Claridge's in the Olympic summer of 2012, with the dedication and that extra level of confidence that makes everything seem so effortless. I learned such a great deal about hospitality, team spirit and working together, especially witnessing the way that chef Martyn Nail approaches leadership: he is a very fair chef and calm leader. The success of this approach is clear inside the kitchen, where everything runs efficiently and smoothly despite the fact that they cater to every request and serve anything under the sun. I'm absolutely baffled by something as simple as the eggs; how can they serve as many eggs as they do and make them taste so delicious? I began every morning with fried eggs (with crispy edges) and a little bowl of cooked vegetables.

In working with Martyn and the rest of the team, I realized the ways I could improve my own leadership back home. It was the seed of how we began to plan our human resources and innovational training for Noma. The experience fuelled our confidence to travel to Japan, Australia and Mexico. It opened us up to taking risks and it sparked a strong desire for adventure in our team and in me, showing us how much we have to gain by exploring beyond the comforts of our everyday routine in Copenhagen. Most importantly, our time with Claridge's totally clarified that at the end of the day it is not about who has the softest or biggest bed, the poshest lobby or dining room, it's the people you put within these frames. Simply put, it is the people at Claridge's – and for us that started with those in the kitchen – who elevate the restaurant and the hotel itself. Without them, these are just soulless luxury experiences of which the world has way too many already.

Thank you so much Claridge's, congratulations on this amazing book and, for sure, see you next time in London!

Right: Chef René Redzepi from Copenhagen's Noma; multiple time 'World's Best Restaurant' recipient.

Introduction

by Meredith Erickson

It has been said that one's stay at Claridge's begins in the taxi, when seated and looking ahead, and the words 'take me to Claridge's' are uttered. This is when that feeling strikes: the anticipation that something extraordinary is about to happen.

This was the case for me, driving past Hyde Park and into Mayfair on a rainy, cold November night. Upon arriving at the red brick building on Brook Street, where doormen in handsome grey flannel await, I was whisked through the revolving door towards the chequered-floor Lobby – gliding past a porter tending the fireplace – and into the Foyer.

Oh, how I wish I was staying for longer than just dinner.

Soon a large white menu with violet illustrations was placed in my hand, along with an oh-so-welcome glass of Champagne from what may be *the* most desirable oak Champagne trolley. My waiter talked me through the du jour menu, but my eyes had already fixated on the Claridge's Chicken Pie. I ordered, relaxed into my chair and breathed a sigh of relief, the rain and the day fading away. In a corner of the room sat one of my favourite British novelists. In another, a great fashion designer from New York. Drinking it all in, I came down to earth as a gentleman at the table beside me struck up conversation. He told me his age, 82, and that he had first come to Claridge's when he was 5. 'There is something magical in the air here,' he said. I joked that 'Yes indeed, and it smells delicious.' 'No, it is something you cannot recreate anywhere else. For 77 years, I've been coming here and the energy is still as intoxicating.'

The waiter arrived with a large silver tray, carrying mashed potatoes, tied French green beans and a pie topped with a golden cloud of puff pastry. What happened next was a bit of a blur, but I can say that the chicken was succulent, the sauce was velvety suprême, there were bacon lardons and a singular quail egg that felt like a treasure, à la Galette des Rois. At some point, I may have been deliriously dipping the mashed potatoes in the pie.

Upon leaving, I asked my waiter for the Claridge's cookbook and he responded that at the time they did not have one. I enquired when the next order would be arriving. 'No ma'am, it does not exist at all.'

As I walked to the Davies Street exit, I noticed a tall, ornate glass door leading to an alluringly confessional enclave with royal purple velvet banquettes. A small bar – complete with shelves of rare Lalique decanters – twinkled below mirrored signage that read 'The Fumoir'. I sat, ordered a nightcap and struck up conversation with a man I later came to know well: the 'artist in residence' of Claridge's, David Downton. 'I don't think anyone comes up the three steps to Claridge's without a little lift to their heart,' he told me after hearing it was my first time here. 'But of all the places in the hotel, it's in here at "my" table (No. 4) in the Fumoir that I love to meet, interview and draw. It's the best bar in London; timeless both design-wise and literally – the low-lit intimacy of the space means that noon can feel like midnight and midnight can stretch until noon.' He was right. I looked around, noticing no windows, only tables of martinis and guests engaging with George, my new favourite waiter – impeccably dressed in a crushed velvet jacket and bow-tie. David continued...

'Claridge's is Claridge's and everywhere else is everywhere else. London's grandest hotel guards her legacy but wears her legend lightly, her eyes trained on that famous revolving door, noting the next, the new (and the who is who). Here, the ghosts of Sir Winston Churchill, Jackie O and Audrey Hepburn converse with the tech billionaire, the Upper East Side maven and the indie designer who are checking in. At Claridge's there is a continuum. Recently, at dinner in Hollywood, Anjelica Huston's eyes lit up when I mentioned the hotel, "The first place I ever tasted mango!" she exclaimed. Across the ocean, her father – maverick director John Huston – whose portrait hangs in the Reading Room, chuckled like thunder.

'New five-star hotels multiply like cranes on the London skyline. Sometimes, all too soon, they become a "scene". But who wants to live in a "scene"? Better, surely, to let time slip away from you right here in the velvety embrace of the Fumoir or in the hushed and unhurried civility of the dining room, where nostalgia is the late-night side order of choice.'

Utterly inspired, the next morning I called and asked to speak to the chef, Martyn Nail, about a vision I had – a fantasy really – to collect the much-loved recipes from the previous 200 years, along with some anecdotal and storied answers to questions like: How *do you* host dinner for 100? What is *in* that Claridge's Regal cocktail? What *is it* that makes room service so special and perhaps, most importantly, How *do you* make that puff pastry?

And so, a venture that began selfishly – I really wanted that pie recipe – turned into a complete love affair with a hotel , its chef and its restaurant. The result of which, many years later, is this very tome.

Where did we start? In the kitchen, of course. Recipe by recipe, plate by plate.

One thing about the Claridge's kitchen: it's a steamship on full throttle. Spending time there, you feel like you're travelling at warp speed 365 days a year, 24 hours a day – all with a bit of Willy Wonka theatrics thrown in, thanks to the pastry department and their renowned afternoon tea creations. The kitchen is reminiscent of a scene from Wes Anderson's *The Grand Budapest Hotel* and has the charm of Escoffier – copper pots, gas ovens, a handsome engraved Parisian Rorgue salamander (indeed the menu at Claridge's was written in French until the 1990s) – alongside the latest gadgets, such as a smoker and the beloved evo-grow herb cabinet (that allows chefs to grow and harvest herbs such as sorrel, chervil and Mexican marigold in the dark underground recesses of the kitchen). It also *feels* as equally cosmopolitan in the kitchen as it does in the dining room. It's a smaller ecosystem of the London just outside: a tourier from Dijon; a pastry chef from Costa Brava, and a small army of excited young chefs, fresh graduates from British cooking schools.

Martyn Nail, the captain of this ship, is a complete anomaly. In a city where restaurant cookbooks are penned a mere year after opening, Martyn has been an integral part of the culinary direction at Claridge's for more than 30 years. This is a rarity in the restaurant world, and that record speaks volumes. On any given day, Martyn manages a team of 60 chefs plus service staff, over breakfast, lunch, afternoon tea and dinner, ultimately overseeing up to 2,000 diners a day, all whilst conducting an orchestra of special events, and, of course, always time for a menu review with an excited bride-to-be. One would think he actually has a room upstairs, but surprisingly, he does go home.

The kitchen is the engine of Claridge's, it turns, turns, turns...and never stops. To capture this, we aimed to fill these pages with the recipes that our guests love, and the ones that give us joy, too. We sifted and sorted through menus so vintage they felt like parchment in our hands. Ultimately, we have included a mix of the classics and newer additions: all relevant for today. They may inspire you to bake (Lemon Drizzle Cake; *see* page 116), to curl up and read (The Art of Carving; *see* page 86), or to make a reservation for a celebratory afternoon tea (Blueberry Crème Fraîche Mousse; *see* page 126).

If you have ever stayed at Claridge's, you will know that what stays with you when you return home is an all-encompassing experience that you cannot fully recreate. But with a turn of each page, we want you to be that much closer.

After a 200-year history, it is clear: the Epicurean spirit and the art of hospitality lives, breathes and thrives at Claridge's.

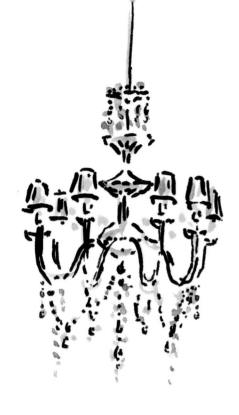

A Brief History of Claridge's

Mivart's is where it all began. In 1812 the Mivart family opened a single Brook Street house as a guesthouse and gradually extended into other properties over the following years. In 1854 they sold the guesthouse to Mr and Mrs William Claridge, owners of a smaller, adjacent hotel. For some years, the new establishment was known as 'Mivart's at Claridge's' before becoming simply Claridge's: a name in need of no further embellishment. For 50 years the hotel flourished and expanded both in length and depth, over several adjacent addresses, all of this at a time when the USA was only 31 states and Napoleon was still fighting a war.

It was in the 1860s when Claridge's social success was sealed, with Empress Eugenie of France staying in the hotel and Queen Victoria visiting her. As Claridge's reputation grew, so did the trend of royal visits: Prince Albert and members of the extended British Royal Family followed Victoria, and the hotel soon became a favourite of heads of state and royalty throughout Europe. Indeed, legend has it that on more than one occasion when a caller would ring Claridge's and request to speak with the King, the response was often 'Certainly Sir, may I ask which one?'.

In the 1890s, The Duke of Westminster approved a revision of Claridge's building plans. This involved a four-year complete rebuild of the hotel, designed by C W Stephens (also responsible for designing Harrods). In 1893, the impresario and hotelier Richard D'Oyly Carte bought Claridge's and financed a redesign and development of the hotel. He consulted the famous Swiss hotelier César Ritz and French Chef Auguste Escoffier (before Ritz went on to open his own London hotel in 1905). Claridge's then reopened towards the end of 1898. At this time, the original Claridge's entrance was through two arches on Brook Street, where the main entrance is today. In the days before the motor car, horse and carriage would enter on one side (through what is now the Front Hall) and exit through the other. Another large-scale change came in the 1920s, when British architect Oswald Milne – a pioneer of the Art Deco movement – was commissioned to transform the Lobby to the Deco style of the era, under the direction of designer Basil Ionides. The carriage entrance was removed and the canopy and revolving door you see today installed, which at once welcomed the bright young things of London. Simultaneously, the Ballroom and the Mirror Room were added with a further set of guest rooms being built on five floors above this new wing.

Now to the heart of this very book you hold in your hands: the Foyer and Reading Room. The original Claridge's Restaurant was a vast space, stretching from the Drawing Room all the way around to the Foyer and Lobby. The restaurant was able to accommodate some 250-plus guests at any moment. The Foyer itself was essentially a large cocktail lounge with two gold standing columns, buttery yellow walls and a mix and match of chairs in floral and brocade. The Reading Room was a snug retreat where waiters were dressed in red livery with knee-length velvet breeches, white stockings and black patent shoes.

In 1986 an ambitious kitchen refurbishment programme took place and a restaurant kitchen was added to the ground floor of the hotel, taking the space from the Drawing Room nearly all the way to Davies Street. A decade later, it was the dining room that was refurbished, with designer Thierry Despont leading a complete restoration of the Foyer and Reading Room. Out went the Baroque and in came the Art Deco. The walls remained the same pale yellow but the furnishings were replaced with sumptuous leather green banquets and chairs with bold geometrics in rich fabrics. Despont also used archived photographs of famous guests at Claridge's – including Audrey Hepburn, Jackie Onassis and Yul Brynner – as inspiration, but also framed and hung the pictures in the Reading Room. The final touch was the Dale Chihuly chandelier as a centrepiece.

The three facades to Claridge's: Brook Street, Davies Street and Brooks Mews, have become a landmark of London and the doormen of Claridge's are famous bastions of Mayfair. What the walls hold inside, is a history spanning over 200 years – a narrative that could fill hundreds of books with millions of secrets.

1853:

The Times claims there are just three first-class London hotels: Mivart's, The Clarendon (Bond Street) and Thomas's (Berkeley Square). Mr James Mivart retires, and the hotel passes to William and Marianne Claridge, who own the adjacent building. In 1856 'Mivart's at Claridge's' becomes simply: Claridge's.

1860

As Claridge's reputation grows it is visited by Queen Victoria and Prince Albert. The hotel soon becomes a favourite of heads of state and royalty throughout Europe.

1893–7.

The hotel is bought by Richard D'Oyly Carte, owner of The Savoy, and closed for five years to allow for a redesign by C W Stephens – the man responsible for Harrods. The hotel reopens in 1898.

1920s

Oswald Milne, a pioneer of the Art Deco movement, transforms the Lobby. The Ballroom is added and, after the First World War, Claridge's is the place for the bright young things of London to drink, dine and dance.

1940s.

During World War II, the hotel is a refuge for dignitaries and exiled heads of state. The Kings of Greece, Norway and Yugoslavia remain there for the duration. At the request of Sir Winston Churchill (who also spent his post-defeat election days at Claridge's), suite 212 is declared Yugoslavian territory so that Prince Alexander II can be born on his own country's soil.

1950s–70s

Hollywood stars and leaders in fashion and finance adopt Claridge's as their London residence. Cary Grant, Katharine Hepburn, Audrey Hepburn, Yul Brynner, Bing Crosby, Spencer Tracy, Elizabeth Taylor and Aristotle and Jackie Onassis are all guests.

1990s.

Renovation and restoration of both restaurants by Thierry Despont. Creation of the Fumoir with original mirrors by Basil Ionides, and the Claridge's Bar by the late David Collins. Guy Oliver, who was also responsible for works to the Drawing Room, French Salon and Ballroom, designs a number of rooms and suites throughout the hotel.

2012

Long-time friend of Claridge's, David Linley, completes his work on 25 suites. David Downton continues as Claridge's first artist-in-residence, drawing such notable guests as Sir Paul Smith, Diane von Furstenberg and Sarah Jessica Parker.

2017.

Claridge's publishes its first cookbook. The hotel continues to evolve, always staying relevant and looking forward to the future.

Claridge's by the Numbers

HOW MANY GUESTS DO WE WELCOME?

87,711 per annum

HOW MANY BREAKFASTS DO WE SERVE?

69,625 per annum

HOW MANY BOTTLES OF CHAMPAGNE DO WE OPEN?

43,983 per annum

HOW MANY DELIVERIES DO WE RECEIVE?

20,000 per annum

HOW MANY PLATES DO WE WASH?

2,000,000 per annum

HOW MANY AFTERNOON TEA REQUEST CALLS DO WE RECEIVE?

22,000 per annum

HOW MANY EGGS DO WE USE?

518,640 per annum

HOW MUCH BUTTER DO WE COOK WITH?

29,600kg (65,257lb) per annum

HOW MUCH GOLD LEAF DO WE USE IN THE KITCHEN?

52 books per annum

HOW MUCH CHOCOLATE DO WE GET THROUGH?

4,250kg (9,370lb) per annum

HOW MUCH SUSTAINABLE CAVIAR IS CONSUMED?

24.6kg (54lb) per annum

HOW MANY FRESH TRUFFLES ARE EATEN?

13.2kg (29lb) per annum

HOW MANY ORANGES DO WE SQUEEZE?

298,667 per annum

HOW MANY LOAVES OF BREAD DO WE SLICE FOR AFTERNOON TEA SANDWICHES?

57,792 per annum

HOW MANY HEADS OF STATE HAVE STAYED AT ANY ONE TIME?

15

HOW MANY EMPLOYEES DO WE HAVE?

456

HOW MANY NATIONALITIES DO WE HAVE ON OUR TEAM?

43

Breakfast

Croissants

The profession of the tourier — someone who creates pastries made from yeast-leavened dough — is becoming more and more of a lost art, and one that you only find in the world's grandest hotels. Too often, viennoiseries such as croissants and pastries are bought in from other bakeries, and are often made with vegetable fat, rather than butter. Not so at Claridge's. Our own tourier, François Grange, has been working the night shift (midnight to 10am) for 35 years (and counting), keeping the dough rolling and taking the pastry to the perfect level of puff. A word of warning: beyond pure tastiness, another by-product of this recipe is that your entire house will smell like a French bakery. Once you've mastered this classic, turn to page 26 to see how we complete our full breakfast basket offering...

MAKES 1KG (2LB 4OZ) CROISSANT DOUGH OR 12 CROISSANTS

NOTE:
This is a 3-day recipe.

YOU WILL NEED:
stand mixer fitted with the dough hook
2 sheets of baking paper, at least 30cm
    (12 inches) square
rolling pin
pastry scraper
pastry brush
2 trays, 1 lined with baking paper
2 baking trays, lined with baking paper

FOR THE FERMENTED DOUGH STARTER:
125g (4½oz) strong flour
125ml (4½fl oz) lukewarm water
pinch of instant yeast or fresh yeast

FOR THE CROISSANT DOUGH:
375g (13oz) strong white flour, plus extra
    for dusting
70g (2½oz) caster sugar
10g (¼oz) sea salt
1 large egg
100ml (3½fl oz) milk
10g (¼oz) instant yeast or 25g (1oz) fresh
    yeast, crumbled
1 x quantity Fermented Dough starter
    (*see* above)
250g (9oz) cold unsalted butter (in a 8 x 8
    x 4cm/3¼ x 3¼ x 1½ inch block), plus
    extra for greasing
1 egg, beaten with a pinch of salt, for the
    eggwash

DAY ONE

In the morning, start by making the fermented dough starter. In a 1 litre (1¾ pint) container or medium bowl, combine all the ingredients with a fork or wooden spoon. Cover the bowl or container with clingfilm and leave to stand at room temperature for a minimum of 12 hours.

In the evening, after 12 hours have elapsed, make the croissant dough. In the stand mixer, combine the flour, sugar and salt. In a separate bowl, gently whisk the egg, milk and yeast to combine and dissolve the yeast. Pour the egg mixture into the mixer bowl, and add the pre-fermented dough. Mix on low speed for 2 minutes. Stop the machine, pull the dough off the hook and place it back in the mixer bowl, then resume mixing for another 2 minutes.

Transfer the dough to a clean, flour-free surface and roll up your sleeves! Knead the dough, using the ball of your hand to stretch it away from you, then fold it back in over itself towards you. Turn the dough a quarter-turn and repeat this back-and-forth motion followed by a quarter-turn in a calm and rhythmic fashion for 10 minutes, until a smooth elastic dough has formed. Set a timer and just enjoy the activity! The dough will become firm and smooth, and the proper kneading will help with the final layers and flakiness of the croissants. Transfer the dough to a lightly greased bowl, cover with clingfilm and refrigerate overnight, or for at least 5 hours.

Lay the butter block down in the centre of 1 sheet of the baking paper. Place the other sheet of paper on top of the butter block, then gently and slowly pound the block with your rolling pin. The butter will start to soften up slightly and to yield under pressure. Keep tapping away evenly all over until the butter is 20cm (8 inches) square and about 6mm (¼ inch) thick. You can use a pastry scraper to encourage straight edges and corners. Refrigerate overnight, or for at least 2–3 hours, until very firm.

DAY TWO

In the morning, remove the dough from the refrigerator. If it feels a little dry to the touch, you can brush it with a tiny amount of water to moisten slightly.

On a lightly floured surface, roll out the dough – you want to end up with a rectangle that's about 20–22cm (8–8½ inches) wide and 42–45cm (16½–17½ inches) long. Make sure you keep the corners square and edges as straight as possible by pressing a palette knife or pastry scraper against them to assist with that shaping as needed between rolls (though you'll be trimming any extra dough, so don't fret too much). Lift the dough occasionally to make sure it isn't sticking; flour the work surface under the dough again if necessary and sprinkle with more flour as you go, dusting away any excess with a pastry brush. The dough »

may need to rest for a few moments before you can roll it out further. Refrigerate for a minimum of 20 minutes to firm up.

You're now ready to start creating those buttery layers in the dough! Transfer the rectangle of dough to a lightly floured surface. If the dough feels dry at all, brush it very lightly with water. Using a pizza wheel or a sharp knife, trim the edges of the dough to obtain a 20 x 42cm (8 x 16½ inch) rectangle. Lay the cold square of butter in the centre of the rectangle, then fold the edges of the dough over the butter. Brush some water on one edge of the dough and press down the other edge to form a seal.

Rotate this square of dough-encased butter 90 degrees, so that the seam is parallel to you and the edge of your work surface. Working quickly but gently, start rolling out the dough into a long rectangle shape. As you work, the butter will be warming slightly and yielding to your pressure; it should not, however, be oozing out of the dough (if that happens, refrigerate the dough for 20 minutes before proceeding) or cracking. Keep rolling until the rectangle is about 26 x 54cm (10½ x 21 inches). Trim the edges to make an even rectangle shape of that size (this will help achieve beautiful final layers in the croissants).

Next, fold the bottom quarter of the dough up towards the centre of the rectangle, and the top quarter of the dough down towards the centre of the rectangle. You should have a thick square of dough. Next, fold the bottom half of the square over the top half. You should now have a rectangle about 26 x 12cm (10½ x 4½ inches). In the world of laminated dough and puff pastry, this is referred to as a double-turn. Transfer the dough to a tray, wrap it tightly in clingfilm and refrigerate for a minimum of 2 hours.

Repeat the double-turn of dough: lay the chilled dough on to a lightly floured surface, short end facing you and the exposed edges of the dough facing right – imagine it as a book, so the 'spine' is to your left. If it feels a little dry, brush very lightly with water. Roll out the dough into another 26 x 54cm (10½ x 21 inch) or so rectangle, then repeat the folding: fold the bottom quarter of the dough up towards the centre of the rectangle, then the top quarter of the dough down towards the centre of the rectangle to make a thick square of dough. Next, fold the bottom half of the square over the top half. Wrap tightly and refrigerate for another 2 hours (the dough can rest longer in the refrigerator, as needed).

Roll out the dough lengthways (again with the edges of the dough facing right and the short end facing you) into a 20 x 50cm (8 x 20 inch) rectangle. Trim any errant edges. Rotate the rectangle so the long side is facing you. It's now time to cut out triangles of dough and shape some croissants! Starting from the top left corner of the rectangle, measure 3.5cm (1½ inches) to the right and make a notch in the top edge of the dough with a knife. From the bottom left corner of the rectangle, measure 7cm (2¾ inches) to the right and make a notch there. Cut diagonally from the bottom left corner of the dough up to the 3.5cm (1½ inch) notch, discarding the scrap of dough to the left. Next, cut from the 7cm (2¾ inch) notch up to the 3.5cm (1½ inch) notch. You have your first triangle of dough. Transfer to the tray lined with baking paper.

For the next triangle, starting in the (new) top left corner, measure 7cm (2¾ inches) to the right. Cut diagonally from the 7cm (2¾ inch) mark down to the (new) bottom left corner. You have your next triangle. Set aside. Measure 7cm (2¾ inches) from the bottom left corner, then cut through to the top left corner: this is your third triangle. Repeat accordingly until you have 12 triangles of dough. Each triangle should be about 7cm (2¾ inches) wide at the base and 20cm (8 inches) high.

To shape the croissants, roll up each triangle of dough fairly tightly, starting at the base of the triangle and ending at the point. Make sure to tuck the point underneath as you transfer the croissants to the prepared baking trays. Press down on the top of each croissant gently with the palm of your hand to help the seal. The croissants can now be covered with clingfilm and refrigerated overnight – you'll need to take them out of the refrigerator to prove at least 2 hours before baking them. (They can also be frozen for up to 1 month. Defrost in the refrigerator on the prepared baking trays for several hours or overnight, then proceed to Day Three as outlined on page 24.) »

DAY THREE

Gently paint the croissants with eggwash. Generously grease 2 large pieces of clingfilm with butter and lay them on top of the croissants. Leave to prove in a warm kitchen for about 2 hours, or until the croissants have almost doubled in size and feel yielding to the touch.

Arrange the oven racks: one in the top third of the oven, the other in the bottom third. Preheat the oven to 220°C (425°F), Gas Mark 7 for about 30 minutes before the croissants are ready to bake.

Discard the clingfilm from the croissants, then bake them for 15–17 minutes, until their exterior is deep golden brown and the layers of dough look nice and airy. Serve warm. These are best eaten on the same day they are baked.

**CROISSANTS AREN'T
MADE IN A DAY**

*To take away some domestic guess work,
here's a proposed schedule:*

To serve croissants on a Saturday morning, start Thursday morning with pre-fermenting the dough, then Thursday evening, finish the dough and pound your butter. Refrigerate. Friday morning, roll out the dough and wrap the butter in it. Refrigerate. Roll out and turn the dough. Friday late-afternoon, roll out and turn the dough again. Refrigerate. Later Friday evening, roll out the dough, then cut and shape the croissants. Refrigerate overnight. Early Saturday morning, get up and set the croissants out to prove for 2 hours (preheating your oven now will also warm up the kitchen); go back to bed. Wake up 2 hours later and bake the croissants!

Breakfast Basket

We always have plain Croissants (see page 20), pains aux raisins, Pains au Chocolat (see page 28), almond croissants and brioches in our breakfast basket selection. Along with these classics, we offer four pastries that change as fruits of the season become available. I think all of the pastry chefs have a favourite; some love the buttery simplicity of the croissants, someone else loves the pains aux raisins and is always a little sad when there aren't any leftovers from the breakfast service. Our pastry chef Kimberly Lin's favourite is this Vanilla Danish (see below), with the Blueberry Bun (see page 28) as a close second: 'Blueberries are abundant in coastal British Columbia, and I grew up with the sticky sweet aroma of baking blueberries wafting around our kitchen during the summer months.' The Blueberry Bun consists of vanilla cream and snappy blueberries on top of our butter-rich croissant dough – a dreamy breakfast pastry. It's simple yet completely comforting and moreish.

Vanilla Danish

MAKES 15

YOU WILL NEED:
rolling pin
8cm (3¼ inch) plain pastry cutter
baking tray, lined with baking paper
stand mixer fitted with the paddle
    attachment
piping bag fitted with a 13mm (½ inch) plain
    piping tip
pastry brush

FOR THE PASTRIES:
1 x quantity Pastry Cream (*see* below)
strong white flour, for dusting
1 x quantity cold Croissant Dough (*see* page
    20)
1 egg, beaten with a pinch of salt, for the
    eggwash
150g (5½oz) nappage pastry glaze or Apricot
    Glaze (*see* page 114)
fresh berries, to decorate

FOR THE PASTRY CREAM:
250ml (9fl oz) milk
½ vanilla pod, split lengthways and seeds
    scraped
60g (2¼oz) caster sugar
25g (1oz) cornflour
60g (2¼oz) egg yolks (about 3 yolks)
25g (1oz) unsalted butter

To make the pastry cream, combine the milk and vanilla pod and seeds in a medium saucepan over a medium heat, then bring to the boil.

Meanwhile, combine the sugar and cornflour in a medium heatproof bowl by whisking gently. Add the egg yolks and whisk vigorously to combine, dispersing any lumps.

Remove the milk from the heat, discard the vanilla pod and pour a small amount into the sugar and egg mixture, whisking to combine/temper. Gradually pour in the rest of the hot milk, whisking all the while. Return to the saucepan.

Over a medium-high heat, bring the pastry cream to the boil – it will start thickening – then reduce the heat and simmer it for 2 minutes, whisking continuously, to cook the flour and eggs without curdling them. Remove from the heat and stir in the butter until smooth and completely incorporated. Cover the surface with clingfilm. Transfer to a container and refrigerate until cold.

On a lightly floured surface, roll out the croissant dough to a thickness of 2mm (1⁄16 inch). Cut out 15 circles with the plain pastry cutter and transfer to the prepared baking tray.

Using the stand mixer, mix the cold pastry cream on low-medium speed to loosen it up. Transfer to the prepared piping bag. Pipe a generous bulb of pastry cream into the centre of each circle, leaving an edge of about 1.5–2cm (5⁄8–¾ inch). Brush the pastry edges with eggwash. Leave the pastries to prove for about 1 hour, until the dough has puffed up (when you press your finger gently into the dough, the impression of your finger should remain).

Preheat the oven to 200°C (400°F), Gas Mark 6 for 20 minutes before the pastries are ready to bake.

Bake for 10 minutes, then reduce the heat to 180°C (350°F), Gas Mark 4, and continue to bake until the pastry is golden brown, about 10 minutes.

While the pastries are baking, warm the glaze until runny. Brush the glaze over the entire pastries to coat. Decorate each Danish with fresh berries, then glaze the berries. These are best served warm on the day they are made.

Fig Danish

MAKES 15

YOU WILL NEED:
rolling pin
8cm (3¼ inch) plain pastry cutter
baking tray, lined with baking paper
stand mixer fitted with the paddle
    attachment
piping bag fitted with a 13mm (½ inch) plain
    piping tip
pastry brush

FOR THE PASTRIES:
1 x quantity Fig Pastry Cream (*see* below)
strong white flour, for dusting
1 x quantity cold Croissant Dough (*see*
    page 20)
15 fresh figs, quartered
1 egg, beaten with a pinch of salt, for the
    eggwash
150g (5½oz) nappage pastry glaze or Apricot
    Glaze (*see* page 114)
pistachio nibs, to decorate

FOR THE FIG PASTRY CREAM:
125g (4½oz) fresh figs, puréed
35g (1¼oz) caster sugar
12g (½oz) cornflour
30g (1oz) egg yolks (about 1–2 yolks)
12g (½oz) unsalted butter

To make the fig pastry cream, bring the fig purée to the boil in a medium saucepan over a medium heat.

Meanwhile, combine the sugar and cornflour in a medium heatproof bowl by whisking gently. Add the egg yolks and whisk vigorously to combine, dispersing any lumps.

Remove the fig purée from the heat and pour a small amount into the sugar and egg mixture, whisking to combine/temper. Gradually pour in the rest of the purée, whisking all the while, then return to the saucepan.

Over a medium-high heat, bring the fig cream to the boil – it will start thickening – then reduce the heat and simmer it for 2 minutes, whisking continuously, to cook the flour and the eggs without curdling them. Remove from the heat and stir in the butter until smooth and fully incorporated. Cover the surface with clingfilm. Transfer to a container and refrigerate until cold.

On a lightly floured surface, roll out the croissant dough to a thickness of 2mm (1⁄16 inch). Cut out 15 circles with the plain pastry cutter and transfer to the prepared baking tray.

Using the stand mixer, mix the cold pastry cream on low-medium speed to loosen it up. Transfer to the prepared piping bag. Pipe a generous bulb of fig pastry cream into the centre of each circle, leaving an edge of about 1.5–2cm (5⁄8–¾ inch). Top each Danish with 2 fresh fig quarters, reserving the remainder. Brush the pastry edges with eggwash. Leave the pastries to prove for about 1 hour, until the dough has puffed up (when you press your finger gently into the dough, the impression of your finger should remain).

Preheat the oven to 200°C (400°F), Gas Mark 6 for 20 minutes before the pastries are ready to bake.

Bake for 10 minutes, then reduce the heat to 180°C (350°F), Gas Mark 4, and continue to bake until the pastry is golden brown, about 10 minutes.

While the pastries are baking, warm the glaze until runny. Brush the glaze over the entire pastries to coat. Decorate each Danish with 2 fresh fig quarters and glaze again, then sprinkle a few pistachio nibs atop each. These are best served warm on the day they are made.

Pains au Chocolat

MAKES 15

YOU WILL NEED:
rolling pin
1–2 baking trays, lined with baking paper
pastry brush

strong white flour, for dusting
1 x quantity cold Croissant Dough (*see* page 20)
30 dark chocolate baking sticks (available online)
1 egg, beaten with a pinch of salt, for the eggwash
unsalted butter, for greasing

On a lightly floured surface, roll out the croissant dough into a 35cm (14 inch) square, about 4mm (⅛ inch) thick. Using a sharp knife or a pizza wheel, trim the edges neatly and discard these scraps (the lamination of the dough tends to be less than perfect along the edges).

Cut the dough into 3 strips about 11cm (4¼ inches) wide, then each strip into 5 rectangles about 6.5cm (2½ inches) wide.

To shape the pains au chocolat, lay the rectangles on a lightly floured surface with the short ends facing you. Place a chocolate stick about 1cm (½ inch) above the bottom edge. Using your fingers, fold the bottom edge of the dough over the chocolate stick and press the dough slightly underneath the stick. Next, place a second chocolate stick directly against the seam, then continue to fold the dough over itself, finishing with the seam on the bottom. Transfer the pain au chocolat to the prepared baking tray, seam facing down. Repeat with the remaining rectangles of dough, using a second baking tray as needed.

Brush the pastries with eggwash. Cover them with buttered clingfilm and leave to prove for 2 hours, or until almost doubled in size (when you press your finger gently into the dough, the impression of your finger should remain).

Preheat the oven to 220°C (425°F), Gas Mark 7 for 20 minutes before the pains au chocolat are ready to bake.

Bake the pains au chocolat for 15–17 minutes, until the pastry is a deep golden brown, the layers look airy and the chocolate has started to melt.

Blueberry Buns

MAKES 15–18

YOU WILL NEED:
rolling pin
palette knife
plastic dough scraper
2 baking trays, lined with baking paper
pastry brush

strong white flour, for dusting
1 x quantity cold Croissant Dough (*see* page 20)
1 x quantity cold Pastry Cream (*see* page 26)
125g (4½oz) fresh blueberries (smaller is better)
1 egg, beaten with a pinch of salt, for the eggwash
unsalted butter, for greasing
150g (5½oz) nappage pastry glaze or Apricot Glaze (*see* page 114)

On a lightly floured surface, roll out the croissant dough into a rectangle about 30 x 50cm (12 x 20 inches) and 3mm (⅛ inch) thick. Arrange the dough with the short side facing you.

Using a palette knife, carefully spread a thin layer of the pastry cream all over the dough, leaving a margin of 3cm (1¼ inches) along the bottom edge, for the seam. Sprinkle the blueberries over the pastry cream.

Using your fingers, fold the top edge of the dough and start rolling it over the blueberries and cream, making the roll as tight as possible: press the dough with your thumbs from left to right and back to obtain the right amount of tension/tightness, and continue like this to fold the dough over itself, trying to roll all of the dough in at once, rather than favouring one end or the other. When you're close to the seam, apply pressure to the margin/seam with a plastic dough scraper to stretch that naked bit of dough out a little, so the seam doesn't puff up and come undone in the oven.

Using a sharp knife, trim the ends as needed, then proceed to cut the roll into 15–18 pieces, each about 2cm (¾ inch) wide (you'll find the log of dough has stretched slightly while you rolled it). Transfer to the prepared baking trays, lying them snail-side down on the paper.

Brush the pastries with eggwash, then cover them with buttered clingfilm and leave to prove for 1–1½ hours, or until almost doubled in size (when you press your finger gently into the dough, the impression of your finger should remain).

Preheat the oven to 200°C (400°F), Gas Mark 6.

Repeat the eggwash a second time. Bake the pastries for 10 minutes, then reduce the heat to 180°C (350°F), Gas Mark 4, and bake for a further 10 minutes, until the pastry is a deep golden brown and the layers look airy.

While the blueberry buns are baking, warm the glaze until runny. As soon as the buns come out of the oven, coat them with glaze.

A Word on Eggs

We're often asked by our guests what makes our eggs not only so tasty, but also why the yolks are so orange. We use the Burford Brown eggs from Clarence Court, where the hens range freely on green pastures that contain plenty of chlorophyll. It's all this greenery that adds to the colour and the richness of flavour. When René Redzepi was here cooking for the Noma pop-up at Claridge's during the London 2012 Olympics, he commented on the flavour, freshness and viscosity of our eggs. The signature dish at Noma is an egg that guests cook themselves at their table, using a timer. Cooking an egg perfectly should not be a luxury but a most basic skill, says René, and we agree. 'When you crack an egg into a pan,' he counsels, 'you want the yolk to sit atop the white like a jockey.' Everyone enjoys their eggs a certain way, and it's our job to remember that. René likes his eggs cooked hot and fast — with crispy white edges and a runny yolk. The Roux brothers like their eggs cooked low and slow. Meredith, the co-author of this book, requested scrambled eggs almost daily during her stay, and wanted to make sure everyone has our method:

FOR ONE PORTION OF SCRAMBLED EGGS:

You will need 3 or 4 eggs depending on how big your eggs are and how hungry you are. Thoroughly whisk the eggs in a heatproof mixing bowl that can sit comfortably over a saucepan of water. Next, bring said pan of water to a simmer; now place the bowl of eggs over the pan, add a good knob of butter and start mixing consistently with a wooden spoon or a spatula. After 2½ minutes the eggs will start to set around the edges of the bowl. Stirring constantly at this stage so the eggs stay smooth, turn off the heat and keep stirring until the texture of the eggs becomes mousse-like. Around the 3½-minute mark, remove the bowl from the pan — remember that eggs will continue cooking even off the heat. When in doubt, always undercook! This method gives the eggs that perfect glossy texture. Serve warm.

Omelette Arnold Bennett

Although we would like to take credit for this little piece of eggy genius, we have to hand this one to The Savoy. That is where, in the 1920s, English writer Arnold Bennett fell in love with this omelette. He loved it so much, in fact, that he insisted on having it made wherever he stayed. For those of you for whom this is a first, it's a flat omelette with smoked haddock and Mornay sauce. Best-quality fish, eggs and a nonstick pan are of upmost importance here, as is the grilling to glaze the sauce (otherwise it's just a cheesy sauce without a glaze and Arnold Bennett would not have had that!).

MAKES 1

NOTES:

This recipe makes 1 omelette but enough Mornay sauce to glaze 4 omelettes. For breakfast for 4, you'll need 12 eggs and 400g (14oz) fish, but you need only increase the milk for poaching the fish to 500ml (18fl oz). Mornay sauce should always be made fresh, never frozen, but will keep in the refrigerator for 3–5 days.

YOU WILL NEED:
sieve
nonstick frying pan

FOR THE MORNAY SAUCE:
250ml (9fl oz) milk
1 onion, peeled and quartered
1 bay leaf
2 cloves
30g (1oz) salted butter
30g (1oz) plain flour
100g (3½oz) mature Cheddar cheese, grated
1 tsp English mustard
1 egg yolk
100ml (3½fl oz) whipping cream, whipped
    until it holds soft peaks
sea salt and freshly ground black pepper

FOR THE SMOKED FISH:
250ml (9fl oz) milk
100g (3½oz) smoked haddock, cubed

FOR THE OMELETTE:
3 eggs
20g (¾oz) salted butter

Begin by making the Mornay sauce. In a small saucepan, over a medium heat, combine the milk, onion, bay leaf and cloves, then bring to the boil. Reduce the heat immediately to low and simmer for 5 minutes.

Meanwhile, in a separate medium saucepan, melt the butter over a medium heat, then stir in the flour with a wooden spoon or spatula until you have a nice smooth paste. Reduce the heat to low. Pass the milk through a sieve (discarding the onion, bay leaf and cloves) into the flour and butter paste. Whisk well to remove any lumps and cook over a very low heat for 2–3 minutes.

Remove from the heat and stir in the grated cheese with a spatula until melted and smooth. Stir in the mustard and season to taste with salt and pepper. Stir in the egg yolk. Cover the sauce to keep warm. (If you're making the Mornay in advance, transfer to an airtight container, laying some clingfilm directly on the surface of the sauce to prevent a skin from forming.) At this point, the sauce should have a velvety consistency but still be spoonable. When you're getting ready to glaze the omelette, you can loosen the Mornay sauce with a little of the fish poaching liquid, as required, and fold in the whipped cream.

To poach the fish, in a medium heavy-based saucepan, bring the milk to the boil and carefully add the haddock. Reduce the heat to low and poach for 5 minutes. You will know the haddock is ready when you pierce it with a sharp knife and encounter no resistance.

While the fish is poaching, make the omelette. First, preheat the oven to 200°C (400°F), Gas Mark 6, or turn on your grill. Then, in a medium mixing bowl, crack the eggs and, using a fork, whisk well until they are nice and foamy. Add pepper. You can add salt, too, but keep in mind the smoked fish will be salty and the Mornay sauce was made with salted butter.

In a medium nonstick frying pan, melt the butter over a medium-high heat, then add the eggs. Let the egg mixture sit untouched for 15–20 seconds and, as it begins to set, use a fork or a spatula to continuously go around the outside, folding the edges towards the centre – to prevent any scorching – while also, every so often, shaking the pan back and forth over the heat, which will ensure your egg mixture is spread out across the pan and your omelette sets evenly (to an untrained eye, it might look like you're scrambling the eggs). About 3 minutes into this, stop fiddling with it and let the omelette finish setting in the pan for a few moments. Eggs continue to cook after they come off the heat, so undercook slightly!

Using a spatula, fold the omelette into a half-moon, carefully slide it on to an ovenproof plate, then gently unfold it back to its full-moon shape. (If you're making more than one omelette, make the remaining omelettes now.)

Using a slotted spoon, remove the haddock from the milk. Place it on to the omelette and gently flake it into smaller pieces. Carefully spoon about a quarter of the Mornay sauce over the haddock to cover it completely. Transfer your plate to the oven or grill and bake or grill for 2–3 minutes until the Mornay sauce is golden and browned in spots. The glaze should look like a light and airy sheet of golden paper rather than a baked lasagne. Serve warm.

Kippers

More than an actual recipe, kippers are a state of mind. As lobster or oysters were half a century ago, kippers were an abundant staple. Today, they've become a luxury item. They are simultaneously alarming yet also steadying. When I see an order for kippers, I'm always intrigued as to whom the guest could be. You will not see kippers on the regular Claridge's menu, but they are available upon request 24 hours a day, 7 days a week, 365 days of the year.

SERVES 1
(BECAUSE, LET'S FACE IT: KIPPERS
ARE OFTEN A SOLO ENDEAVOUR)

YOU WILL NEED:
baking tray

**1 herring, salted, hung and smoked
50g (1¾oz) unsalted butter**

TO SERVE:
**1 lemon wedge
slices of buttered bread**

Preheat the grill to high for 5 minutes.

Cut off the tail and remove the head from the fish: this is done by cutting a V on either side of the head and removing it gingerly.

Place the fish on a baking tray with a good dollop of butter on top. Grill for 4 minutes until it shrinks in size slightly. Remove from the heat, and using a small knife, gently lift out the spine, starting at the tail end, then carefully remove the rib bones.

Transfer to a warm plate and serve with a lemon wedge and buttered bread.

Right: 4th October, 1950. Sir Frederick Bell, Chairman of the Herring Industry Board, with kippers at a Kipper Breakfast at Claridge's. The aim of the breakfast was to introduce the Scottish kipper to the American market. On the right is US broadcaster and kipper connoisseur Professor Dennis Brogan.

Vanilla Brioche French Toast

The charm of room service, at least for us, seems especially magnified at breakfast time: you're in a Claridge's white robe, the trolley is rolled in, carrying the Guy Oliver-designed china, and, for a moment — hopefully longer — you can still shut out the rest of the world. If you're going to go for it, go big, we say. Our toast is made with brioche, and its thickness is perfect to drench up the maple syrup and clotted cream.

SERVES 4

6 brioche slices, crusts removed
6 eggs
100ml (3½fl oz) milk
80g (2¾oz) icing sugar
1 vanilla pod, split lengthways and seeds scraped
a pinch of ground cinnamon
2 pats salted butter (we use Buttervikings – *see* page 108 – but any best-quality butter will do)

TO SERVE:
120ml (4fl oz) maple syrup (we use Vermont or Quebec syrup)
200g (7oz) clotted cream
200g (7oz) berries of your choice

Cut each brioche slice in half to make 2 triangles. In a large bowl, whisk the eggs, milk, icing sugar, vanilla seeds and cinnamon together.

Add half of the butter to a large frying pan over a medium-high heat. While the butter is melting, dip and dredge the brioche triangles in the egg mixture.

When the butter is foaming, reduce the heat to medium and fry 6 of the brioche triangles (being sure to drain off any excess egg mixture before adding to the pan) until golden brown. Set aside to keep warm. Repeat with the remaining butter and triangles.

Serve the French toast immediately with the maple syrup, clotted cream and berries.

Welsh Rarebit

This simple but serious cheese dish is very much something that would be featured as a savoury course in a formal British dinner, served after pudding but before port. Louis Saulnier's Le Répertoire de la Cuisine, a reference guide to Escoffier's longer work, has been an invaluable staple for me as chef, as I hope it is for many working in grand hotels around the world. This pocket gem records 52 recipes in its 'Savourie' section — and I often use it as a reference when planning menus for those interested in multi-course meals. That said, there is no reason why a Welsh rarebit, on a cold day, can't stand alone.

SERVES 4

NOTES:
We recommend making the rarebit mix in advance and storing it in the refrigerator ready to spread on to toasted sourdough and browned under a hot grill whenever the mood strikes. It will keep for up to 4 days. Rarebit can be served as a canapé, for high tea or as a main course (though the portion is a little reserved). More recently, it has featured on our breakfast menu, and is served with heirloom tomatoes and a poached Clarence Court egg.

FOR THE RAREBIT MIX:
490ml (18fl oz) Guinness, or any dark ale
75ml (2½fl oz) milk
175g (6oz) Gruyère cheese, grated
175g (6oz) Quicke's mature Cheddar
      (or your favourite mature Cheddar)
      cheese, grated
25g (1oz) fresh breadcrumbs
25g (1oz) plain flour
1 tsp English mustard
3½ tsp Worcestershire sauce
2 eggs, plus 2 egg yolks

6 slices of sourdough, toasted, to serve

In a wide saucepan or frying pan, bring the Guinness or ale to the boil over a high heat, then reduce the heat. Reduce until you have about 125ml (4fl oz) syrup, about 45–60 minutes.

In a large heavy-based saucepan, bring the milk to the boil. Remove from the heat, add the cheeses and mix until smooth. Fold in the reduced Guinness or ale, breadcrumbs, flour, mustard and Worcestershire sauce. Pour into a bowl and leave to cool slightly.

When cool, beat the eggs and egg yolks together, then fold into the mix. Refrigerate for 30 minutes.

Spread the rarebit mix on to the toasted bread, then brown under a preheated hot grill for 4 minutes.

Quinoa & Flaxseed Porridge

Because you can't have room service bring you French toast every day. In keeping with a disciplined state of mind, this recipe calls for water, but you can, of course, use milk (or soya, almond or coconut milk), adding honey for a bit of richness.

SERVES 4

240g (8½oz) white quinoa
160g (5¾oz) steel-cut oats
¼ tsp salt
1.25 litres (2 pints) water

TO SERVE:
a handful of flaxseeds and pumpkin seeds
a handful of berries (optional)
milk (optional)
honey (optional)

Combine the quinoa, oats, salt and measured water in a large heavy-based saucepan, then bring to the boil over a high heat.

Reduce the heat to medium-low and simmer gently, uncovered, for a good 25–30 minutes, stirring occasionally, allowing the grains to plump up, thicken and release their starch. If, after 25 minutes, the water has been completely absorbed but the grains are not yet fully cooked, add a splash more water to finish cooking through and to loosen the consistency of your porridge.

Divide among 4 bowls, then top with the seeds and berries, if liked. Serve accompanied by a small jug of milk and some honey as you see fit.

Bircher Muesli

Originally devised by Swiss doctor and nutritionist Maximilian Bircher-Benner as healthful fortification for a vigorous day ahead, we've adopted (and adapted) the recipe for the very same purpose. Ours is a steadying mix of oats, fresh apples, dried fruit, yogurt and a splash of orange juice and honey for some sweetness. On offer on our Claridge's all-day menu, it's the healthy choice, yes, but also one of the tastiest. It's actually delicious as is (the oats have a nice toothsomeness and do feel soaked not dry), but adding some yogurt when you serve it, for a person to stir in themselves, will make it look like all those mueslis enjoyed on the sunny Alpine slopes.

MAKES ABOUT 1.5KG (3LB 5OZ) OR 10–12 SERVINGS

NOTE:
Don't hesitate to customize your muesli with additions of sliced almonds, dates or even granola. If you can't find flaked hazelnuts, replace them with roughly chopped and toasted hazelnuts.

450g (1lb) rolled oats
50g (1¾oz) sultanas
50g (1¾oz) ready-to-eat dried apricots, roughly chopped
50g (1¾oz) dried sour cherries
200g (7oz) flaked hazelnuts, toasted
100ml (3½fl oz) semi-skimmed milk
40ml (1½fl oz) freshly squeezed orange juice
50ml (2fl oz) natural yogurt, plus extra to serve
100ml (3½fl oz) honey
2 green apples, peeled, cored and cut into small dice
fresh blueberries or strawberries, to serve (optional)

Using your hands, combine the dry ingredients in a large bowl. Add the milk, orange juice, yogurt and honey and stir well, using a wooden spoon or spatula. Transfer to a smaller bowl and cover. Alternatively, seal in a 2 litre (3½ pint) glass jar with a lid. Leave the oats to soak for at least 6 hours or overnight in the refrigerator.

In the morning, transfer the soaked oats and fruit to a mixing bowl, add the diced apple and stir well to combine.

Serve each portion with a generous dollop of yogurt and top with fresh berries, if liked.

This muesli will keep for 1 week covered and refrigerated.

Cocoa Espresso Energy Snacks

On the sixth floor of Claridge's lies our gym, and to the guilt of many of us, it's often busiest in the mornings, with guests on treadmills taking in the view of Mayfair as they begin their day. On offer, post-workout, are these energizing bites. Our pastry chef Kimberly Lin created these when she was training for a marathon: 'I tried many varieties of commercial energy snacks: too sweet, too chewy, not actually healthy, too artificial. The list goes on and on. After intense training sessions or long runs, it felt impossible to chew on a thick, glucose-packed energy snack. These are easy to eat, taste great, they're packed with natural sugars, fibre and protein and no junk. Training is hard enough; snacking should be the easy part.'

MAKES 12

YOU WILL NEED:
food processor

4–6 Medjool dates, pitted and any stems removed
125g (4½oz) cashew nuts
100g (3½oz) whole raw almonds
50g (1¾oz) smooth or crunchy no-added-sugar peanut butter
10g (¼oz) cocoa powder
1 tsp instant coffee granules
30ml (1fl oz) coconut oil
25g (1oz) desiccated coconut

In a food processor, combine the dates, cashews and almonds until you have a fairly fine meal. If your dates are particularly soft, you might have a paste: this is fine.

Transfer the nut and date blend to a medium bowl, then add the remaining ingredients. Combine well using a spatula or your hands – messy but easiest!

Once all the ingredients have come together, divide into 12 pieces (30–35g/1–1¼oz each, if you wish to measure out) and roll each into a ball.

These can be eaten straight away, but are best chilled until needed. They will easily keep in an airtight container for up to 1 week in the refrigerator.

Coconut Lime Protein Snacks

For this recipe, if you can't find rich and velvety coconut cream, use the thick cream that settles at the top of a tin of coconut milk and save the watery milk for smoothies.

MAKES 12

100g (3½oz) coconut cream
150g (5½oz) desiccated coconut, plus extra for coating (optional)
30g (1oz) vanilla whey protein powder (or any non-dairy vanilla protein powder)
zest and juice of 2 limes
50g (1¾oz) raw almonds, finely chopped or pulsed in a food processor
pinch of Stevia (optional)
splash of coconut or almond milk (optional)

In a medium bowl, combine the coconut cream, desiccated coconut, protein powder, lime zest and juice and almonds, mixing well. If you wish for a sweeter mix, add a pinch of Stevia. If you find the mix is too dry and won't come together, add in a splash of coconut or almond milk: it should hold together like cookie dough.

Divide into 12 pieces (30–35g/1–1¼oz each, if you wish to measure out) and roll each into a ball. You can now roll each ball in desiccated coconut, if using.

These can be eaten straight away, but are best chilled until needed, and will easily keep in an airtight container for up to 1 week in the refrigerator.

Our Fresh Juices

In the deepest recesses of the cold section of our kitchen you'll find Vlad the Reviver. Vlad is singlehandedly responsible for rejuvenating our guests, with vitamins and alkalizers, which are served in shockingly delicious concoctions. On the menu we offer several options, including the popular Carrot, Apple & Ginger Juice. These juices boost the immune system, positively ward off any travel fatigue and energize you for the day ahead.

EACH MAKES 1 LITRE (1¾ PINTS)

YOU WILL NEED:
juicer or juice extractor

FOR THE BEETROOT, CARROT & ORANGE JUICE (*PICTURED OPPOSITE, LEFT*):
1kg (2lb 4oz) carrots
1kg (2lb 4oz) oranges (about 6)
400g (14oz) red beetroot

FOR THE SUPERGREEN JUICE (*PICTURED OPPOSITE, CENTRE*):
4 green apples, peeled and cored
1 cucumber, roughly chopped
200g (7oz) green grapes
50g (1¾oz) kale, torn
500g (1lb 2oz) spinach, torn
juice of 1 lemon
200g (7oz) celery stalks
8g (¼oz) fresh root ginger

FOR THE CARROT, APPLE & GINGER JUICE (*PICTURED OPPOSITE, RIGHT*):
1.2kg (2lb 12oz) carrots
1.2kg (2lb 12oz) apples, peeled and cored
40g (1½oz) fresh root ginger

In a strong juicer, process all the ingredients for your juice of choice.

Serve within 10 minutes of making.

A Note on Room Service

Whether it's a consommé for one or canapés and champagne for ten, room service is always a seductive option. Ensuring you have what you want, when you want it. At Claridge's the answer is always 'yes'.

Breakfast at 3pm? Certainly. Dinner for one and your favourite glass of red at 11pm? Strongly encouraged. There are times when checking into Claridge's means drinks in the Fumoir at 7pm sharp, followed by dinner in the Foyer with friends and family. There are other times, when true indulgence is to be found in the refuge of your room, embraced by a pillow-y robe and the sweet knowledge of no further obligations. For a little while at least.

If you are coming to Claridge's for romance you can dine with every indulgence of the Foyer menu without stepping out of your robe. One can ring up their suite butler and say, 'For dinner we would like sole and the remainder of the bottle of white wine from last night,' and of course, like that, it would be done. If heading to the Tate for the afternoon the team would prepare the room for the evening – knowing your personal preference from memory.

At Claridge's the comfort of a room warms you, the details of a suite inspire you. Staying in a suite is like a fantasy, experiential and rewarding; a touchable sense of magic. Even if you don't venture onto the streets of Mayfair you *know* that you are in London. How could you forget? The personality of the city is accentuated by British signature touches, from the Burberry trench coats in the wardrobes, to the iconic Linley tub chairs and the appropriately named Brook Street china specially designed for room service.

Our team know that when working the night shift, either as duty manager or as waiter, you are sharing a particularly intimate relationship with guests and there is no demand too great or unexpected. Indeed many of us know the satisfaction that the 2am club sandwich can bring. In these moments your conduit to the outside world will be one of our in-room dining waiters or butlers. Those of you who have stayed in one of our suites at Claridge's will be familiar with our butler Michael Lynch (who can be seen bearing gifts galore on page 243). If you haven't, you may remember him as the very Irish and very amiable personage from the BBC documentary *Inside Claridge's*. Yes, indeed, 'Is Michael working today?' is a question our team hear often. It was recently posed by three children as they rushed through the doors of Claridge's, flushed with excitement. By the time the family had got to their room, Michael had appeared to screams of, 'It's him! He's here! He's here!' and an ensuing barrage of breathless stories and questions. After calm was restored, the children's mother explained to Michael that they had seen him on the television programme, and having fallen for his smile and charm, decided he could be their very own Mrs Doubtfire. Our guests feel very connected to the familiar faces of this hotel and that connection with room service, especially over many stays, is perhaps the most personal.

'It's my job to offer a highly tailored service that feels very personal. I've always said we have the best guests in the world and that has not changed in my 40 years here'.

Elevenses

Peanut Butter Sesame Biscuits

Everyone has a favourite biscuit. Our pastry chef Kim's favourite is this one right here: her Canadian grandmother's recipe. Mine is my grandmother's Chocolate Sandwich Biscuits, but that's another story (see page 62). We serve these Peanut Butter Sesame Biscuits for elevenses, alongside our classic Shortbread Biscuits (see page 54), with tea or coffee.

MAKES 30

YOU WILL NEED:
stand mixer fitted with the paddle
    attachment
2 baking sheets, lined with baking paper
wire rack

125g (4½oz) unsalted butter, softened
75g (2¾oz) light brown sugar
75g (2¾oz) caster sugar
1 tsp vanilla extract
2 tsp honey
2 eggs
125g (4½oz) crunchy peanut butter
250g (9oz) plain flour
1 tsp bicarbonate of soda
½ tsp salt
50g (1¾oz) mixed black and white
    sesame seeds

Using the stand mixer, cream the butter, sugars, vanilla and honey on low speed. Add the eggs, one at a time, mixing well after each addition. Add the peanut butter and continue mixing until you have a smooth batter, about 30 seconds.

Add the flour, bicarbonate of soda and salt and mix until well incorporated. Cover and refrigerate the dough for a minimum of 4 hours until firm enough to handle.

Spread the sesame seeds out on a small tray or a flat plate. Remove the dough from the refrigerator and divide it into 2 pieces, then, on a work surface, form each into a log about 16cm (6¼ inches) long and 4cm (1½ inches) in diameter. Roll the logs' sides in the sesame seeds until well coated. Refrigerate for 20 minutes. (If you wish to only make 15 biscuits at this point, you can freeze one of the logs for up to 2 months. Just defrost the dough logs in the refrigerator before proceeding to the next step.)

Preheat the oven to 180°C (350°F), Gas Mark 4.

Cut each log into 1cm (½-inch) thick rounds. Transfer to the prepared baking sheets, spacing the biscuits at least 3cm (1¼ inches) apart. Bake for 12–15 minutes, until golden and crisp.

Transfer to a wire rack to cool. These will keep in an airtight container for up to 5 days.

WHY ELEVENSES?

The tradition of elevenses started out as a cup of tea and a biscuit to keep workers going, in an era when the day started very early — a welcome pause in the morning's work to satisfy you until lunch. At Claridge's, elevenses is an opportunity to showcase our pastry team's biscuits and, on special occasions, our doughnut trolley. There is that moment where the Foyer begins to empty after breakfast and there is a quiet pause. This is when the croissants and Danish pastries make way for biscuits, frangipane tarts, fruit cakes and Eccles cakes...

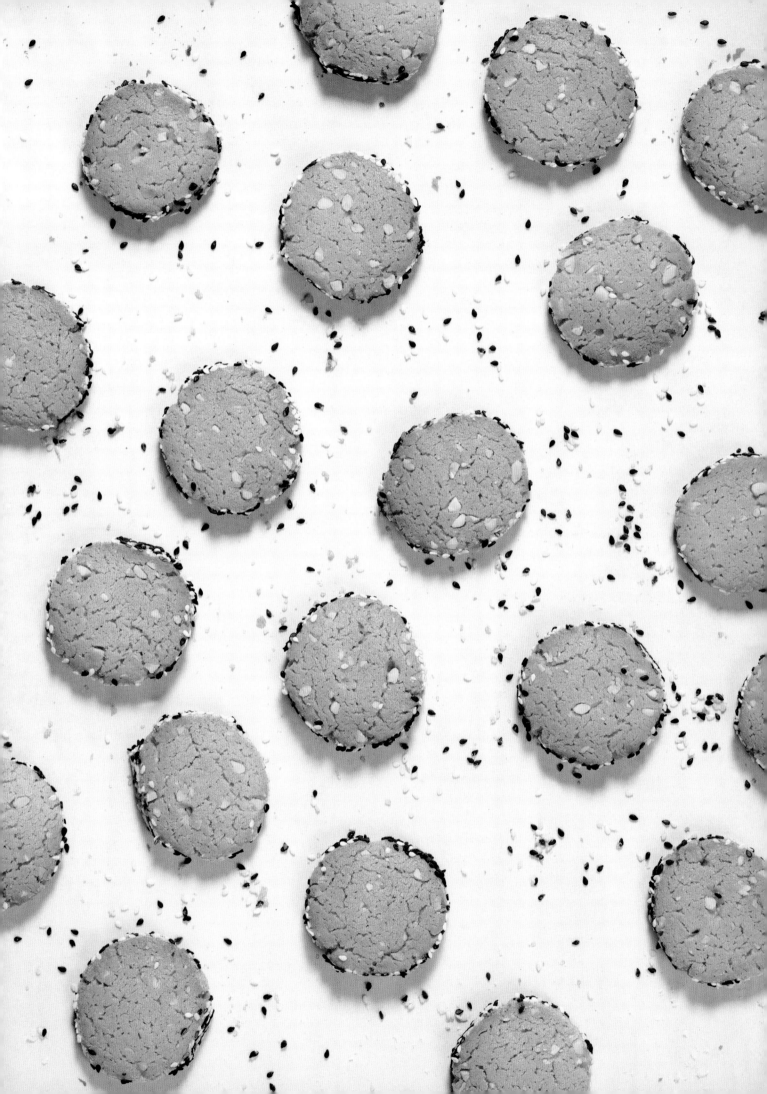

Shortbread Biscuits

At Claridge's, shortbread should always be had with a cup of tea. We make all kinds: caraway and lemon, chequerboard, almond or these simple vanilla ones. In fact, we cut over 7,000 vanilla shortbread a month. Ours is not the most buttery shortbread – rather, it's more mellow in flavour and ends with a good crunch. A particular favourite of our regular breakfast guest Gerry Parker and also of Glenn Piper, our Foyer Director, who, with his team, takes such great care of our guests and helps to make Claridge's Foyer the special place that so many people know and love.

MAKES ABOUT 30

YOU WILL NEED:
stand mixer fitted with the paddle
    attachment
baking sheet, lined with baking paper

200g (7oz) unsalted butter, softened
½ vanilla pod, split lengthways and seeds
    scraped
½ tsp vanilla extract
70g (2½oz) icing sugar
250g (9oz) strong white flour
caster sugar, for dusting

Using the stand mixer, combine the butter, vanilla seeds and vanilla extract on medium speed for 1 minute. Stop the mixer and scrape down the sides and bottom of the bowl with a spatula. Add the icing sugar, then cream on low speed for 1 minute. Scrape the sides and bottom of the bowl once more, then add the flour. Mix on low speed until the flour is completely incorporated.

Divide the dough into 2 pieces. Roll each piece into a log about 20cm (8 inches) long and 3–4cm (1¼–1½ inches) in diameter, pushing the dough together if it feels crumbly, then wrap in baking paper or clingfilm. Refrigerate until firm, about 40 minutes or so. (The dough can also be frozen at this stage for up to 2 months. Just defrost the dough logs in the refrigerator before proceeding to the next step.)

Preheat the oven to 180°C (350°F), Gas Mark 4.

Cut each log into 1cm (½-inch) thick rounds. Transfer to the prepared baking sheet, spacing them 2cm (¾ inch) apart.

Bake for 20 minutes or so, until very pale golden around the edges. Remove from the oven and immediately dust the biscuits generously with caster sugar (this will ensure that the sugar sticks to the shortbread). Leave to cool completely on the sheet.

Once the shortbread has cooled, shake off any excess sugar and pack away in an airtight container. These biscuits can be stored for up to 5 days.

Sourdough Doughnuts

Every once in a while, some type of pastry will have its moment in the spotlight: the cupcake, the éclair, the macaron. . . At Claridge's, we're not impervious to a tasty trend — as a gift to a departing guest a few years ago, we decided to make a few doughnuts. We may have gone overboard, and a dozen doughnuts quickly turned into a trolley piled high with 250 doughnuts in all flavours, shapes and sizes. It caused a sensation. Since then, we like to put together a full trolley when people least expect it. We're including our pastry chef's 'hands-down, all-time' favourite doughnut glaze: 'It has the sweet earthiness of vanilla but the zing of lemon and crème fraîche.'

MAKES A BAKER'S DOZEN

NOTES:
This recipe needs to be started at least 24 hours ahead: leaving the dough to rest in the refrigerator helps to develop a light sourdough flavour. If you don't have a table-top deep-fryer, use a heavy-based saucepan large enough so that when you add the oil to it, it is no more than half full; be vigilant about keeping the oil temperature at 180°C (350°F) throughout the cooking process so that the doughnuts cook evenly and don't burn.

YOU WILL NEED:
stand mixer fitted with the dough hook
baking sheet
6cm (2½ inch) pastry cutter
2cm (¾ inch) pastry cutter (optional)
2 litres (3½ pints) vegetable oil, for
    deep-frying
table-top deep-fryer or large, deep,
    heavy-based pan (*see* Note above)
deep-frying thermometer
tray, lined with kitchen paper
wire rack fitted over a baking tray with sides

FOR THE DOUGH:
500g (1lb 2oz) strong white flour, plus extra
    for dusting
4 eggs
60g (2¼oz) caster sugar
15g (½oz) fresh yeast, crumbled, or 6g (¼oz)
    instant yeast
7.5g (¼oz) salt
75ml (2½fl oz) milk
75ml (2½fl oz) buttermilk
100g (3½oz) unsalted butter, cold but
    softening, cut into 10g (¼oz) pieces,
    plus extra for greasing

Using the stand mixer, combine all the dough ingredients except for the butter, mixing on low speed. Once the dough has formed, increase the speed to medium and mix for 5 minutes, until nicely smooth and starting to come away from the sides. Add the butter one piece at a time, continuing to mix on medium–high speed for 5–10 minutes – you'll actually see the strands of gluten developing – until all the butter is incorporated and the dough looks shiny and elastic.

Turn the dough out on to a lightly floured surface. It'll be soft and sticky. Form into a smooth ball and place in a well-greased bowl or plastic container. Leave the dough out to ferment, until it's doubled in size, about 1–1½ hours, depending on how warm your kitchen is. Punch the gas out of the dough, then cover with clingfilm or a lid and refrigerate for 24 hours. You may notice the dough ferment further in the refrigerator, puffing up – it's okay to punch it down once and re-cover it. (The dough will keep for up to 3 days in the refrigerator, although the finished doughnuts will not be as fluffy.)

It's time to make doughnuts. Generously grease the baking sheet, then turn the chilled dough on to a floured surface. Using a rolling pin, gently roll out the dough to an even thickness of 2–3cm (¾–1¼ inches). Leave it to relax for 5–10 minutes. Dust the pastry cutters with flour, then gently but decisively cut out the doughnuts using the 6cm (2½ inch) cutter, taking care not to stretch or tug on the dough as you cut it or remove it from the cutter, and then, if you wish, cut the centre out with the small cutter – these doughnuts 'holes' can be fried as well. Transfer the doughnuts to the baking sheet as you work, leaving space in between for them to prove. Do the same with any 'holes'.

When you've cut out as many doughnuts as you can, gather up the remaining scraps of dough into a ball, knead it a few times, then roll out the dough and cut out doughnuts one more time.

Cover the doughnuts with clingfilm or a clean tea towel. Place in a warm area and leave the doughnuts to puff up – this can take up to 2 hours or more. Touch the doughnuts with your finger: a properly proved doughnut will maintain the indentation without collapsing. If the indentation springs back, the doughnut needs more time. If, however, the dough collapses, it is over-proved. The proving time will vary depending on the time of year and how warm or humid it is in your kitchen. Be patient!

When the doughnuts have about doubled in size, heat the oil to 180°C (350°F) in a deep-fryer or pan (*see* Notes). When the oil reaches 180°C (350°F), carefully drop 2–4 doughnuts (depending on the size of your fryer) into the oil – don't overcrowd the pan. When the doughnuts have a nice deep golden colour on the first side, about 1½ minutes, use a metal spatula or fish slice to flip them over and fry for a further 1½–2 minutes. Lift them out with a slotted spoon and transfer to the lined tray. Repeat with the remaining doughnuts. Doughnut holes will cook a lot faster, about 1–1½ minutes. **»**

FOR THE VANILLA CRÈME FRAÎCHE GLAZE:
1 vanilla pod, split lengthways and seeds
    scraped
200g (7oz) icing sugar
50g (1¾oz) crème fraîche
juice of ½–1 lemon

To make the glaze, stir the vanilla seeds into the icing sugar in a small bowl, then whisk in the crème fraîche and lemon juice to create a smooth glaze with the consistency of runny honey. Add a little more lemon juice or a splash of water as needed.

When the doughnuts have cooled to the touch, about 15–20 minutes, dip them one at a time in the glaze, turning them over to coat completely, or just dipping their tops if you prefer. Lift the doughnuts out of the glaze using your fingers or a small spatula and place on the wire rack over the baking tray to catch any drips. Repeat until all the doughnuts have been dipped. Leave the doughnuts to stand at room temperature until the glaze has set...or eat straight away! Serve with the doughnut holes on the side.

Doughnuts are best kept at room temperature and eaten on the day they are made.

Coffee Almond Biscuits

Warning: these cookies might be the sleeper hit of this tome of recipes you're holding right here in your hands. They have a sablé consistency, they taste like coffee ice cream and they're quite gorgeous with their demerara sugar robe.

MAKES 25–30

YOU WILL NEED:
**stand mixer fitted with the paddle
      attachment**
pastry brush
2 baking sheets, lined with baking paper
wire rack

1 tsp hot water
2 tsp instant coffee granules
140g (5oz) unsalted butter, softened
80g (2¾oz) icing sugar
1 egg, separated
200g (7oz) plain flour
**40g (1½oz) flaked almonds, roughly but
      evenly chopped**
50g (1¾oz) demerara sugar, for coating

In a small cup or bowl, mix together the hot water and instant coffee to make a thick syrup. Set aside.

Using the stand mixer, lightly cream the butter and icing sugar on low speed. Scrape down the sides and bottom of the bowl, then add the egg yolk and the coffee syrup. Mix well. Next, add the flour, mixing on low speed until incorporated. Add the flaked almonds, mixing slowly and gently until they are distributed throughout – you may need to stop the mixer and stir them in manually, so the nuts don't get crushed.

Divide the dough into 2 pieces, then roll each piece into a log about 15cm (6 inches) long and 4cm (1½ inches) in diameter. Wrap in clingfilm or baking paper and refrigerate until firm, about 45 minutes.

Preheat the oven to 180°C (350°F), Gas Mark 4. Spread the demerara sugar on to a tray or flat plate.

Lightly beat the egg white to loosen it. Unwrap the logs of dough. Brush each all over with the egg white, then roll each log in the sugar. Press gently to ensure it sticks to the dough.

Slice the dough into 1cm (½-inch) thick pieces and transfer to the prepared baking sheets, spacing them 2cm (¾ inch) apart. (If you wish to only make 15 or so biscuits at this point, you can freeze one of the logs for up to 2 months. Just defrost the dough logs in the refrigerator before proceeding to the next step.)

Bake for 17–20 minutes, until lightly golden. Transfer to a wire rack to cool.

These biscuits will keep in an airtight container for up to 5 days.

Chocolate Sandwich Biscuits

These were the favourite biscuits of Jack and Norma Melchor, who were guests of the hotel for many decades (you may remember them from the Inside Claridge's documentary series). Over the years, they tried almost all of our biscuits, but their particular favourite was this chocolate sandwich: crisp but chewy biscuits with a chocolate ganache, inspired by my grandmother's buttercream chocolate sandwich recipe, and so very easy to make.

MAKES 60 BISCUITS/30 SANDWICHES

NOTES:
You can make the ganache up to 3 days ahead of time. At Claridge's, we make all our ganaches the day before we need to use them and let them crystallize at room temperature, which helps give the ganache an ultra-silky texture! In lieu of liquid invert sugar, you can use honey in a pinch, a natural invert sugar.

YOU WILL NEED:
2 piping bags, each fitted with a medium plain piping tip
2 baking sheets, lined with baking paper

FOR THE CHOCOLATE GANACHE:
75g (2¾oz) dark chocolate (at least 55% cocoa solids), broken into pieces
90ml (3fl oz) whipping cream
8g (¼oz) liquid invert sugar
30g (1oz) unsalted butter, softened

FOR THE BISCUITS:
2 eggs
190g (6¾oz) demerara sugar
250g (9oz) dark chocolate (at least 55% cocoa solids), broken into pieces
50g (1¾oz) unsalted butter
50g (1¾oz) strong white flour
¼ tsp baking powder
pinch of salt

Make the ganache. Melt the chocolate in a medium heatproof bowl placed over a saucepan of simmering water, or simply in the microwave. In a small saucepan, bring the cream and invert sugar to the boil over a medium heat, then remove from the heat. Pour one-third of the hot cream into the melted chocolate. Using a spatula, stir briskly to incorporate the cream. The chocolate might look grainy and split at this point – don't worry! Repeat twice more, adding another third of the cream at a time. The chocolate should now be smooth and glossy. Add the butter and stir well.

Using the spatula, clean the sides of the bowl, scraping any errant ganache back into the mix. Place a sheet of clingfilm directly on to the surface of the ganache to prevent a skin from forming. Leave to set at room temperature for 12–24 hours.

The next day, make the biscuits. In a medium bowl, whisk the eggs and sugar together until just combined – the sugar does not need to be dissolved. Leave this to rest for 20 minutes.

Over a low heat, melt the chocolate and butter together in a pan, stirring until well combined. Whisk the melted chocolate into the egg and sugar mixture. Once incorporated, stir in the dry ingredients. Cover with clingfilm directly touching the surface until the mixture sets, about 10–20 minutes, depending on how warm your kitchen is (a cooler spot will work well but do not be tempted to refrigerate!).

Preheat the oven to 180°C (350°F), Gas Mark 4.

Transfer the biscuit mixture to the prepared piping bag. Pipe the mixture on to the prepared baking sheets in mounds 3cm (1¼ inches) in diameter (about the diameter of a 50p coin) – about 30 per sheet, depending on the size of your baking sheets. Use a wet finger or the back of a spoon to smooth the tops of the mounds as needed.

Bake for 10 minutes, or until the biscuits feel crisp on the edges but are still soft in the middle. Their surfaces will look cracked: that's normal! Leave to cool completely on the baking sheets.

To assemble, match the biscuits in equal-sized pairs. Fill the second piping bag with the ganache and pipe about 1 teaspoon of ganache on to the centre of the flat side of half of the biscuits. Then top with the remaining biscuits and gently press to push the ganache to the edges.

These biscuits will keep for 3 days at room temperature in an airtight container.

Inset right: Jack and Norma Melchor celebrating their golden wedding anniversary at Claridge's.

Lunch

Lobster, Langoustine & Crab Cocktail

As a chef, marrying the style of your food to the place and time in which it's served is key. The grand history and decor of the hotel prompts us to look back along our long culinary timeline. The arrival of a new Martini glass in the Fumoir caught the eye of former sous-chef Ewan Simpson, who loved to research everything about a dish. He immediately thought of prawn cocktail, popular in the 1970s, which can actually be traced back to Escoffier (whose portrait looks down on us from my office wall). Here, the prawns are replaced with British crab, langoustines and lobster, combined with our Marie-Rose sauce, and topped with quail eggs and caviar. This dish led to a mysterious shortage of Martini glasses in the Fumoir...

SERVES 4

YOU WILL NEED:
4 Martini glasses or small shallow bowls

FOR THE COCKTAIL:
160g (5¾oz) Gem lettuce, shredded
400g (14oz) cucumber, peeled and thinly
    sliced
1 x quantity Marie-Rose Sauce (*see* below)
12 small round lettuce leaves
1 cooked Cornish lobster, about 1kg (2lb 4oz),
    removed from the shell
250g (9oz) cooked Cornish white crab meat,
    thoroughly picked
16 cooked peeled Cornish langoustines

FOR THE MARIE-ROSE SAUCE:
150g (5½oz) Mayonnaise (*see* page 108), or
    use your favourite store-bought brand
50g (1¾oz) tomato ketchup
¼ tsp Tabasco sauce
¼ tsp Worcestershire sauce
½ tsp brandy
sea salt and freshly ground black pepper

FOR THE GARNISH:
4 quail eggs, soft-boiled and shelled (*see*
    Note on page 94), left whole
2g (1/16oz) caviar d'Aquitaine or another
    sustainably farmed sturgeon caviar
    (optional)
crème fraîche
4 blanched cherry tomatoes
16 pea shoots
20 leaves of red veined sorrel
4 edible pansy flowers

To make the Marie-Rose sauce, in a medium bowl, combine all the ingredients well and season to your liking.

This dish is all about the final assembly. To go the Martini glass route, place the shredded lettuce in the bottom of the Martini glasses. If that's too OTT for you, small shallow bowls will work well. Now line the inside of each glass or bowl with the cucumber slices. Dollop one spoonful of Marie-Rose sauce on each bed of lettuce, then add 3 round lettuce leaves to the side of each glass. Arrange the lobster, crab and langoustines neatly on top of the sauce.

Top each cocktail with a quail egg, crème fraîche and the caviar. Add 1 cherry tomato to each, then arrange the herbs and flower petals over the top. Divide the remaining Marie-Rose sauce into quarters and add a dollop to one side of each glass, where there is space.

Cornish Crab Salad

A chef's pride at buying the best produce is never more evident than when sourcing the biggest, meatiest crabs. We get ours from Portland in Dorset, and every day the crabs are cooked and cracked and the succulent flesh meticulously picked to remove all traces of shell.

SERVES 4

NOTE:

If you're having trouble finding brown crab meat, ask your fishmonger for a nice 1kg (2lb 4oz) brown (Cornish) crab or a Jonah crab. To cook, boil it in heavily salted water for 12 minutes. Leave it to cool, then crack it and get picking! You should have enough meat, white and brown, for this recipe.

YOU WILL NEED:

tray, lined with kitchen paper
stick blender
small disposable piping bag (no tip needed, just cut the bag)
7cm (2¾ inch) ring mould

FOR THE SPICED CRUMBS:

113g (4oz) salted butter
1½ tsp cayenne pepper
1 tbsp ground mace
1 tbsp mixed spice
½ sheet nori (roasted seaweed), finely chopped
100g (3½oz) white breadcrumbs

FOR THE BROWN CRAB EMULSION:

150g (5½oz) brown crab meat
2 tsp Worcestershire sauce
1 tsp Tabasco sauce
20ml (¾fl oz) brandy
40g (1½oz) white breadcrumbs, plus extra if required
2g (1⁄16oz) sea salt
1 tbsp water, if required

FOR THE CRAB:

50g (1¾oz) crème fraîche
10g (¼oz) chives, finely chopped
zest of ½ lemon
280g (10oz) picked white crab meat
lemon juice (optional)
sea salt and freshly ground black pepper

FOR THE SALAD:

1 cucumber, peeled and thinly sliced
16 small round lettuce leaves
2 radishes, thinly sliced
4 cherry tomatoes, halved
4 quail eggs, soft-boiled and shelled (*see Note on page 94*), left whole

FOR THE GARNISH:

lemon oil
chervil, pea shoots and rock samphire

Start by making the spiced crumbs. In a medium saucepan, heat the butter over a medium-high heat until foaming, then stir in the spices and nori and cook until fragrant, about 2 minutes. Stir in the breadcrumbs and cook until the butter has been absorbed and the crumbs have turned golden brown. Transfer the crumbs to the lined tray, spreading them out flat. When cool, transfer to an airtight container – the recipe will make more than you need, but these crumbs are great for a little spicy kick/topping.

Next, make the brown crab emulsion. Using the stick blender, process the brown crab meat until smooth, adding the sauces and brandy after 30 seconds. Continue mixing until perfectly smooth. Transfer to a small bowl and gently stir in the breadcrumbs until well incorporated. Season with the salt. Depending on the time of year, the emulsion may need more breadcrumbs or water to arrive at a consistency that can be piped or spooned. Transfer to the piping bag and set aside. (You'll have more sauce than you need, but it's difficult to make in smaller amounts.)

Now onto the crab. In a medium bowl, combine the crème fraîche with the chives and lemon zest. Add the white crab meat and stir gently to coat. Season to taste, adding a squirt of lemon juice, if you so desire.

To assemble the salad, begin by laying out 4 plates on a work surface. Place the ring mould in the centre of the first plate. Spoon one-quarter of the white seasoned crab meat into the mould, using the back of the spoon to pat the crab down evenly before removing the mould. Arrange one-quarter of the cucumber slices in a circle around the crab to form a 'crown'. Next, artfully lay 4 lettuce leaves, one-quarter of the radish slices, 2 cherry tomato halves and 1 quail egg around and atop the crab. Repeat with the other 3 plates.

To finish, carefully pipe a few small dollops of the brown crab emulsion around each plate, then sprinkle 1 tablespoon of the spiced crumbs in a few places. Drizzle a little lemon oil around the cucumber and finish with a few plumes of chervil, pea shoots and samphire.

Warm Pretzel, Goats' Cheese, Butternut Squash

Not exactly a sandwich, more like the perfect comfort snack, typically these pretzels sit on a wooden board and can often be seen shared by two people in the Fumoir with late-afternoon drinks. A note to pretzel aficionados around the world: this is not technically a pretzel because the recipe doesn't include a bicarbonate of soda or lye bath before baking. For the sake of ease, we have skipped the alkaline bath and have gone straight to the baking. The pretzel will be a little less chewy than you might expect from an authentic pretzel, but just as tasty.

SERVES 8 (MAKES 4 PRETZELS)

YOU WILL NEED:
stand mixer fitted with the dough hook
2 baking sheets, lined with baking paper
pastry brush
wire rack
baking tray
potato ricer
electric hand mixer

FOR THE PRETZELS:
500g (1lb 2oz) plain flour, plus extra for
    dusting
250ml (9fl oz) ice-cold water
20g (¾oz) fresh yeast, crumbled, or 6g (¼oz)
    instant yeast
14g (½oz) coarse sea salt
25g (1oz) cold unsalted butter, cubed, plus
    extra for greasing
1 egg, beaten with a pinch of salt, for the
    eggwash

FOR THE SQUASH:
1 tbsp vegetable oil
240g (8½oz) butternut squash, peeled,
    deseeded and roughly diced
25g (1oz) sage, finely chopped
sea salt

FOR THE GOATS' CHEESE MOUSSE:
240g (8½oz) goats' cheese, rind removed,
    crumbled with your fingers
80g (2¾oz) cream cheese
a dash of freshly ground white pepper

Start by making the pretzel dough. Combine the flour, measured water, yeast, salt and butter in the stand mixer. Mix on low-medium speed until a dough begins to form, about 3 minutes, adding small spritzes of water as needed if the dough looks too dry and crumbly.

This dough needs to be kneaded by hand, so transfer it to a clean, flour-free surface and knead, using the ball of your hand to stretch it away from you, then fold it back in over itself towards you. Turn the dough a quarter-turn and repeat this back-and-forth motion followed by a quarter-turn in a calm and rhythmic fashion for 10 minutes, until a smooth elastic dough has formed. Set a timer and just relax into the kneading! Transfer the dough to a lightly floured bowl, cover with clingfilm and leave to rest 15 minutes.

Divide the dough into 4 equal pieces, using a knife or a pastry scraper. Cover 3 of the 4 pieces with clingfilm so a skin doesn't form on the surface, making it harder to work with.

Shape the first piece of dough into a ball shape. Working with the ball of dough resting on a clean surface, gently curl your fingers over the ball and begin to roll the dough in circles to form a tight smooth ball: push the ball with the palm of your hand as you roll away and, as you roll back, curl your ring finger and little finger around the base of the ball of dough, gathering it in, until, eventually, after a few complete circles, a seamless ball has formed. (If you find the ball of dough slipping on your work surface, oil the surface very slightly to cause some friction.) Wrap the ball with clingfilm and set aside. Repeat the shaping with the remaining balls, again covering with clingfilm.

Next, shape each of the balls into logs: turn the first ball you shaped upside down so the seam is now facing up, press the ball down on the surface with your palm to flatten it, then bring the top part of the circle into the middle and press down, then roll it over the bottom part of the circle, forming a log. Roll a few times like you rolled playdough as a child, using the palm of your hands and the base of your fingers to roll the log back and forth, until the log is about 20cm (8 inches) long. Cover with clingfilm and leave to rest while you shape the remaining balls into logs.

Take the first log you shaped and roll it out into a rope of dough about 90cm (35 inches) long, leaving the central part a little thicker than the rest of the rope (this is the 'belly' of your pretzel). Be patient, you want to be gradually stretching the dough out using only pressure applied from the top, not pulling the dough out to the sides.

To shape the pretzel, hold up each end of the rope in each hand, letting the 'belly' of the rope rest on the work surface, then twist the ends of the rope around each other once and lower them on to the rest of the pretzel, pressing the ends on either side of the 'belly'. Transfer to a prepared baking sheet and make any necessary adjustments to round out the pretzel. »

100g (3½oz) Tomato & Chilli Jam (*see* below)
a handful of Crispy Shallots (*see* page 88)
20 watercress pluches (leaves only)

Repeat with the remaining logs. Cover the pretzels with a well-buttered sheet of clingfilm, then leave to prove in a warm place for 45–60 minutes – the timing will depend on how quickly you worked the dough, how much it warmed up while you worked on it and how warm your kitchen is. Now's a good time to preheat the oven to 220°C (425°F), Gas Mark 7. To test if the pretzels are proofed, poke one gently with your index finger: if the dough bounces back slowly when pushed in a little, and feels light and airy, it's ready for baking. Discard the clingfilm. If the pretzel stills feels dense to the touch, wait a little longer.

Using a sharp serrated knife, make a slash in the outer part of the pretzels' bellies (which will give them a nice spring in the oven), then gently brush the pretzels with the eggwash. Bake for 25 minutes, until golden brown. Transfer to a wire rack to cool.

While the pretzels cool, cook the butternut squash. Reduce the oven temperature to 180°C (350°F), Gas Mark 4. Heat the oil in a pan, add the squash and fry until golden brown. Transfer to a baking tray, cover with foil and cook for 30 minutes, or until soft. Remove from oven and using a ricer, mash the squash, then season to taste with salt. Scatter the sage atop.

To make the goats' cheese mousse, combine the goats' cheese and cream cheese in a bowl, then beat until smooth using an electric mixer. Mix in the pepper.

To bring it all together, slice the pretzels with a serrated knife. Dollop a few spoonfuls of the goats' cheese mousse onto 4 pretzel bottom halves (you could also pipe it, as we do, if you're feeling fancy). Dab a little of the chilli jam next to the mousse. Fill the gaps with the squash mash. Top with the Crispy Shallots and watercress leaves. Arrange the remaining 4 pretzel tops at a jaunty angle and serve – this is as rustic as we get!

Tomato & Chilli Jam

John Williams, Executive Chef at Claridge's from 1994 to 2004, started a tradition of giving cookery books as gifts to the kitchen brigade. This tradition lives on here and in the kitchens of The Ritz, which John now leads. In 1997, John gave me Peter Gordon's Sugar Club Cookbook, and we've used this recipe ever since. From the moment I first tried it, I knew I had to have a jar of it in the refrigerator at all times, hence we're giving you more than you need for the pretzel recipe (see above and page 70). This jam is great on fried eggs, lamb or pork, in a Montgomery Cheddar sandwich, or brushed over bruschetta with some pungent slices of just-melted goats' cheese.

MAKES 500ML (18FL OZ)

YOU WILL NEED:
blender
500ml (18fl oz) sterilized jar

750g (1lb 10oz) very ripe organic tomatoes
2 long red Thai chillies or fresh cayenne
    peppers
4 garlic cloves, peeled
2 thumbs of fresh root ginger, peeled and
    roughly chopped
285g (10oz) unrefined golden caster sugar
90ml (3fl oz) red wine vinegar

Dice half the tomatoes into very small pieces, skin and all, and set aside. In a blender, purée the remaining tomatoes, the chillies, garlic and ginger until smooth. (I recommend you don't strain the purée to remove the tomato seeds because they provide the pectin that will help the jam set, while the chilli seeds add some necessary heat.)

Combine the tomato purée, sugar and vinegar in a tall-sided pot or saucepan, then bring to the boil over a medium heat, stirring slowly and continuously. When it comes to the boil, reduce the heat to low and add the reserved tomatoes. Skim off any foam and cook gently for at least 1 hour, and up to 1½ hours, stirring every so often to release the solids that settle on the bottom of the pan. Be sure to scrape the sides of the pan during cooking so that the entire mass cooks evenly. The jam is cooked when it looks thick and is no longer runny – it should sit firmly on a cold plate.

Transfer to the sterilized jar of your choice and cool to room temperature before refrigerating for later use. It will keep for up to 2 months.

Chicken Elixir

We receive nearly 90,000 guests over a year, and of those guests, there will be some who check in feeling unwell. We strive to make you feel your best, even when you're feeling the worst. We therefore always make sure to have this restorative elixir on offer. Making consommé from scratch is a three-day process for us, because we start by making the chicken stock and proceed from there. After the stock has cooled and been clarified, we heat the proteins in the broth carefully to create the famous 'raft' that will sift away all the impurities, before gently straining the consommé through a refining muslin cloth. There is a long line of chefs who have stood by our 10-gallon pot of consommé, nervous or confident depending on their level of experience. It is by the side of this old pot that chefs have had some of their proudest moments, when great flavour and clarity emerge from the clarification raft of minced chicken legs, vegetables and so many egg whites.

MAKES 1 LITRE (1¾ PINTS), SERVES 4

NOTE:
For the winter garnish, you'll need to pickle mushrooms ahead of time. To do so, bring 150ml (5fl oz) water, 100ml (3½fl oz) white wine vinegar and 30g (1oz) salt to the boil in a medium saucepan; add 200g (7oz) diced button mushrooms. Boil until the mushrooms are softened, about 2 minutes. Pour the mushrooms and liquid into a small jar and leave to cool, then refrigerate overnight.

YOU WILL NEED:
food processor
large, deep saucepan or stockpot
fine-mesh sieve lined with a muslin cloth

FOR THE CONSOMMÉ:
45g (1½oz) minced chicken legs
40g (1½oz) onion, cut into small dice
35g (1¼oz) leek, cut into small dice
35g (1¼oz) carrot, cut into small dice
260g (9¼oz) egg whites (from about 8–9 eggs), whisked to foam
1.5 litres (2¾ pints) Double Chicken Stock (*see* page 76)
coarse sea salt

FOR A WINTER GARNISH:
240g (8½oz) cooked spelt
200g (7oz) pickled mushrooms (*see* Note)
20 celeriac discs (of 2cm/¾ inch diameter), cooked in 200ml (7fl oz) Madeira until tender
200g (7oz) cooked chicken breast, diced
4 tsp chopped chives
chervil pluches

FOR A SUMMER GARNISH:
240g (8½oz) cooked orzo
80 small tomato dice
60 mini green and yellow courgette balls
200g (7oz) cooked chicken breast, diced
4 tsp chopped chives
chervil pluches

Combine the minced chicken, onion, leek and carrot in the food processor, blitzing until well combined and very finely minced. Transfer this mixture to the large saucepan or stockpot and whisk in the foamy egg whites.

Pour in the stock, mix well and slowly bring to a very gentle simmer over a medium-low heat, whisking very regularly to prevent any of the chicken and egg mixture sticking to the bottom of the pot. Reduce the heat to low and continue to simmer, without stirring now – the proteins will coalesce to form a 'raft' on top of the simmering stock. When the raft is fully formed, carefully poke a hole in the centre of it, using the handle of a spatula or wooden spoon, so you can see the stock simmering very gently. Cook for a further 30 minutes or so.

Strain the consommé: ladle the stock through the hole in the raft directly into the prepared sieve over a bowl, working one ladleful at a time and leaving the raft undisturbed. Transfer to a clean saucepan, season to taste with the salt and keep warm until ready to serve. (While consommé can be brought to the boil and reheated, one must be very careful because if it over-boils, it will become irreversibly cloudy. It can be refrigerated for up to 3 days, or frozen for up to 1 month.)

To serve, pack the spelt or orzo into a tidy mound in the centre of each shallow bowl. Next arrange the vegetable garnishes and chicken in each bowl. Pour 250ml (9fl oz) hot consommé into each bowl and garnish with chives and chervil. At Claridge's, we ladle the consommé table-side – be it in your room or in the Foyer.

Double Chicken Stock

A properly extracted and full-flavoured stock requires many steps and takes two days to make in the Claridge's kitchen. We realize you don't have our hefty turn-of-the-century copper stockpot or perhaps the patience to tend to bones and aromatics over several stages, so we're including this abbreviated recipe to get you the kind of chicken stock that will forever stop you from purchasing ready-made stock at the supermarket. Like any classic stock, it's free of salt, which allows you to reduce it and concentrate the flavours without over-seasoning your sauces. It's the basis for the Claridge's Chicken Pie, the Chicken Elixir, the Lobster Risotto and the Vichyssoise (see pages 168, 74, 80 and 78). If you have the room in your freezer and a second stockpot, you can confidently double this recipe and feel quietly smug about your reserves.

MAKES 5 LITRES (9 PINTS)

YOU WILL NEED:
large, deep stockpot
fine-mesh sieve
5 x 1 litre (1¾ pint) containers

1.5kg (3lb 5oz) chicken bones
1 large chicken, about 2kg (4lb 8oz)
1kg (2lb 4oz) onions, peeled and quartered
500g (1lb 2oz) celery, roughly chopped
500g (1lb 2oz) carrots, roughly chopped
3 bay leaves
2 thyme sprigs
20 peppercorns
bunch of flat-leaf parsley, washed
6 litres (10½ pints) water

Combine all of the ingredients with the measured water in a large, deep stockpot. Over a medium heat, bring to a very gentle simmer, then immediately reduce the heat to the lowest possible setting and simmer for 6 hours or overnight, uncovered. Skim any foam or impurities off the top of the stock at regular intervals. It's important, especially if you are going to be making Chicken Elixir (see page 74), for the stock never to come to a rolling boil.

Remove and discard the bones, chicken meat and aromatics. Strain the stock gently through a fine-mesh strainer into a large bowl, then transfer to the containers, leaving some space at the top for the stock to expand when frozen. Leave it to cool slightly, before refrigerating to cool completely. Once the fat cap has formed and risen to the top of the containers of stock (likely overnight), remove and discard the fat. The stock is now ready to be frozen until further use. It can be kept frozen for up to 3 months.

Right: The moment of truth. Checking the clarity of the chicken consommé pouring out of the spigot of our 10-gallon stock pot.

Vichyssoise with Smoked Eel

This is the classic potato and leek soup, served cold, but can also be served hot. We elevate it with smoked eel, lemon verbena oil and buttery rye croutons. When I first started at Claridge's, this soup would be presented in a large terrine on ice, rolled into the dining room on a grand wooden trolley. Today, we source our eel from Severn & Wye, a smokery in Gloucestershire that harvests the eels from the banks of the mighty Severn and Wye rivers. Their smoker is powered by a wind turbine. So there you have it: a classically French soup, topped with a sustainable British product. Très Claridge's kitchen.

SERVES 4–6

YOU WILL NEED:
high-speed blender
ice baths
coffee filter or muslin cloth

FOR THE LEMON VERBENA OIL:
100g (3½oz) fresh lemon verbena leaves
100ml (3½fl oz) neutral oil, such as
    grapeseed

FOR THE RYE CROUTONS:
300g (10½oz) goats' butter
4 x 1cm (½-inch) thick slices of dark rye
    bread, crusts removed and cut into
    1cm (½ inch) cubes

FOR THE VICHYSSOISE:
25g (1oz) salted butter
1 onion, finely chopped
400g (14oz) trimmed, cleaned and sliced
    leeks
400g (14oz) peeled Maris Piper potatoes,
    diced
400ml (14fl oz) Double Chicken Stock
    (*see* page 76), plus extra if needed
    (optional)
50ml (2fl oz) double cream
1 tsp sea salt
½ tsp freshly ground black
    pepper

FOR THE GARNISH:
100g (3½oz) smoked eel, skinned and
    excess fat removed, cut into small
    pieces
10g (¼oz) chives, finely chopped

To make the lemon verbena oil, bring a large pan of water to the boil, then plunge the verbena leaves into the hot water and blanch them for no more than 30 seconds. Drain and shake off any excess water. Combine the leaves with the oil in the blender and purée well.

Transfer the verbena oil to a bowl and rest it in the ice bath – this will set the chlorophyll and ensure the finished oil is a vibrant green. Refrigerate the oil mixture for 4 hours to infuse it, then strain through the coffee filter or muslin cloth and reserve. The herb oil can be made in advance and stored for up to 1 week.

For the croutons, heat the goats' butter in a frying pan over a medium heat. When it's foaming, add the bread cubes and cook until golden and crisp, about 5 minutes. Remove from the pan with a slotted spoon and drain and cool on kitchen paper.

Now for the vichyssoise. In a large heavy-based saucepan, heat the butter until foaming, then add the onion and leeks. Cover and sweat the vegetables until soft and translucent, about 8–10 minutes. Add the potatoes, stirring to combine, then pour in the stock and cream, add the salt and pepper and bring to the boil over a medium-high heat. Reduce the heat to low and simmer for 20–30 minutes until the potatoes are tender.

Transfer the soup to the (cleaned) blender and purée until smooth, adding water or stock as needed to adjust the consistency. Pour the soup into a large bowl set over a fresh ice bath, stirring occasionally. When the soup is no longer hot, refrigerate until completely chilled.

Ladle the soup into shallow bowls and garnish with the smoked eel, rye croutons, chives and a dash of verbena oil. You also, like us, could pour the vichyssoise table-side.

LEMON VERBENA

We started growing lemon verbena in our herb cabinet to be cut in front of guests for fresh tea. My chefs soon started stealing it to make lemon verbena oil (see above), or to give a true taste of spring and summer to any savoury (also see page 172). This herb actually flourishes in anyone's garden and will survive gaps of watering between days off. Fantastic combined with peas and mint.

Lobster Risotto

A mainstay of the menu for the last 30 years, this dish works both in winter (because of the creamy rice) and summer. It's decadent, warming and — besides the Claridge's Chicken Pie (see page 168) — it's our most popular dish. You'll need to make a lobster sauce before starting the risotto, but the sauce will keep refrigerated for up to two days. The lobster sauce recipe makes a little more sauce than you need, which only means that it will be there to be sopped up with bread for a midnight snack. You'll also need to have some Madeira sauce already made and tucked away in the freezer. If you don't have homemade chicken stock on hand, purchased stock is okay as long as it is sodium-free.

SERVES 4

NOTE:
You can either buy cooked lobster meat and shells from a fishmonger or buy 2 live lobsters and cook the meat and shell them yourself.

YOU WILL NEED:
**fine-mesh sieve lined with a muslin cloth
stick blender**

FOR THE LOBSTER SAUCE:
**180g (6½oz) lobster shells and legs (leftover
    from a cooked 670g/1lb 8oz lobster),
    cracked into even-sized pieces
2 tbsp vegetable oil
60g (2¼oz) unsalted butter, cubed
70ml (2½fl oz) brandy
90ml (3fl oz) white wine
70g (2½oz) mix of carrot, onion and celery,
    cut into small dice (mirepoix)
230ml (8fl oz) Double Chicken Stock (see
    page 76)
470ml (16½fl oz) double cream
sea salt and freshly ground black pepper**

FOR THE TRUFFLE SAUCE (MAKES
100ML/3½FL OZ):
**25g (1oz) salted butter
20g (¾oz) fresh black truffle, finely chopped
50ml (2fl oz) tawny port
50ml (2fl oz) Malmsey Madeira
50ml (2fl oz) Madeira Sauce (see page 207)**

FOR THE RISOTTO:
**1.6 litres (2¾ pints) Double Chicken Stock
    (see page 76)
1 tbsp vegetable oil
140g (5oz) unsalted butter**

To make the lobster sauce, in a heavy-based saucepan, roast the shells and legs in the oil over a medium-high heat until lightly caramelized, about 2 minutes. Add the butter and stir well. After about 1 minute, the butter will begin to foam. When it does, add one-third of the brandy and stir the shells a few times. Add the next third of brandy, stir for 1 minute, then add the final third. This helps the shells absorb the alcohol and pick up the flavour. When the brandy has almost completely evaporated, about 2–3 minutes, add the white wine all at once and cook over a medium heat until reduced, about 4 minutes.

Add the mirepoix of vegetables and stir for 1 minute. Add the stock and bring to the boil, then reduce the liquid by half, about 7 minutes. Next, add the cream and simmer gently, skimming the red fat from the sauce (or else it will be too greasy) every so often, and cook until just before coating consistency, about 12 minutes. Gently simmer for 3 minutes and leave to cool. Pass through the prepared sieve into a medium bowl. Discard the shells and aromatics. Buzz with the stick blender for 1 minute. Season to taste and set aside. You should have about 680ml (24fl oz) lobster sauce. (The sauce can be made ahead of time and will keep in the refrigerator for up to 2 days.)

Next, make the truffle sauce. In a small saucepan, heat the butter over a medium-low heat until foaming. Add the truffle. Reduce the heat to low and sweat for 4 minutes. Add the port and Madeira, then reduce slowly to half the original amount, about 10 minutes. Stir in the Madeira sauce, remove from the heat and cover.

Continue on with the risotto. First, pour the stock into a saucepan and bring to the boil, then reduce the heat to low.

Place a large heavy-based saucepan over a medium heat. Pour in the oil and 80g (2¾oz) of the butter. When the butter is foaming, add the onion and stir to coat, sweating until translucent, about 4 minutes. Add the rice, stirring it to glaze completely. Reduce the heat to medium-low and cook for a minute or so, stirring all the while, before adding a first generous ladle of stock. Once the liquid has been absorbed, add another ladle of hot stock, and keep stirring with each subsequent addition. Cook until the rice is tender, the mixture seems creamy and almost all of the stock has been incorporated, about 25 minutes or so. Reduce the heat to low.

Prepare the lobster emulsion. In a medium saucepan, combine the butter and measured water over a medium heat, whisking every once in a while. Keep warm over a low heat. Gently immerse the lobster meat in the emulsion and reheat for 2–3 minutes.

Next, add a small ladle of lobster sauce to the rice and stir. Stir in the Parmesan, remaining butter and salt and pepper, stirring until well combined, a further minute or so. The cheese will naturally thicken the risotto, so you may need to add a little more stock to loosen the risotto at this point.

70g (2½oz) onion, cut into small dice
400g (14oz) Arborio rice
100g (3½oz) Parmesan cheese, grated

FOR THE LOBSTER EMULSION:
226g (8oz) unsalted butter
250ml (9fl oz) water
2 whole lobsters, about 670g (1lb 8oz) each,
    cooked, tail meat and claws reserved,
    or about 500g (1lb 2oz) lobster meat
    in total

FOR THE GARNISH:
10g (¼oz) or 1 tsp finely chopped chives
12 pieces of picked rock samphire

Warm the lobster sauce, and, using the (cleaned) stick blender, blend until foamy. Warm the truffle sauce.

Divide the risotto among 4 shallow bowls. Drain the lobster meat and add equal amounts of lobster pieces to the rice. Ladle about 100ml (3½fl oz) foamed lobster sauce over and around the risotto in each bowl. Spoon the truffle sauce atop the lobster to finish, then garnish with a sprinkling of chopped chives and the samphire stalks.

Sunday Lunch
Roast Beef, Yorkshire Pudding, Creamed Leeks, Potatoes & Beef Jus

For as far back as anyone can remember, roast beef was carved on the trolley at Claridge's on Wednesdays, and, of course, for Sunday lunch. Although this tradition is now offered only upon request, we always keep cold roast beef as a larder item for sandwiches and cold cuts, so the skill of roasting large joints is still very much part of Claridge's daily repertoire. Our 'Cooking the Perfect Sunday Roast and Carving' masterclass is always in high demand, and it's a task I've handed over to Adam Peirson, my executive sous chef who hails from Yorkshire, so he naturally runs this workshop with great pride. It's only when I joined his family for lunch one day that I realized what serious business Yorkshire pudding is: the generations gathered around the table in anticipation of the 'Yorkshires' served straight from the oven before the beef 'so you get them at their best and really appreciate the flavour of the beef gravy,' Adam's grandmother explained. The roast beef is then carved at the table, served with beef jus, creamed leeks, roast potatoes, horseradish cream and, of course, more Yorkshires.

**SERVES 6, WITH LEFTOVERS
FOR SANDWICHES**

NOTES:
While the meat is resting, you have time to roast the potatoes. The Yorkshires can be cooked in the last 15 minutes before serving.

YOU WILL NEED:
roasting trays
digital thermometer with a probe
3cm (1¼ inch) deep, 20cm (8 inch) square baking tin or 4-hole Yorkshire pudding tray (for large puddings), or a 12-hole deep muffin tin (for individual puddings)

FOR THE ROAST:
4kg (9oz) rib of beef
150ml (5fl oz) vegetable oil
3 onions, halved
sea salt and freshly ground black pepper

FOR THE YORKSHIRE PUDDING:
250g (9oz) plain flour
5 large eggs
350ml (12fl oz) milk
beef dripping (from the roast)

FOR THE HORSERADISH CREAM:
80g (2¾oz) horseradish root, peeled and finely grated
160ml (5½fl oz) double cream

First, remove the beef from the refrigerator and let it come to room temperature while you prepare the batter for the Yorkshire pudding. In a large mixing bowl, whisk the flour, eggs and one-third of the milk to a smooth thick paste before gradually adding the rest of the milk (the mixture should lightly coat the back of a spoon). Give it a quick whisk and put it in a jug just before you need it so it's ready to pour into the tins. This can now rest at room temperature until go time – the longer it sits, the higher it will rise!

For the horseradish cream, stir the horseradish into the cream, then add salt to taste and mix well. Leave to stand for at least 15 minutes to thicken. Keep cool, or refrigerate if it's a warm day.

Preheat the oven to 150°C (300°F), Gas Mark 2.

Season the beef generously with salt and pepper and seal in the oil in a hot frying pan on all sides until browned. Place the onion halves in the roasting tray and sit the beef on top. Roast for 1 hour 40 minutes, or until the core temperature reaches 38°C (100°F) on the meat probe (which should be inserted into the thickest part of meat), then remove from the oven and leave to rest for 1 hour in a warm place while the internal temperature slowly rises to 54°C (129°F), aka medium-rare. If you prefer your meat medium-well, cook to 48°C (118°F), then rest while the temperature rises up to 65°C (149°F).

While the beef is roasting, start the beef jus. In a sauté pan, colour the beef trimming in the oil until well browned, then add the shallots and caramelize. Add the thyme and bay leaf, then the veal jus and gently simmer for 1 hour.

After removing the beef from the oven, increase the oven temperature to 220°C (425°F), Gas Mark 7. Then discard the onion and pour off most of the excess fat (the dripping) from the roasting tin and set aside for the roast potatoes and Yorkshires, reserving a little in the tin for flavour. Next, strain the beef jus base directly into the tin, discarding the trimmings, shallots and herbs. Over a medium heat on the hob, use a spatula to scrape off the roasting sediment on the base of the tin, and reduce the jus for 4–5 minutes. If the sauce seems too thin, add the cornflour and water paste to thicken slightly.

Bring the potatoes to the boil in a large pan of water over a high heat, then cook until the edges are soft, about 15 minutes. Drain and fluff up the edges of the potatoes by gently shaking the pan back and forth, then transfer the potatoes to a roasting tray and add half **»**

FOR THE BEEF JUS:

120g (4¼oz) beef trimmings

1 tbsp oil

40g (1½oz) shallots, sliced

1 thyme sprig

½ bay leaf

200ml (7fl oz) Veal Jus (*see* page 206)

1 tsp cornflour, mixed with a splash of water
(optional)

FOR THE POTATOES:

400g (14oz) Maris Piper potatoes, peeled
and cut into 2.5cm (1 inch) cubes

beef dripping (from the roast)

FOR THE CREAMED LEEKS:

30g (1oz) unsalted butter

120g (4¼oz) leeks, trimmed, cleaned and
thinly sliced

30g (1oz) plain flour

50ml (2fl oz) Double Chicken Stock (*see*
page 76)

50ml (2fl oz) double cream

40g (1½oz) peeled cooked carrots, halved
and then sliced

of the reserved beef dripping. Roast the potatoes until crispy and browned, about 35 minutes, shaking and turning them at the halfway mark.

While the potatoes are roasting and the meat is resting, make the leeks. Heat the butter in a heavy-based pan over a medium-high heat, add the leeks, cover with a lid and reduce the heat to low. Sweat until softened, about 5 minutes. Stir in the flour and cook for a further 5 minutes, then slowly stir in the chicken stock followed by the cream. Gently cook for 15 minutes, stirring regularly. Add the sliced cooked carrots, adjust the seasoning and keep warm.

When the potatoes are roasted, remove from the oven and set aside in a warm place. Increase the oven temperature to 250°C, or as high as your oven will go. The time has come to bake the Yorkshire puddings!

Pour the remaining half of the reserved beef dripping into the baking tin, pudding tray or muffin tin. Ensure they are evenly placed on the tray. Place in the oven until the fat starts to smoke, about 4 minutes. Carefully retrieve the tray from the oven and quickly divide the batter into your tin, filling to three-quarters of the way up with a good finger's-width left at the top for the rise. You'll hear the batter sizzle as it hits the hot fat. Immediately return to the oven.

Reduce the oven temperature to 180°C (350°F), Gas Mark 4. Bake for 15 minutes, until golden and risen: they should be baked enough to hold their structure but not too crisp. They are a joy served straight from the oven.

To serve, carve the meat (*see* page 86). Plate all together, and spoon the horseradish cream as a sauce for the beef.

The Art of Carving

At one time a gentleman's education would not be complete until he had mastered the art of carving. At Claridge's, we see nobility in both the butcher's and carver's roles: as there is nothing to carve if the meat is not of good quality or hasn't been cooked properly. Our advice to you about butchering meat is to defer to a local butcher whom you trust, someone you can ask for the appropriate cut, as outlined below. But back to carving. Once or twice a year we hold a Carving Masterclass in our kitchen. It is booked almost immediately, and the guests are often husbands whose wives have sent them, or wives whose husbands have sent them, or wives whose wives have sent them, or husbands whose husbands have sent them: we all want a partner who can carve the roast as we raise our glass and smile across the table. Here's how you can fulfil that duty with the deftness of a knight.

1 Select an appropriate cut of meat. This is where our friend the butcher comes in. Choose larger cuts of meat since they will be firmer, easier to carve and will lose fewer juices when cut. Meat with most of (or all) the bones removed will be easier to cut.

2 Let all roasts rest for at least 10 minutes before carving. This will not only increase the flavour of the meat, but also allow the roast to firm up.

3 Remove strings, skewers and so on in the kitchen, before you head out into the limelight.

4 Have your tools in order. It is best to use 2 knives: a long-bladed one for slicing and a short-bladed one for trimming and separating joints. Have a warm platter at the ready, and a pair of kitchen scissors. There you are, ready to go, knife in hand and all eyes on you.

5 Allow elbow room at the table. Always stand, never sit.

6 Carve uniform, attractive slices perpendicular to the grain of the meat.

Roast Beef Sandwich

This sandwich is the perfect consequence of Sunday Lunch (see page 82), if there are any leftovers.

MAKES 4

NOTES:
Both the brown butter (beurre noisette) and the Bordelaise butter are very useful to have on hand in your refrigerator: they can be used at any time to finish a sauce or risotto and add additional layers of flavour to the most simple of recipes, like scrambled eggs, for instance. Gram flour is a gluten-free flour made from chickpeas. We use it to dredge the shallots because it yields the crispiest and lightest of coatings.

YOU WILL NEED:
table-top deep-fryer or large, deep, heavy-based pan (*see* Notes on page 56)

8 brioche slices
10g (¼oz) sorrel leaves, shredded
750g (1lb 10oz) roast beef, thinly sliced
10g (¼oz) watercress, leaves picked

FOR THE BROWN BUTTER:
250g (9oz) salted butter, cubed
juice of ½ lemon

FOR THE BORDELAISE BUTTER:
500ml (18fl oz) red wine
300ml (10fl oz) beetroot juice
1 tbsp red wine vinegar
40g (1½oz) shallots, finely chopped
10g (¼oz) green peppercorns, finely chopped

FOR THE HORSERADISH CREAM:
100ml (3½fl oz) whipping cream
25g (1oz) horseradish root, peeled and finely grated
juice of ½ lemon
sea salt

FOR THE CRISPY SHALLOTS:
vegetable oil, for deep-frying
30g (1oz) shallots, thinly sliced
gram flour, for dredging

TO SERVE (OPTIONAL):
fried onions
mustard

First, make the brown butter. Heat the butter in a hot saucepan and cook it to the noisette stage (until it turns a light brown and releases a nutty scent). Remove from the heat and stir in the lemon juice, then transfer to a jar or container.

Next, make the Bordelaise butter. Heat the wine, beetroot juice, vinegar and chopped shallots in a saucepan over a high heat until reduced to a syrup consistency, about 5 minutes. Add the peppercorns to the reduction, then fold everything into the brown butter. Refrigerate for up to 2 weeks until needed.

To make the horseradish cream, carefully whip the cream in a small bowl just until it starts to leave a trail. Fold in the horseradish, lemon juice and salt. The acidity of the juice will also thicken the cream at this stage, so be careful not to over-whip and split the cream.

To make the crispy shallots, heat the oil to 150°C (300°F). Roll individual shallot strands in gram flour, then deep fry in the oil until golden and crisp, about 5 minutes. Remove with a slotted spoon and drain on kitchen paper.

Lightly toast the brioche. Spread Bordelaise butter on each slice of toast and cover with the horseradish cream. Add the shredded sorrel and layer the seasoned roast beef over the top, as thick as you like. Finish with the picked watercress leaves and the crispy shallots (not pictured but absolutely essential). Serve with fried onions and mustard, if liked.

Puff Pastry

We're not going to lie to you: making puff pastry is labour-intensive and requires care to weave the alternating layers of dough and butter. At Claridge's, it's the job of one man, our tourier François Grange, to make all the puff we need, and we need a lot (see page 20 for more on this). At a very busy time of the year like Christmas, we will make 145kg (320lb) of plain puff pastry per week. This doesn't include the 60kg (132lb) of puff for a week's worth of Parmesan Bar Snacks (see page 156) or special events. Don't be daunted: making your own puff pastry will absolutely yield a distinctly superior crust, and once you go through the process of making it and tasting it, you'll gain the confidence to make it again and again. This recipe makes a decent amount of puff because a number of our recipes call for it (Claridge's Chicken Pie, Venison Wellington, Salmon en Croûte, Mille-Feuille...see pages 168, 198, 94 and 130) and the dough can be portioned into smaller amounts that will keep for 3 months in the freezer.

MAKES 2.6KG (5LB 12OZ)

NOTES:

Making puff pastry is time-consuming because the dough needs plenty of resting and chilling time between the rolling and folding processes, which is key to great puff. As such, we recommend you start it the night before you need it (though it can be done from start to finish over a 12-hour period if you absolutely have to). You'll need a fairly large work surface for the rolling out of this amount of dough – a kitchen island or long counter are ideal.

YOU WILL NEED:

stand mixer fitted with the paddle
        attachment
palette knife or pastry scraper
sheet of baking paper or clingfilm, at least
        24cm (9½ inches)
rolling pin
pastry brush
23 x 33cm (9 x 13 inch) baking tray

FOR THE DÉTREMPE (PASTRY LAYER):
235g (8¼oz) cold unsalted butter, cut into
        1cm (½ inch) cubes
920g (2lb 1oz) strong white flour, plus extra
        for dusting
32g (1oz) sea salt
375ml (13fl oz) cold water

FOR THE BEURRAGE (BUTTER LAYER):
830g (1lb 13oz) unsalted butter, cold but
        softening, cut into 1cm (½ inch) cubes
280g (10oz) strong white flour

DAY ONE

Prepare the détrempe. Using a food processor or your fingertips, combine the butter, flour and salt together until the mixture resembles coarse breadcrumbs. Add the measured water and combine, kneading lightly to bring the dough together. Transfer the dough to a sheet of clingfilm and shape into a 20cm (8 inch) square, about 4cm (1½ inches) thick, then score the dough all over to prevent shrinking when you roll it out. Wrap tightly and refrigerate overnight or at least until chilled, about 2 hours.

Make the beurrage. In the stand mixer, on low speed, mix the butter and flour until completely combined, about 1 minute. Using a rubber pastry spatula or a short palette knife, transfer the plain flour and butter mixture to the sheet of baking paper or clingfilm. Using a pastry scraper or your spatula, shape the mixture into a thick, neat 23cm (9 inch) square. Wrap in the paper and refrigerate overnight or until chilled, about 2 hours.

DAY TWO

An hour before you intend to roll, remove the beurrage square from the refrigerator to soften slightly. Take the détrempe square out 10 minutes before rolling time.

On a lightly floured surface, roll the dough square into a larger 35cm (14 inch) square. Place the butter square diagonally in the centre of the dough square. Fold the corners of the dough square over the butter square: they should meet neatly in the middle of the butter square. You can sprinkle a little water on the seams to seal this dough packet.

Lightly dust the length of your work surface with flour. Gently tap the dough packet all over with a rolling pin to soften it up slightly, then begin gradually rolling the pastry out away from you to a rectangle almost 3 times as long as it is wide, about 35 x 80–85cm (14 x 32–34 inches). Make sure you keep the corners square and edges as straight as possible by pressing a palette knife or pastry scraper against them to assist with that shaping as needed between rolls. Lift the dough occasionally to make sure it isn't sticking; flour the work surface again if necessary and sprinkle with more flour as you go, dusting away any excess with a pastry brush.

Fold the dough in thirds, like you would a business letter: take the short edge of the pastry furthest away from you and fold it down a third, then fold the bottom edge up a third to cover the first fold. Turn this rectangle of dough 90 degrees clockwise, which will bring the seam side to your right. »

Repeat the rolling out process, from top to bottom of the rectangle, making sure that the dough doesn't stick to the surface when rolling and that you're keeping the corners square and the edges straight, until the dough is about 3 times as long as it is wide. Again, fold as you would a business letter and rotate clockwise. The dough has now been rolled out and folded twice and is considered to have had 2 'turns'. Wrap tightly in clingfilm, place on the baking tray and refrigerate for at least 30 minutes, until firm again, but not so firm that it will impede your rolling. When you're working with puff pastry dough, it should always feel cool to the touch, and not start to become soft. If it does, return it to the refrigerator for 15 minutes or so to firm it back up.

Give the dough 2 more rolls and folds, making sure you rotate it 90 degrees clockwise between turns. (If you're finding the dough hard to roll out to a long rectangle, leave it to sit at room temperature for a few minutes until it becomes more docile.) Wrap and rest in the refrigerator for at least 1 hour, if not overnight.

If you've chilled the dough overnight, remove it from the refrigerator for 45–60 minutes before giving it a single turn. The puff pastry has now had 5 turns and can be portioned into smaller amounts (see individual recipes for specifics), wrapped tightly and frozen until ready to use; it will also keep in the refrigerator for 3–4 days, if you're planning on using it in the short term.

Salmon en Croûte

In the original Claridge's Restaurant, which was located adjacent to Davies Street, this sumptuous dish would be the Trolley du Jour meal every Friday lunch. We also served it for grand buffets in the Ballroom. Today, Claridge's Salmon en Croûte has a more formal and refined look; hens' eggs have been replaced with quail eggs, mushrooms turned into a creamy duxelles. The challenge, beyond the final assembly of the dish, is in the precision and uniformity of cuisson: to serve lovely crisp pastry, but keep the salmon pink and moist, and the quail eggs soft-boiled. While this is time-consuming to make, it can be assembled ahead of time and chilled overnight, then baked as your guests arrive. It remains a perfect dish to serve for a luncheon accompanied by copious amounts of Champagne.

SERVES 8–10

NOTES:

Success with this dish resides in the careful and steady preparation of the different components needed for the final assembly. You can complete your mise en place while food processor bowl and blade are in the freezer. To soft-boil quail eggs, bring water to the boil in a medium saucepan, gently lower the eggs into the boiling water, reduce the heat and simmer for 2 minutes 15 seconds. While the eggs are cooking, fill a large bowl with cold water and ice. Using a slotted spoon, transfer the eggs immediately to this ice bath.

YOU WILL NEED:

rolling pin
lattice pastry cutter
baking tray, lined with baking paper
food processor
ice baths
piping bag fitted with a plain piping tip
sheet of baking paper, cut to 10 x 24cm
    (4 x 9½ inches)
sheet of clingfilm, cut to about 13 x 30cm
    (5 x 12 inches)
offset spatula or palette knife
large sheet of baking or greaseproof paper
small tray
small baking tray, lined with baking paper
fine-mesh sieve
pastry brush
digital meat thermometer with a probe

First things first: on a lightly floured work surface, roll out both pieces of puff pastry to about 2mm (1/16 inch) thick: you should have a 35 x 50cm (14 x 20 inch) rectangle to wrap the salmon in, and a 20 x 30cm (8 x 12 inch) rectangle for the lattice. Cut the lattice pattern into the dough now. Transfer the 2 pieces of dough to the lined tray and refrigerate until needed, at least 2 hours.

Next, place your food processor bowl and blade in the freezer for 20 minutes.

In the meantime, if you haven't already, complete your mise en place: blanch the 150g (5½oz) and 250g (9oz) spinach leaves separately in a pan of boiling salted water, then transfer to an ice bath to cool. Squeeze dry and set aside. Soft-boil the quail eggs (see Notes, left), blanch the root vegetables, slice the mushrooms for the sauce...

Make the salmon mousse. Retrieve the food processor bowl from the freezer. Blitz the salmon cubes and egg white until completely smooth. Transfer the food processor bowl with the salmon to sit over a bowl of iced water and chill for 10 minutes.

Start the mushroom duxelles. Pat and squeeze the diced mushrooms hard in kitchen paper. Next, over a medium-high heat, sauté the mushrooms and shallots in a little oil and cook until much of the moisture has evaporated, stirring regularly, about 10–15 minutes.

Return to the salmon mousse: add the salt, white pepper and cayenne, and return to the processor base. With the motor running, slowly pour in the cold cream: the salmon should turn into a smooth mousse. Pulse in the chopped herbs and the small-diced vegetables. Transfer to the piping bag and refrigerate.

For the duxelles, in a medium saucepan, bring the cream to a boil and, over a low heat, reduce the cream by half, about 7 minutes. Combine the mushrooms and shallots with the cream, then adjust the seasoning as needed. At this stage, the duxelles mix should be firm. Transfer to a bowl and chill over an ice bath or refrigerate.

Lay the 10 x 24cm (4 x 9½ inch) sheet of baking paper down on a clean work surface with the long edge facing you. Next, place the cut sheet of clingfilm directly over the paper rectangle. Carefully arrange and overlap the 150g (5½oz) blanched spinach leaves to cover the baking paper rectangle. Using an offset spatula or palette knife, gently spread the mushroom duxelles over the spinach. Top and tail the quail eggs with a sharp paring knife, then arrange them in a tight line along the long bottom edge of the spinach and mushroom rectangle. Using the clingfilm for support, carefully roll up the spinach over the eggs to form a tight roll, about 24cm (9½ inches) long. Refrigerate for at least 20 minutes. »

plain flour, for dusting
1kg (2lb 4oz) + 600g (1lb 5oz) cold Puff
 Pastry (see page 90)

FOR THE SALMON MOUSSE:
150g (5½oz) salmon fillet, skinned, boned,
 cubed and chilled
1 egg white
¼ tsp sea salt
¼ tsp freshly ground white pepper
¼ tsp cayenne pepper
250ml (9fl oz) chilled double cream
5g (⅛oz) each of chives, chervil and tarragon,
 chopped
15g (½oz) mixed root vegetables (such as
 carrot, parsnip and swede), diced very
 small, blanched, drained and patted dry

FOR THE MUSHROOM DUXELLES:
250g (9oz) button mushrooms, finely diced
 (or blitzed in the food processor)
100g (3½oz) shallots, finely chopped
grapeseed or vegetable oil for frying
125ml (4fl oz) double cream

FOR THE QUAIL EGG, MUSHROOM AND
SPINACH ROLL:
150g (5½oz) large-leaf spinach, washed,
 stalks removed, blanched and patted dry
10 quail eggs, soft-boiled (see Notes on page
 94), shelled

FOR THE FINAL ASSEMBLY:
800g (1lb 12oz) piece of centre-cut, skinned
 and boned Atlantic salmon, about 24cm
 (9½ inches) long
6 sheets of spring-roll pastry (available in the
 freezer at Asian supermarkets)
250g (9oz) large-leaf spinach, washed, stalks
 removed, blanched and patted dry
2 egg yolks, beaten, for the eggwash
sea salt and freshly ground black pepper

FOR THE CHAMPAGNE SAUCE:
200g (7oz) sole bones, cleaned and chopped
 (ask your fishmonger to set these aside;
 you may need to call ahead)
50g (1¾oz) salted butter
200g (7oz) shallots, chopped
300g (10½oz) button mushrooms, sliced
300ml (10fl oz) dry white wine
200ml (7fl oz) Double Chicken Stock (see
 page 76)
200ml (7fl oz) double cream
handful of parsley stalks
60ml (2fl oz) Champagne

While the egg, mushrom and spinach roll is chilling, prepare the salmon for assembly. Cut the piece of salmon down its middle into 2 long equal pieces. Season the fillets. In a large nonstick frying pan, very quickly seal the pieces of salmon over a medium-low heat –you're not trying to cook it, just to have it shrink to final size somewhat. This can also be done in a steamer over boiling water. Drain on kitchen paper and refrigerate.

Now it's finally time to assemble! Lay a large sheet of baking or greaseproof paper on to the work surface. Arrange 6 overlapping sheets of spring-roll pastry on this to form a 30cm (12 inch) square. Lay the remaining spinach over the pastry sheets. Place one piece of salmon in the centre. Retrieve the salmon mousse from the refrigerator and pipe a line of mousse on to the salmon following the bottom length, and then repeat a line of mousse along the top length of the salmon fillet.

Carefully unwrap and discard the clingfilm from around the spinach, mushroom and quail egg roll, then lay this roll along the centre of the salmon between the 2 lines of mousse. Pipe more mousse over the top of the roll and then, using a palette knife, smooth the mousse all over to encase the roll. Lay the remaining salmon fillet carefully on top. Next, pipe a fair amount of mousse on to the top salmon fillet and then spread it into a thin layer.

With a sharp knife, cut 1 square out of each corner of the spring-roll pastry square (you're making flaps at each end of the salmon brick, which you can pull up over the salmon at each end). Lift the paper to lift up the spring-roll pastry to cover the salmon along one side, then repeat this on the other side to completely cover the whole thing. Flip on to a small tray and refrigerate, so it can firm up before being wrapped in puff pastry.

Lay out the larger sheet of cold puff pastry on a lightly floured surface, with the long side parallel to the bottom section of your surface. Remove the paper wrapping from around the salmon log, then place in the centre of the rectangle of puff pastry, with the long side of the log parallel to the bottom edge of your surface. Using a sharp knife, cut out the corners of the pastry so that you have two long sides and two short ends ready to wrap around the salmon log. Using the paper, fold one long side of the pastry up to the centre of the log and then lift the other side up to meet it. Brush the edges on each end of the log with the eggwash and fold in the ends of pastry to completely encase the salmon log. Flip over slowly so that the seam is on the underside of the log.

Next, gently stretch open the lattice dough, and use it to cover the log. Trim off any excess lattice if necessary. Transfer to the prepared baking tray and refrigerate for at least 2 hours.

To make the Champagne sauce, sweat the fish bones in the butter in a medium saucepan over a medium-low heat. Add the shallots and sliced mushrooms and cook until translucent but not browned. Add the wine and cook over a medium-high heat until reduced by half, about 5–7 minutes. Add the stock and simmer to reduce by half, a further 7 minutes or so. Add the cream and gently simmer over a low heat until the sauce coats the back of a spoon, about 20 minutes. Remove from the heat, add the parsley stalks and leave to rest for 20 minutes. Strain the sauce, stir in the Champagne and keep warm until serving time.

Preheat the oven to 260°C, or as high as your oven will go. For the final step before cooking, brush the dough with eggwash. (For extra browning, you can return the salmon to the refrigerator for 10 minutes, then eggwash a second time.) Insert a meat probe into the centre of the salmon en croûte before placing in the oven.

Bake for 15 minutes. Reduce the oven temperature to 190°C (375°F), Gas Mark 5, and continue to cook until the internal temperature has reached 38°C (100°F), about 30–35 minutes. Remove from the oven and leave to rest until the internal temperature rises to 52–55°C (126–131°F), about 20 minutes.

Slice the salmon en croute into 3cm (1¼-inch) thick portions and serve with the warm Champagne sauce on the side.

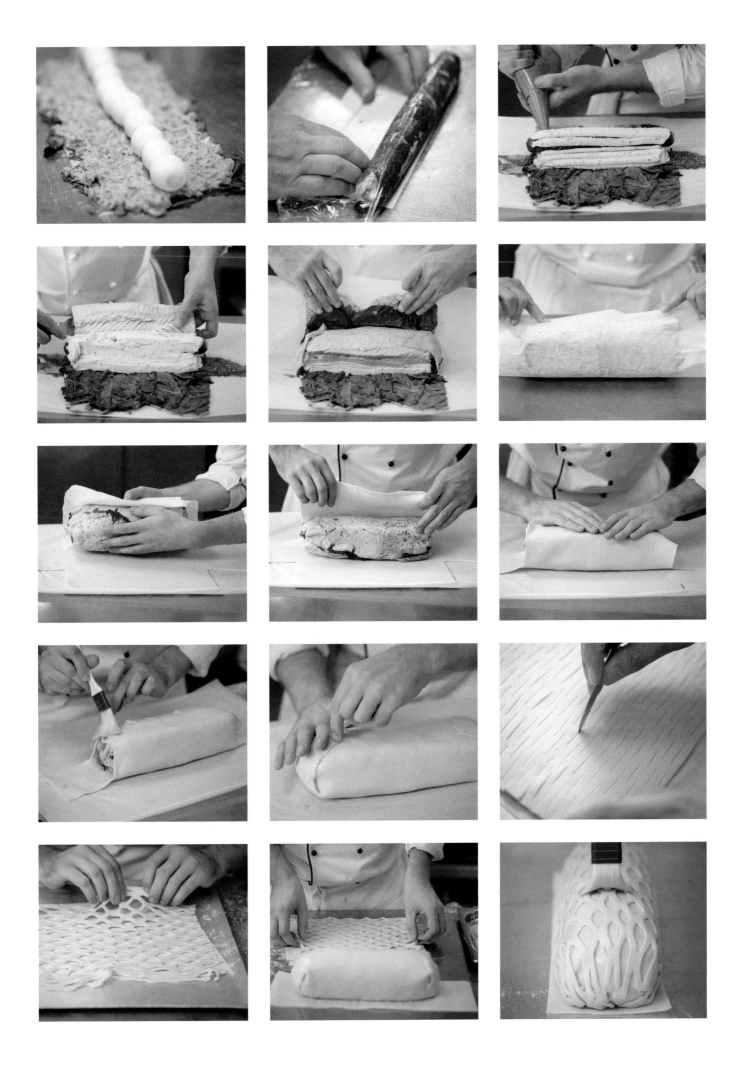

Roast Duck Breast
Red Cabbage & Quince
with Confit Duck Pies

The best duck, in my opinion, comes from La Dombes in southeastern France: it's corn-fed, has a beautiful even layer of yellow fat, cooks perfectly and consistently pink and is, of course, delicious. British producers do a great job of producing duck, but a La Dombes duck is, if you'll pardon the analogy, the Rolls-Royce of ducks. If you have trouble sourcing the duck, look for an equivalently sized Moulard duck or Muscovy duck. You can serve this with the goats' butter-roasted celeriac (see page 204), cut into small wedges.

SERVES 4

NOTES:

If you cannot beg, steal or borrow a press for the duck carcass and legs, place the rare meat and bones in several layers of muslin, squeeze very tight and press them manually, using a heavy pot. This recipe requires a total of 700ml (1¼ pints) Veal Jus (*see* page 206).

YOU WILL NEED:

fine-mesh sieve
food mill/mouli or potato ricer
roasting tray
digital thermometer with a probe
4 x 9cm (3½ inch), 200ml (7fl oz) ovenproof
    ramekins (we use mini copper
    saucepans)
large piping bag fitted with a star piping tip
meat cleaver and/or poultry shears
vegetable press (or *see* Notes above)
baking sheet

FOR THE BRAISED RED CABBAGE:

200g (7oz) red cabbage, finely shredded
80ml (2¾fl oz) red wine
20ml (¾fl oz) ruby port
90g (3¼oz) onion, grated
90g (3¼oz) apple, peeled and grated
1 tbsp cider vinegar
dash of ground cinnamon
60g (2¼oz) redcurrant jelly
sea salt and freshly ground black pepper

FOR THE CONFIT DUCK PIES:

2 duck legs
coarse sea salt
500ml (18fl oz) Veal Jus (*see* page 206)
500g (1lb 2oz) peeled Maris Piper potatoes,
    cubed
200–300ml (7–10fl oz) double cream

Let's begin with the cabbage, which needs long, slow braising. Combine all of the ingredients except for the redcurrant jelly in a heavy-based saucepan. Bring to the boil, then cover, reduce the heat to low and simmer, stirring every once in a while, until the cabbage is tender, about 2 hours.

Get the duck pies started. Season the duck legs liberally with salt, then place them in a flameproof casserole and cover with the veal jus. Bring to the boil over a medium-high heat, then reduce the heat to low and simmer until tender, about 1½ hours. Turn off the heat and leave the meat to rest in the sauce for a further 1 hour.

While the duck legs are braising and resting, boil the potatoes in a pan of salted boiling water until tender. In a small saucepan, bring 200ml (7fl oz) of the cream and 100g (3½oz) of the butter to the boil, then set aside. Drain the potatoes and pass through the food mill or potato ricer to mash. Gently fold the cream and melted butter into the potatoes, stirring well. Depending on the time of year and the age of your potatoes, these may need more or less cream to achieve mashed greatness. The texture should be smooth, velvety and able to hold its shape when piped. Add more cream as needed. Set aside.

Next, sauté the cèpes or porcini and shallots in the remaining butter until gently coloured. Stir in the parsley and set aside.

Preheat the oven to 250°C, or as high as your oven will go.

Start the caramelized quince. Peel and core the quince, then place in cold water mixed with the lemon juice. In a medium saucepan, bring the measured water and sugar to the boil and cook until the sugar is dissolved, about 2 minutes. Reduce the heat to low and add the lemon zest. Quarter the quince, add to the syrup and poach for 20 minutes, until tender. Remove with a slotted spoon. Set aside.

Now, place the whole duck in a roasting tray and insert the thermometer probe into the thickest part of the breast. Roast for 12 minutes in the hot oven. Reduce the heat to 190°C (375°F), Gas Mark 5, and roast for a further 10 minutes, or until the internal temperature registers 55°C (131°F). Remove from the oven and set aside in a warm place to rest for 40 minutes.

Continue with the duck pies. Lift the duck legs out of the veal jus, and using a fork or your fingers, pick away and remove the leg meat from the bone. Discard the bones and skin, but keep the braising liquid. In a medium bowl, mix the sautéed cèpes, shallots and parsley with the small cubes of foie gras and braised duck meat to combine. Portion into the ramekins, then spoon 2 tablespoons of the duck braising liquid over each.

Fill the piping bag with the mashed potato and pipe small rosettes to top each ramekin completely. Set aside. »

130g (4½oz) unsalted butter

50g (1¾oz) fresh or frozen cèpes, or 10g
    (¼oz) dried porcini, rehydrated

15g (½oz) shallots, minced

15g (½oz) flat-leaf parsley, finely chopped

30g (1oz) deveined foie gras, cubed

FOR THE CARAMELIZED QUINCE:

1 quince

strips of zest and juice of 1 lemon

500ml (18fl oz) water

500g (1lb 2oz) granulated sugar

2 tbsp salted butter

FOR THE DUCK BREASTS AND SAUCE:

1 La Dombes duck, about 2–2.5kg (4lb
    8oz–5lb 8oz)

2 tbsp vegetable oil

80g (2¾oz) shallots, minced

100ml (3½fl oz) red wine

150ml (5fl oz) brandy

100ml (3½fl oz) ruby port

8 green peppercorns

200ml (7fl oz) Veal Jus (*see* page 206)

10g (¼oz) deveined foie gras, cubed

TO SERVE:

Celeriac (*see* page 204)

Kale (*see* page 192)

Place the whole duck on a chopping board. Using a sharp knife, remove the legs at the hip joints and set aside. Carefully remove the breasts from the chest plate, angling the knife at a right angle to the bird and working in gentle strokes, using the breastbone as your guide. Set aside to keep warm.

Using the meat cleaver or poultry shears, break down the breastless carcass into pieces small enough to fit the vegetable press; separate the legs at the joint, then break them into smaller pieces. Working in batches, press the duck pieces to release their juices and blood. Skim any fat off the top of the bloody juices. Set aside.

Start the sauce. In a medium frying pan or saucepan, heat the oil over a medium heat, then cook the shallots until lightly coloured, about 5 minutes. Pour in the red wine, stirring to get any little crispy bits off the bottom of the pan. Add the brandy and reduce the heat to low; when the brandy is warm, light a match and carefully toss it into the pan. Stand back while the brandy is burning out, then remove the match. Add the port and bring to the boil. Next, add the peppercorns and the veal jus. Reduce by half over a medium-low heat, about 10 minutes. Set aside.

You're now in the home stretch. To finish the cabbage, fold in the redcurrant jelly, seasoning to taste. Keep warm.

Place the duck pies on a baking sheet and bake for 15 minutes, or until hot, then turn on the grill and brown the potato topping until golden and crisp. Set aside in a warm place.

While the duck pies are baking, finish the caramelized quince. Melt the butter in a sauté pan, add the quince quarters and sear over a medium-high heat until caramelized, about 5 minutes. Keep warm in the pan.

Bring the sauce for the duck back to the boil, then, over a medium heat, whisk in 125ml (4fl oz) of the duck blood until the sauce thickens slightly and becomes cloudy, looking almost like hot chocolate. Whisk in the foie gras cubes until dissolved. Check and adjust the seasoning. Reduce the heat to low. This sauce cannot be brought to a boil again because the blood will coagulate and turn it lumpy.

To serve, spoon a small amount of red cabbage into the centre of each plate, then lay 1 piece of caramelized quince next to the cabbage. Cut the duck breasts in half lengthways, on the bias. Arrange each half duck breast on top of the cabbage. Indulge with as much sauce as you like. Add a wedge of celeriac and a pile of kale and accompany each with a duck pie.

Right: Our Claridge's duck press. A marvellous piece of equipment that was first introduced to the world in the 19th century at La Tour d'Argent, Paris, where Canard à la presse is still served.

Afternoon Tea

Tea Sandwiches

At Claridge's, we've been observing this delightful aspect of our nation's culinary heritage for the best part of 150 years. For a century or more, all of the Executive Chefs have remained faithful to the classic combination of finger sandwiches, scones served warm and sweet pastries, accompanied by a remarkable selection of the world's finest loose leaf teas curated by our tea guru Henrietta Lovell. So we won't stop now. We're not providing sandwich recipes here, really, seeing as the two key aspects to a good sandwich are sourcing the product – the best-quality eggs, meat and breads – and cutting the sandwiches. Well, perhaps the cutting part is most key for us as we're serving 180 people per day. Please note, the quality and freshness of the bread is paramount and should always be your first consideration. Picking different breads to pair with your fillings also gets exciting: rye, malt, granary, brown, onion, plain white…these are just some of the breads we regularly use.

Claridge's Five Sandwich Rules:

1   A sharp serrated knife is crucial for cutting sandwiches. You'll need a knife with teeth that aren't too large (these will tear the bread). Something like a Victorinox 26cm (10½ inch) pastry knife is ideal.

2   A palette knife or spreader knife is crucial for spreading butters and jams.

3   Never let the bread dry out. Keep the slices covered at all times. We stack the sandwiches as we make them, placing the crust slices of the bread on the bottom and top of the pile to keep the bread just right. You could use clingfilm, or a damp clean tea towel.

4   The one-third rule! The perfect afternoon tea sandwich should be two-thirds bread and one-third filling.

5   Keep it even, keep it neat! We slice our loaves of bread lengthways (horizontally) into long rectangular slices, rather than vertically. This makes it easier to cut into rectangular fingers and reduces wastage. The bread should be evenly sliced, evenly topped with the freshest of fillings, then evenly cut and trimmed.

Poached Var Salmon, Garden Herb Mayonnaise on Rye Bread

Due to the volume of salmon we require, our fresh salmon is farmed. However, it is farmed by three brothers on the Faroe Islands between Scotland and Iceland, famed for being the finest salmon breeders in the world. The natural habitat, with exceptionally strong currents to swim against, provide the most real conditions with the highest welfare standards. For our Mayonnaise recipe, see right.

English Cucumber, Cream Cheese, Rocket on White Bread

Our cucumbers are grown organically in the heart of England, under glass or in the great outdoors, depending on the weather. As is traditional, the cucumber sandwich comes on a soft white bread, recalling the time when white bread was a culinary sensation thanks to 19th-century milling techniques.

FOR CLARIDGE'S CREAM CHEESE:
30g (1oz) cream cheese
5g (⅛oz) dill, chopped
3g (¹⁄₁₆oz) horseradish root, peeled and
   finely grated

Mix the cream cheese with the dill and horseradish. A nice flavouring for a mild vegetable such as cucumber.

Corn-Fed Chicken, Lemon & Thyme Mayonnaise, Walnut on Malted Bread

The chickens are naturally reared Cotswold White birds, which are given space and time to develop to produce a meat with great flavour and texture, perfect for our sandwiches. Once roast and carved, the chicken is lightly seasoned and served on malted bread with lemon and thyme mayonnaise (see right) and chopped toasted walnuts.

Breckland Brown & Clarence Court Egg Mayonnaise on White Bread

Both eggs are soft-boiled, then chopped by hand, turned with our homemade mayonnaise and finished with a good twist of pepper and pinch of mustard cress. The sandwich is served on fresh creamy white bread that is soft, yielding and very moreish.

FOR CLARIDGE'S MAYONNAISE:
1 large egg yolk
2 tsp Colman's mustard powder
3 pinches of salt, plus extra to taste
1 tbsp white wine vinegar
500ml (18fl oz) vegetable oil or rapeseed oil
dash of cayenne pepper

In a glass bowl, combine the egg yolk, mustard powder, salt and vinegar and whisk briefly to dissolve the salt. Whisking rapidly, add small drops of oil bit by bit, allowing the egg and oil to emulsify. Once you have added about one-quarter of the oil, the mixture will have begun to look like mayonnaise and you can add more oil faster. Add the cayenne pepper and adjust the seasoning to taste.

This mayonnaise can be used plain or further flavoured, such as with the addition of chopped chervil, tarragon and chives for pairing with salmon (see Poached Var Salmon, left) or lemon juice and chopped thyme to complement roast Corn-fed Chicken (see below left).

Dorrington Ham, Smoked Tomato Chutney, Watercress on Onion Bread

We purchase our hams directly from a small butcher in Dorrington, near Shrewsbury in Shropshire. Darren Sadd sources the pork from local farms. I first met Darren when visiting some friends in Shrewsbury who have an allotment, and I was so impressed with the flavour of the ham they had bought from Darren, that we had to go and visit. Any good-quality tomato chutney is a perfect pairing for ham. We also often serve our ham with a tarragon and mustard mayonnaise and a sliced tomato.

FLAVOURED BUTTER

We make a few flavoured butters for our sandwiches, such as mustard and redcurrant butter. We process cubed butter in the food processor until almost whipped but not quite. We then transfer it to a stand mixer fitted with a paddle attachment, add a little warmed/softened redcurrant jelly and some freshly toasted mustard seeds, and mix until incorporated. The butter will keep for up to 1 month refrigerated. I should state that we're starting with the best base, the handmade butter of Patrik Johansson and Maria Håkansson at Buttervikings. They use an ancient Swedish method of butter-making and it was during the Noma pop-up in 2012 that I was first introduced to them. They have since moved to the Isle of Wight and we are delighted to have them closer.

Claridge's Scones

This recipe is our timeless classic, carefully refined in our kitchen over generations. We offer two options: plain and with raisins. What makes the perfect scone is a much-debated topic around the UK: How big should it be? What's the ideal texture? What's the timing on the rise? Cracks or no cracks on the sides? The Devon way (cream first) or the Cornish way (jam first)? We serve more than 150,000 scones a year in the morning and at teatime, with Cornish clotted cream and Marco Polo tea gelée (a lip-smacking preserve of bergamot, strawberry, vanilla and pepper, made by our Parisian friends at Mariage Frères). And by the way, in our view, the cream goes on first followed by a teaspoon of jam. Of course, this is just our opinion, and the order of ceremony should always be to the guest's taste.

MAKES 12

NOTE:
We recommend you start this recipe the night before, so the flour and butter mix can be thoroughly chilled overnight.

YOU WILL NEED:
stand mixer fitted with the paddle
**   attachment**
rolling pin
5cm (2 inch) pastry cutter
baking tray, lined with baking paper
pastry brush

330g (11½oz) plain flour, plus extra for
**   dusting**
60g (2¼oz) caster sugar
1½ tbsp baking powder
¼ tsp salt
90g (3¼oz) cold unsalted butter, cubed
70g (2½oz) raisins (optional)
110ml (3¾fl oz) buttermilk
90ml (3fl oz) milk
1 egg, beaten with a pinch of salt, for the
**   eggwash**

In a large bowl, combine the flour, sugar, baking powder and salt, then add the butter and rub into the flour mixture with your fingers until you have a fine crumb (you could also pulse this 5–6 times in a food processor to achieve the same sandy texture, but it's almost as fast to work by hand). If you're making raisin scones, stir the raisins in now. Transfer to a smaller container, cover and leave to rest in the refrigerator overnight, or until thoroughly chilled.

The next morning, preheat the oven to 240°C (475°F), Gas Mark 9.

Transfer the butter and flour mixture to the stand mixer. Slowly mix in the buttermilk and milk until the dough comes together.

On a lightly floured surface, roll out the dough to form a circle, about 21cm (8¼ inches) in diameter and 2cm (¾ inch) thick, then cut out 12 scones using the pastry cutter. Transfer the scones to the prepared baking tray.

Using a pastry brush, carefully brush the tops with the eggwash. We like to let our scones sit out for 20 minutes at room temperature to give the baking powder a chance to activate before we bake them.

Bake until evenly golden, about 12–13 minutes. Leave to cool for 5 minutes, then serve warm.

We strongly suggest serving these only on the day of baking. Leftover scones can be frozen and will remain good for up to 3 weeks: as needed, defrost completely, then reheat in a preheated 180°C (350°F), Gas Mark 4 oven for 3 minutes.

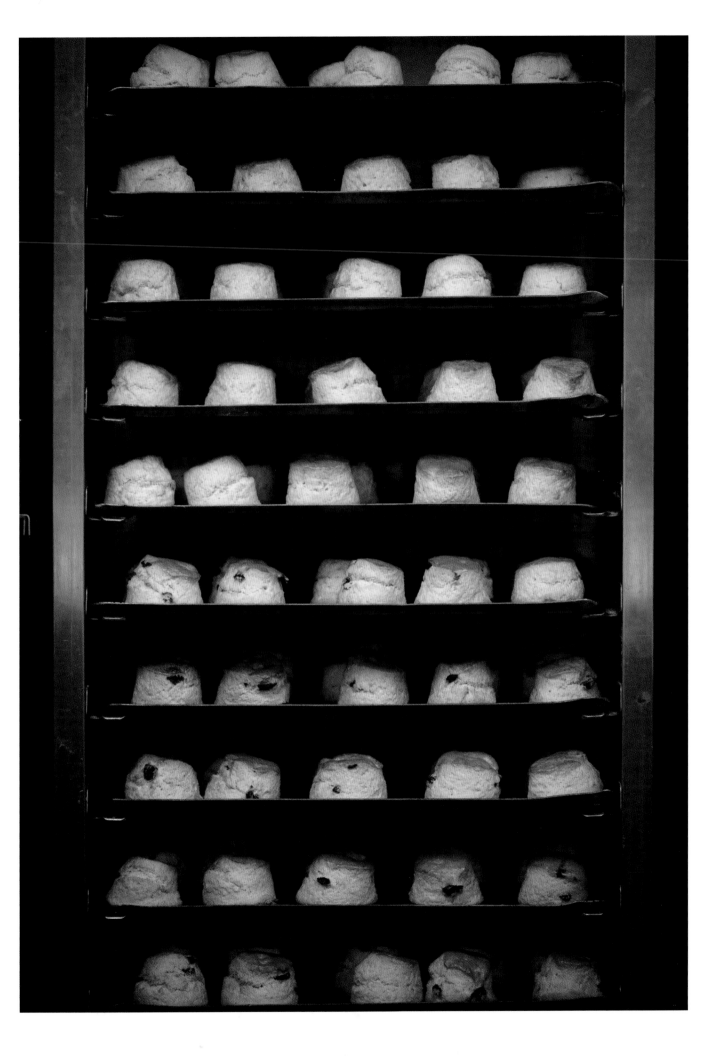

Marco Polo Bakewell Tart

This classic English tart is traditionally made with a sweet shortcrust pastry, a moist frangipane filling and raspberry or strawberry jam. But, at Claridge's, we love using a thin layer of Marco Polo tea gelée instead, and serve the tart with a dollop of Chantilly cream. This dessert comes together faster than you might think, because — contrary to popular belief — the pastry case does not need blind baking. The dough, pastry cream and frangipane can all be made ahead of time and refrigerated until you're ready to assemble the tart.

MAKES A 20CM (8 INCH) TART, SERVES 10–12

YOU WILL NEED:
stand mixer fitted with the paddle attachment
20cm (8 inch) tart ring or loose-bottomed tart tin
baking sheet, lined with baking paper
fine-mesh sieve
pastry brush

FOR THE SWEET SHORTCRUST PASTRY:
150g (5½oz) unsalted butter, cold but softening
90g (3¼oz) icing sugar
35g (1¼oz) ground almonds
1 egg
250g (9oz) strong white flour, plus extra for dusting

FOR THE PASTRY CREAM:
60g (2¼oz) egg yolks (about 3 yolks)
60g (2¼oz) caster sugar
10g (¼oz) pastry cream powder or custard powder
10g (¼oz) cornflour
200ml (7fl oz) milk
½ vanilla pod, split lengthways and seeds scraped
20g (¾oz) unsalted butter, softened

FOR THE FRANGIPANE:
125g (4½oz) unsalted butter, softened
125g (4½oz) icing sugar, sifted
280g (10oz) Pastry Cream (*see above*)
2 eggs
150g (5½oz) ground almonds
15g (½oz) pastry cream powder or custard powder
15ml (½fl oz) rum

Start by making the sweet pastry dough. Using the stand mixer, lightly cream the butter on low speed just to soften, about 1 minute. Add the icing sugar and ground almonds. Cream on low speed until combined. Add the egg. Mix until completely incorporated, stopping the machine to scrape the sides and bottom of the bowl with a spatula as needed. Next, add the flour and mix on low speed until it's almost completely incorporated.

Turn the dough out on to a clean work surface. At this point the dough may still seem a little crumbly: bring the crumb together and gently knead a few times until smooth – resist the urge to add flour if the dough feels sticky. Pat the dough flat into a disc that's about 3cm (1¼ inches) thick. Wrap tightly in clingfilm and refrigerate for at least 1 hour until firm. (The dough can be made up to 3 days ahead and refrigerated, or frozen for 2 months.)

While the dough is resting, proceed with the pastry cream and frangipane.

For the pastry cream: in a medium heatproof bowl, whisk the egg yolks, sugar, pastry cream powder and cornflour until smooth and lump-free.

In a medium saucepan, combine the milk, vanilla pod and seeds. Bring to the boil over a medium heat, then quickly remove from the heat. Discard the vanilla pod.

Slowly pour one-third of the milk into the egg mixture while whisking continuously. Pour the combined egg and milk mixture back into the saucepan with the rest of the vanilla-infused milk and whisk to combine. Bring to the boil over a medium heat, whisking constantly. As this custard starts to thicken, whisk vigorously to eliminate any lumps. Once the custard has started to boil, remove from the heat and whisk in the butter until smooth and completely incorporated.

Transfer to a clean bowl or container and place clingfilm directly on the surface to prevent a skin from forming as it cools. Refrigerate for an hour or more, until cooled. (The pastry cream can be made up to 3 days in advance.)

For the frangipane: in the (cleaned) stand mixer, lightly cream the butter and icing sugar for 1–2 minutes on low speed until just lightened. Add the pastry cream and mix until combined, stopping the machine to scrape the sides and bottom of the bowl with a spatula as needed. Next, gradually add the eggs and mix well at low speed until just combined. Add the ground almonds and pastry cream powder. Mix for 1 minute on low speed, again stopping the machine to scrape the sides and bottom of the bowl with a spatula as needed. Finally, pour in the rum and mix for a few moments longer. (The frangipane can be refrigerated for up to 3 days or frozen for up to 2 months.)

To assemble the Bakewell tart, place the tart ring on the prepared baking sheet. (If you're using a loose-bottomed tart tin instead, simply place the tin directly on to the baking sheet.)

On a floured surface, roll out the pastry dough into a 24cm (9½ inch) circle, large enough to fit the tart ring or tin. Lay the dough inside the tart ring or tin. Gently press the dough to the »

FOR THE FILLING:
70g–75g (2½–2¾oz) Marco Polo tea gelée, or any jam of your choosing
50g (1¾oz) flaked almonds

FOR THE APRICOT GLAZE:
150g (5½oz) apricot jam
2 tbsp water or lemon juice

FOR THE CHANTILLY CREAM:
250ml (9fl oz) double cream
75g (2¾oz) icing sugar, plus extra for dusting (optional)
½ vanilla pod, split lengthways and seeds scraped

sides, making sure the sides stand straight and the base lies completely flush on the baking paper or base of the tin. Using a sharp paring knife, trim any excess dough hanging over the edge. Refrigerate or freeze for 15–20 minutes, until firm.

Preheat the oven to 190°C (375°F), Gas Mark 5.

Using a spoon or palette knife, spread the jelly or jam evenly in the bottom of the chilled tart case. Next, spread over the frangipane, smoothing the top: the filling should just about reach the top of the sweet pastry case. Lay the flaked almonds artfully on top of the frangipane.

Bake for 30–35 minutes, until the frangipane is a light golden brown colour all over.

While the tart is baking, make the apricot glaze. In a small saucepan, melt the jam with the measured water or lemon juice over a medium heat, about 3–4 minutes. Strain the warm, now-liquid jam through the sieve to remove any pieces of fruit. Return the glaze to the saucepan to keep warm.

When the tart is cooked and still warm, using a pastry brush, generously paint the surface with the glaze. (Any leftover glaze will keep refrigerated for months.)

To make Chantilly cream, whip the cream with the sugar and vanilla seeds until soft peaks form (you can do this by hand or in the stand mixer). Refrigerate until ready to serve.

Serve the tart at room temperature, edges dusted with icing sugar if you wish. Remove the tart ring or tin, then cut into pieces and serve with a generous dollop of Chantilly.

Far right: Actress Merle Oberon overseeing our events team behind the scenes.

Lemon Drizzle Cake

A classic lemon cake, moist with the fragrant oil from the zest. We have included a recipe for two small loaves or three two-person round cakes (as pictured), mainly because it's practically impossible to not slice into the first right after baking. These cakes are versatile and can be served morning, noon or night, making them a constant not only in our Foyer but also in room service. We urge you to buy the best-quality lemons here. We love Italian Amalfi lemons that tend to be large and hence generous with the juice. We also love the fragrance of the lemons, which fills our kitchens while making this recipe.

MAKES 2 X 450G (1LB) LOAF CAKES OR 3 X 350G (12OZ) ROUND CAKES

NOTE:

The key to the moisture of this cake is zesting the lemons over the sugar and letting the oils from the peel infuse the sugar overnight, or for at least 6 hours. It's life-changing. Or at least, cake-changing. So...if you want to enjoy this cake with your tea, zest the night before.

YOU WILL NEED:

Two x 14 x 9 x 5cm (5½ x 3½ x 2 inch) loaf
    tins or three x 10cm (4 inch) diameter,
    7cm (2¾ inch) deep cake tins
baking paper (optional)
fine-mesh sieve
plastic dough scraper (you can use a knife but
    the scraper really works much better)
wire rack

FOR THE CAKE:

440g (1lb) caster sugar
3 lemons
125g (4½oz) unsalted butter, very soft, plus
    extra melted butter, for greasing
6 eggs
190g (6¾oz) crème fraîche
340g (12oz) plain flour, plus extra for dusting
    (optional)
½ tsp salt
1½ tsp baking powder
18ml (¾floz) rum (optional)
icing sugar, for dusting (optional)

FOR THE LEMON SYRUP:

100g (3½oz) caster sugar
100ml (3½fl oz) water
juice from the 3 zested lemons

To start, place the sugar for the cake in a large mixing bowl. Zest the lemons directly over the sugar, cover with clingfilm and leave to infuse for 6 hours or more. As you're zesting the lemons, have a thought for the Claridge's pastry chefs who have to zest 40–45 lemons each morning.

The next day (or later that evening), preheat the oven to 180°C (350°F), Gas Mark 4. Brush all sides of the tins lightly with melted butter, then line with baking paper or dust with flour. Set aside.

Add the eggs and crème fraîche to the mixing bowl with the sugar and lemon zest. Mix with a spatula until combined.

Sift the flour, salt and baking powder together twice. Stir the dry ingredients into the egg and sugar mixture, little by little, until smooth and lump-free.

Once all the flour has been incorporated, stir the very soft butter into the cake mixture. If using, add the rum. Stir the cake mix until smooth.

Divide the mixture evenly between the tins, making sure to leave at least 2-fingers room at the top of the tins. This cake will rise.

Meanwhile, make the lemon syrup. In a small saucepan, combine the sugar, measured water and lemon juice, then simmer over a medium-high heat for 4–5 minutes, until the sugar has dissolved. Do not let the syrup come to a rolling boil.

Using the plastic scraper, dip the edge in melted butter and, pressing down, drag a line across the top of the cake mixture. This helps to create a crack and bump along the cake when it is baking and a more even rise.

Bake for 45–55 minutes, or until a skewer inserted into the centre comes out clean. Remove from the oven and drizzle the cakes with the syrup. Leave to cool slightly in the tins for a few minutes before turning out on to a wire rack to cool completely. Dust liberally with icing sugar, if you wish. This cake will stay moist and fresh for up to 5 days.

Daisy Daisy

The Daisy Daisy is the creation of Nick Patterson, who was our pastry chef from 2002 to 2012. It's an uplifting combination of mascarpone, coconut dacquoise, mango jelly, silver meringues and, of course, those lovely pastillage daisies! The recipe that we used called for more than 30 vanilla pods for just 100 mini mousses. You won't need as many. Again, don't be intimidated — this entremets can be pulled off if you make the components over the course of several sessions.

MAKES ONE 20CM (8 INCH) MOUSSE CAKE, SERVES 10–12

NOTE:
You can order the speciality ingredients and professional pastry moulds from suppliers such as MSK Ingredients and the Home Chocolate Factory.

YOU WILL NEED:
shallow 16cm (6¼ inch) diameter silicone cake mould or Flexipan
mini-sphere silicone mould (with at least 3 indents) (for the jelly balls)
stand mixer, with whisk attachment and paddle attachment
4 baking trays, 3 lined with baking paper
2 piping bags, fitted with a 13mm (⅔ inch) and a 9mm (½ inch) plain piping tip
instant-read digital thermometer
fine-mesh sieve
mesh tea infuser
rolling pin
medium daisy cutter from a PME daisy plunger cutter set (of 3)
10mm (½ inch) plain piping tip
sheet of acetate the same size as the unlined baking tray, plus 1 strip long enough to line the mousse ring (listed below)
20cm (8 inch) metal mousse ring, about 4.5cm (1¾ inches) high
wire rack
spray gun and compressor

FOR THE EXOTIC JELLY:
5g (⅛oz) leaf gelatine
150g (5½oz) mango purée
50g (1¾oz) passion fruit purée
50g (1¾oz) banana purée
10g (¼oz) caster sugar

DAY ONE

To make the jelly, start by soaking the gelatine in cold water for 5 minutes, or until soft and pliable. In a small saucepan, combine the fruit purées and sugar. Bring to the boil, then immediately remove from the heat. Add the soaked and squeezed gelatine and stir until dissolved. Pour the still-warm purée into the silicone cake mould and place in the freezer until firm. Fill 3 indents in the mini-sphere mould with the remaining jelly and freeze.

Next, make the coconut dacquoises. Preheat the oven to 190°C (375°F), Gas Mark 5. Whisk together the icing sugar, desiccated coconut and almonds to remove any lumps. Set aside. In the stand mixer fitted with the whisk attachment, whisk the egg whites to very soft peaks on medium speed, about 3 minutes. Slowly add the caster sugar, continuing to whisk the whites at medium speed until all the sugar is added and you have a stiff meringue, about 5 minutes. Using a pen, trace 2 circles, 16cm (6¼ inches) in diameter, on to the paper lining 1 of the baking trays, then flip the paper over. Fold the icing sugar, coconut and almonds into the meringue and transfer to the piping bag fitted with the large tip. Starting in the centre, pipe a spiral of dacquoise mixture to form each circle: keep in mind the meringue will spread a little as it bakes, so leave about 5mm (¼ inch) to spare when filling the circles. Bake for 18–25 minutes, or until golden and crisp. Leave to cool on the tray. Wrap in clingfilm and keep at room temperature until ready to use.

Make the crème anglaise base for the vanilla mousse. Soak the gelatine in cold water as before. In a medium saucepan, bring the cream and vanilla to a simmer. In a large heatproof bowl, whisk the egg yolks and sugar together until pale yellow. Slowly add the hot cream to the yolks, whisking constantly to prevent scrambling. Return all the mixture to the saucepan and cook, stirring constantly, until the custard reaches 84°C (183°F). Remove the pan from the heat and discard the vanilla pod, then whisk in the soaked and squeezed gelatine. Pass through the sieve into a clean container. Lay clingfilm directly on the surface of the custard to prevent a skin from forming and chill until cool but not completely set, about 1 hour.

When the custard is cool, continue making the mousse. In the (cleaned) stand mixer now fitted with the paddle attachment, mix the mascarpone slowly until smooth, about 5 seconds. With the mixer still running, slowly add the anglaise base, stopping the machine to scrape down the sides of the bowl to ensure the mascarpone is fully incorporated.

DAY TWO

Make the silver meringues. Preheat the oven to 120°C (250°F), Gas Mark ½. Using a stand mixer and whisk attachment, whisk the egg whites until frothy. Add the caster sugar and whisk until the meringue has formed stiff peaks. Fill the second piping bag with the meringue and pipe teardrop shapes of meringue about 2–3cm (¾–1¼ inches) high on to the second paper-lined baking tray: apply a domed circle of meringue, no larger than a 50p coin, then drag the tip out and down to achieve the teardrop shape. When all the meringue is piped, dust lightly with edible silver glitter – a mesh infuser for tea works well for this job. Now dry the meringues in the oven for 40–60 minutes, or until completely dry. »

FOR THE COCONUT ALMOND DACQUOISE:

90g (3¼oz) icing sugar
25g (1oz) desiccated coconut
50g (1¾oz) ground almonds
100g (3½oz) egg whites (about 3–4 whites)
30g (1oz) caster sugar

FOR THE VANILLA MASCARPONE MOUSSE:

9g (¼oz) leaf gelatine
520ml (18fl oz) whipping cream
2 vanilla pods, split lengthways and seeds scraped
108g (3¾oz) egg yolks (about 5–6 yolks)
135g (4¾oz) caster sugar
475g (1lb 1oz) mascarpone

FOR THE SILVER MERINGUES:

50g (1¾oz) egg whites (about 1–2 whites)
100g (3½oz) caster sugar
edible silver glitter

FOR THE DAISY PASTILLAGE:

2g leaf gelatine
2 tbsp hot water
250g (9oz) icing sugar, sifted, plus extra for dusting
25g (1oz) cornflour
⅛ tsp distilled vinegar

FOR THE COATING:

200ml (7fl oz) liquid white cocoa butter, or you can use 200ml (7fl oz) plain cocoa butter melted with 10g (¼oz) fat-soluble white colour and then blitzed with a stick blender to fully dissolve the colour into the cocoa butter

Store in an airtight container.

To make the pastillage daisies, soak the gelatine in cold water as before, then squeeze out and dissolve in the measured hot water. Warm in the microwave if needed. Place the dry ingredients in a bowl, add the vinegar and warm gelatine water and mix together with your hands to create a soft smooth dough. If more water is needed add very sparingly, sprinkle by sprinkle until the correct consistency is reached – this should feel neither sticky nor dry. Knead the pastillage on a work surface to form a smooth dough. Lightly dust the surface with icing sugar, then working quickly, roll out the pastillage very thinly, no more than 3mm (⅛ inch) thick. Dip the daisy cutter in icing sugar before cutting out a daisy shape. Expel the shape on to the paper-lined flat tray, then cut out the circular centre with the 10mm (½ inch) piping tip. Repeat to make 6 daisies (you need 3 but make 6 in case you break any). Place in a dry warm area to dry for at least 24 hours.

To assemble the mousse cake, line the second flat tray with the sheet of acetate – moisten the tray slightly, then lay the acetate on to it, smoothing out any air bubbles. Place the mousse ring on the acetate and line the inside with the long strip of acetate so that it is overlapping. Ladle half of the mascarpone mousse into the ring, using the bottom of the ladle to spread the mousse out evenly. Lay the frozen disc of exotic jelly in the centre of the mousse, gently pressing it down, then lay a dacquoise disc directly on top of the jelly (it doesn't matter which side of the dacquoise is facing up). Ladle most of the rest of the mousse over the dacquoise, or enough to fill the ring just slightly below the top of the acetate. Press the final dacquoise disc into the mousse, bottom side up (don't worry if some of the cream oozes over the sides of the ring) and cover with the remaining mousse. Freeze overnight.

DAY THREE/FINAL TOUCHES

It's spray-painting time. Set up a spraying area as needed.

Unmould the frozen mousse cake from the ring, using your hands to warm up the metal ring to loosen the seal, peeling off the acetate strip. Place on the wire rack and spray with the white cocoa butter to cover completely, following the spray gun manufacturer's instructions.

Decorate the top of the mousse with the mini-sphere jellies and the pastillage daisies. Apply the silver meringues to the sides of the Daisy Daisy, pressing gently until they adhere.

Refrigerate for 2–3 hours to defrost before serving.

Pineapple
Coconut Tarts

Before she came to Claridge's, our pastry chef Kimberly Lin visited a 160-hectare (400-acre) farm on the Caribbean island of St Kitts. The desserts there included a lot of coconut, pineapple and rum, and lots and lots of sugar. Inspired by the experience, she brought this recipe with her to the hotel, and it surfaces on our afternoon tea menu when we're all in need of sunshine. Though Caribbean in flavour, this recipe is no vacation — it includes the following components: coconut frangipane, coconut mousse, pineapple compote, an exotic glaze and toasted meringue. However, if you focus on making a component or two a day, putting this dessert together won't feel stressful. The yield for the pineapple compote is deliberately generous, as it is completely sumptuous on vanilla ice cream.

MAKES 12

NOTE:

You can order the speciality ingredients and equipment from suppliers such as MSK, Classic Fine Foods or Amazon.

YOU WILL NEED:

stand mixer, with paddle attachment and whisk attachment
rolling pin
8cm (3¼ inch) plain pastry cutter
2 small trays, 1 lined with baking paper
instant-read digital thermometer
stick blender
disc of baking paper
4cm (1½ inch) demi-sphere silicone flexi mould (with at least 12 indents)
piping bag fitted with a 9mm (⅜ inch) plain piping tip
2 baking sheets, lined with baking paper
small kitchen blowtorch
fine-mesh sieve
12 x 6cm (2½ inch) tart rings or moulds (we use slope-sided for afternoon tea and straight-sided for buffets and working lunches)
palette knife
wire rack fitted over a baking tray with sides or a plate

FOR THE PASTRY:

1 x quantity cold Sweet Shortcrust Pastry (see page 112)
plain flour, for dusting

DAY ONE

Start by making and chilling the Sweet Shortcrust Pastry dough (*see* page 112).

To macerate the pineapple for the compote, scrape the seeds from the vanilla pod, then toss the pod and seeds well with the pineapple and demerara sugar. Mix well with your hands or a spoon. Cover with clingfilm and refrigerate for 24 hours.

Turn out the rested pastry dough on to a floured surface and gently roll out into a large circle about 3mm (⅛ inch) thick. Cut out 12 discs using the pastry cutter, then place on the lined small tray, cover tightly with clingfilm and refrigerate until ready to assemble.

Make and chill the Pastry Cream for the frangipane (*see* page 112).

DAY TWO

Make the frangipane. In the stand mixer fitted with the paddle attachment, lightly cream the butter and icing sugar for 1–2 minutes on low speed, until just lightened. Add the pastry cream and mix until combined, stopping the machine to scrape the sides and bottom of the bowl with a spatula as needed. Next, gradually add the eggs, and mix well at low speed until just combined. Add the ground almonds, desiccated coconut and pastry cream powder. Mix for 1 minute on low speed, again stopping the machine to scrape the sides and bottom of the bowl with a spatula as needed. Finally, pour in the rum and mix for a few moments longer. (The frangipane can be refrigerated for up to 3 days or frozen for up to 2 months.)

Next, finish the pineapple compote. In a medium saucepan, warm the macerated pineapple with all the juices it has released and the vanilla until lukewarm. Mix the pectin with the caster sugar. Stir the pectin and sugar mixture into the warm fruit. Bring the fruit to the boil and cook it for a few minutes until the temperature reaches 104°C (219°F), stirring frequently to ensure the compote isn't burning. Add the tartaric acid to the fruit and boil a little longer. Remove from the heat and discard the vanilla. Divide the hot compote into 2 containers or bowls, and, using the stick blender, carefully blend half the compote until smooth. Stir the smooth compote back into the chunky compote. Be very careful as you work: jam burns hurt! Place a disc of baking paper directly on the surface of the hot compote to prevent a skin from forming. Chill completely.

For the coconut mousse, soak the gelatine in cold water for at least 5 minutes, or until soft and pliable. Whip the whipping cream to soft peaks and set aside. In a small saucepan, heat half the coconut purée or coconut milk along with the sugar until hot and the sugar has dissolved. Add the soaked and squeezed gelatine and stir to dissolve. Combine the heated purée with the remaining coconut purée or milk. Whisk the crème fraîche into the coconut »

FOR THE PINEAPPLE COMPOTE:

1 Tahitian vanilla pod, split lengthways

500g (1lb 2oz) peeled and cored pineapple,
    cut into 1cm (½ inch) cubes

100g (3½oz) demerara sugar

2 tsp high methoxyl (HM) pectin or yellow
    pectin

16g (½oz) caster sugar

¼ tsp tartaric acid

FOR THE COCONUT FRANGIPANE:

1 x quantity Pastry Cream (see page 112)

125g (4½oz) unsalted butter, softened

125g (4½oz) icing sugar, sifted

93g (3¼oz) whole eggs (1–2 eggs)

100g (3½oz) ground almonds

50g (1¾oz) desiccated coconut

15g (½oz) pastry cream powder or custard
    powder

15ml (½fl oz) coconut rum

FOR THE COCONUT MOUSSE:

5g (⅛oz) leaf gelatine

185ml (6½fl oz) whipping cream

150ml (5½fl oz) coconut purée or coconut
    milk

40g (1½oz) caster sugar

90g (3¼oz) crème fraîche

20ml (¾fl oz) rum

150g (5½oz) unsweetened desiccated
    coconut, to decorate

FOR THE TOASTED MERINGUES:

50g (1¾oz) egg whites (1–2 egg whites)

100g (3½oz) caster sugar

FOR THE EXOTIC GLAZE:

110g (4oz) caster sugar

370ml (13fl oz) water

peel of ½ orange

peel of ½ lemon

½ Tahitian vanilla pod, split lengthways and
    seeds scraped

11g (¼oz) pectin NH or low methoxyl (LM)
    pectin

3 mint sprigs

juice of 1 lemon

purée, then fold in the whipped cream. Lastly, add the rum. Pour the mousse mix into 12 indents in the demi-sphere mould and freeze.

To make the toasted meringues, preheat the oven to 120°C (250°F), Gas Mark ½. Using the stand mixer fitted with the whisk attachment, whisk the egg whites until frothy. Add the caster sugar and whisk until the meringue has formed stiff peaks. Fill the piping bag with the meringue and pipe at least 12 teardrop shapes of meringue about 2–3cm (¾–1¼ inches) high on to 1 of the prepared baking sheets. When all the meringue is piped, lightly toast the meringue using the blowtorch. Now dry the meringues in the oven for 40–60 minutes, or until completely dry. Store in an airtight container.

For the exotic glaze, combine 105g (3¾oz) of the caster sugar, the measured water and the citrus peel in a medium saucepan. Add the vanilla pod and seeds, then warm until lukewarm (or 40°C/104°F). Mix together the remaining sugar with the pectin. Whisk the pectin mixture into the vanilla and citrus syrup and bring to the boil, whisking occasionally. Boil for 2 minutes, then add the mint and lemon juice. Boil for a further 1 minute. Remove from the heat and pass through the sieve into a container. Place clingfilm directly on the surface of the glaze and refrigerate until needed.

DAY THREE/ASSEMBLY

Preheat the oven to 190°C (375°F), Gas Mark 5. Place the tart rings on the second paper-lined baking sheet. (If you're using moulds instead, simply place the moulds directly on to the baking sheet.)

Lay a pastry disc inside each tart ring. Gently press the dough to the sides of the ring, making sure the sides stand straight and the base lies completely flush on the baking paper. Using a sharp paring knife, trim any excess dough hanging over the edges. Refrigerate or freeze for 15–20 minutes, until firm.

Spoon or pipe the frangipane into the prepared tart cases, filling each three-quarters full. Spread evenly and as flat as possible. Bake for 14–18 minutes, or until the tarts are evenly golden brown and the underside of the pastry is golden and crisp. Remove from the oven and leave to cool at room temperature.

When the tartlets have cooled, using a palette knife or a spoon, remove the tart rings, then spread the top of each tart with about 1 teaspoon of the pineapple compote.

Unmould the frozen coconut mousse domes on to the wire rack over the baking tray or plate. Gently reheat the exotic glaze in the microwave or a small saucepan, without boiling, until it is runny and lump-free. Ladle generous amounts of glaze over each dome.

To decorate the mousse domes, spread a generous layer of desiccated coconut on the unlined small tray. Slide a palette knife under each dome and transfer to the tray (flat side down). Using the palette knife, dab the edges around the base of each dome with the desiccated coconut.

Slide the palette knife under each dome and transfer to the top of each tartlet, placing the dome in the middle of each tart

Decorate each tart with a toasted meringue. Leave for about 40 minutes at room temperature or 1 hour in the refrigerator to allow the coconut mousse to defrost before serving.

Right: Our iconic Bernardaud
Galerie Royale china – eau-de-nil
for the Foyer and Reading Room,
and black tulip for tea in the Fumoir.

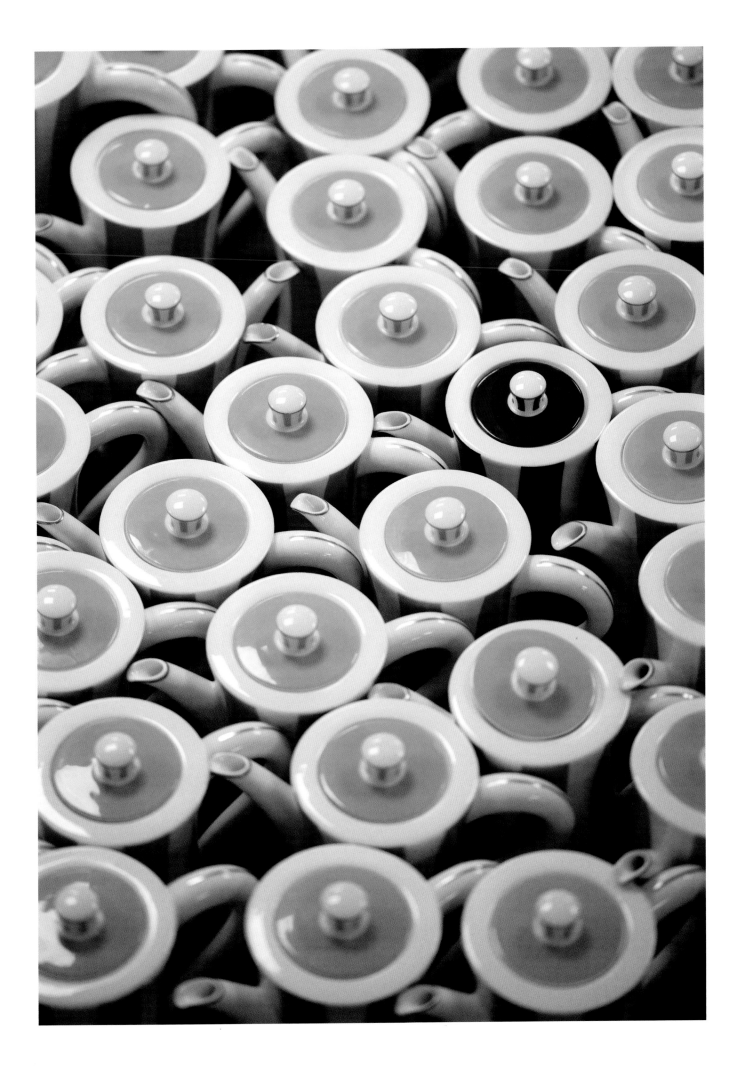

Blueberry Crème Fraîche Mousse

When we were narrowing down what to include in this cookbook, we deliberately chose many recipes that would be doable at home, dishes one could whip up in, say, an afternoon. This is not one of those recipes. In fact, it will take you three days to recreate this showstopper of a mousse cake. Don't be completely put off, though: the cake is made of mousse, jelly and meringue layers. If you pace your preparation and invest in some professional pastry moulds and a few speciality ingredients, you can conquer this mousse.

MAKES 1 X 20CM (8 INCH) MOUSSE CAKE, SERVES 10–12

NOTE:
You can order the speciality ingredients and professional pastry moulds from suppliers such as MSK Ingredients and the Home Chocolate Factory. If you're hesitant about investing in a spray gun, this cake doesn't need to be sprayed with purple cocoa butter. It can be served as a white mousse, decorated as per the picture.

YOU WILL NEED:
16cm (6¼ inch) diameter silicone cake mould or Fleximat
stand mixer, with whisk attachment and paddle attachment
2 baking trays, lined with baking paper
piping bag fitted with a 13mm (½ inch) plain piping tip
instant-read digital thermometer
fine-mesh sieve
flat tray
sheet of acetate the same size as the flat tray, plus one strip long enough to line the mousse ring (listed below)
20cm (8 inch) metal mousse ring, about 4.5cm (1¾ inches) high
wire rack
spray gun and compressor
mesh tea infuser

FOR THE BLUEBERRY VIOLET JELLY:
3 sheets of leaf gelatine
50g (1¾oz) raspberry purée
100g (3½oz) blueberry purée
drop of violet syrup
20g (¾oz) caster sugar

DAY ONE

Make the blueberry violet jelly. Soak the gelatine in cold water for 5 minutes, or until soft and pliable. In a small saucepan, combine the fruit purées, violet syrup and sugar. Bring to the boil, then immediately remove from the heat. Add the soaked and squeezed gelatine, then stir until dissolved. Pour the warm purée into the silicone mould and freeze until firm.

Next, make the dacquoise. Preheat the oven to 190°C (375°F), Gas Mark 5. Whisk together the icing sugar and ground almonds to remove any lumps. Set aside. In the stand mixer fitted with the whisk attachment, whisk the egg whites to very soft peaks on medium speed, about 3 minutes. Slowly add the caster sugar, continuing to whisk the whites at medium speed until all the sugar is added and you have a stiff meringue, about 5 minutes. On 1 of the prepared baking trays, trace 2 circles, 16cm (6¼ inches) in diameter, on to the paper using a pen, then flip the paper over.

Fold the icing sugar and almonds into the whites, then transfer to the piping bag. Starting in the centre, pipe a spiral of dacquoise mixture to form each circle: keep in mind the meringue will spread a little as it bakes, so leave about 5mm (¼ inch) to spare when filling the circles. Bake the dacquoises for 18–25 minutes, or until golden and crisp. Leave to cool on the tray and store at room temperature.

For the blueberry milk crumb, reduce the oven temperature to 135°C (275°F), Gas Mark 1. Mix together 40g (1½oz) of the milk powder, the flour, cornflour, sugar, salt and melted butter in a small bowl. It will be a clumpy, crumbly mix. Spread the crumble on to the second lined baking tray. Bake for 20 minutes. The crumbs should be very pale golden but cooked through. Remove from the oven and leave to cool completely. When completely cool, combine with the remaining milk powder. Gently toss the crumbs and freeze-dried blueberries in the melted white chocolate. Sprinkle the crumbs into a single layer on a piece of baking paper. Leave at room temperature to allow the chocolate to set. When the chocolate is set, store in an airtight container at room temperature.

DAY TWO

Make a crème anglaise base for the crème fraîche mousse. Soak the gelatine as before. In a medium saucepan, bring the cream and vanilla to a simmer. In a large heatproof bowl, whisk the egg yolks and sugar together until pale yellow. Slowly add the hot cream to the yolks, whisking constantly to prevent scrambling. Return all the mixture to the saucepan and cook, stirring constantly, until the custard reaches 84°C (183°F). Remove from the heat, discard the vanilla pod and whisk in the soaked and squeezed gelatine. Pass the custard through the sieve and into a clean container. Lay clingfilm directly on the surface of the custard to prevent a skin from forming and chill until cool but not completely set, about 1 hour. »

FOR THE ALMOND DACQUOISE:
90g (3¼oz) icing sugar
75g (2¾oz) ground almonds
100g (3½oz) egg whites (about 3–4 whites)
30g (1oz) caster sugar

FOR THE BLUEBERRY MILK CRUMB:
60g (2¼oz) milk powder
40g (1½oz) plain flour
12g (½oz) cornflour
25g (1oz) caster sugar
½ tsp Maldon sea salt flakes, crushed
55g (2oz) unsalted butter, melted
10g (¼oz) freeze-dried blueberries, crushed
90g (3¼oz) white chocolate, melted

FOR THE CRÈME ANGLAISE BASE:
9g (¼oz) leaf gelatine
520ml (18fl oz) whipping cream
1 vanilla pod, split lengthways and seeds
    scraped
108g (3¾oz) egg yolks (about 5–6 yolks)
135g (4¾oz) caster sugar

FOR THE CRÈME FRAÎCHE MOUSSE:
245g (8½oz) mascarpone
230g (8oz) crème fraîche

FOR THE COATING AND DECORATION:
200ml (7fl oz) liquid purple cocoa butter,
    or you can use 200g (7oz) plain cocoa
    butter melted with 10g (¼oz) purple
    fat-soluble colour and then blitzed
    with a stick blender to fully dissolve
    the colour into the cocoa butter
crystallized lemon peel
crystallized violets
edible fresh violets
blueberries
edible glitter

When the custard is cool, continue making the mousse. In the stand mixer fitted with the paddle attachment, mix the mascarpone and crème fraîche slowly until smooth, about 5 seconds. With the mixer still running, slowly add the anglaise base, stopping the machine to scrape down the sides of the bowl to ensure the mascarpone is fully incorporated.

To assemble the mousse cake, line a flat tray with acetate – moisten the tray slightly, then lay the sheet of acetate on to it, smoothing out any air bubbles. Place the mousse ring on the acetate and line the inside of the ring with the long strip of acetate so that it is overlapping. Ladle half of the crème fraîche mousse into the ring, using the bottom of the ladle to spread the mousse out evenly. Lay the frozen disc of blueberry violet jelly in the centre of the mousse, gently pressing it down, then lay a dacquoise disc directly on top of the jelly (it doesn't matter which side of the dacquoise is facing up). Ladle most of the rest of the mousse over the dacquoise or enough to fill the ring just slightly below the top of the acetate. Press the final dacquoise disc into the mousse, bottom side up (don't worry if some of the cream oozes over the sides of the ring) and cover with the remaining mousse. Freeze overnight.

DAY THREE/FINAL TOUCHES

It's spray-painting time. Set up a spraying area as needed. Unmould the frozen mousse from the ring, using your hands to warm up the metal ring to loosen the seal, and peel off the acetate strip. Place on the wire rack and spray with the purple cocoa butter to cover completely, following the spray gun manufacturer's instructions.

Decorate the top of the mousse with the blueberry milk crumb, crystallized lemon peel, crystallized violets and fresh violet flowers. Slice the blueberries in half, arrange them on top and dust with edible glitter.

Refrigerate for 2 hours to defrost before serving.

Below right: This emblem on the kitchen tile, dated 1988, marks a significant past refurbishment of the current kitchen at Claridge's.

Mille-feuille

Hélène Darroze — London's grande dame of French dining — can usually be found around the corner from us at her namesake restaurant at The Connaught. She'll occasionally pop in to the Foyer for tea with her daughters and her mother: 'My favourite time to have tea at Claridge's is Christmas with the special ambiance, the Christmas tree in the Lobby, the choir singing carols. . .then there is the Christmas pudding that I always receive as a gift from Martyn. Since arriving in London, I have never missed a Christmas afternoon tea at Claridge's. My daughters and I are crazy about the scones and we can eat a dozen of them! For my mother, the pastry team always makes her favourite, the mille-feuille. The secret to a good mille-feuille is, of course, its freshness, and you can easily see that the one at Claridge's is made à la minute.' A timeless French pastry — a triple-decker of caramelized puff pastry sandwiching rich pastry cream. While our menu showcases some of the best English ingredients, we must include certain continental classics. If you have some puff pastry lying around in your refrigerator or freezer, this treat is actually quite easily put together. These mille-feuille are bigger than those we serve at afternoon tea (pictured), so are perfect for sharing — or not.

**MAKES 6 GENEROUS PASTRIES
(EACH 10 X 4CM/4 X 1½ INCHES)**

YOU WILL NEED:
rolling pin
2 baking sheets, 1 lined with baking paper,
     plus additional sheets of baking paper
fine-mesh sieve
stand mixer fitted with the paddle
     attachment
piping bag fitted with a 13mm (½ inch) plain
     piping tip
small tray
palette knife

FOR THE MILLE-FEUILLE:
plain flour, for dusting
400g (14oz) cold Puff Pastry (*see* page 90)
icing sugar, for dusting
100ml (3½fl oz) whipping cream

FOR THE PASTRY CREAM:
500ml (18fl oz) milk
½ vanilla pod, split lengthways and seeds
     scraped
120g (4¼oz) egg yolks (about 7 yolks)
125g (4½oz) caster sugar
30g (1oz) cornflour
20g (¾oz) pastry cream powder (or custard
     powder)
50g (1¾oz) cold unsalted butter, cubed

Preheat the oven to 190°C (375°F), Gas Mark 5.

On a lightly floured surface, roll out the puff pastry into a rectangle about 25 x 38cm (10 x 15 inches) and 2mm (1/16 inch) thick. Transfer to the lined baking sheet and prick the dough every 1.5cm (approximately ½ inch) with a fork. Place a sheet of baking paper on top of the dough, followed by another baking sheet to 'dock' the pastry; this will prevent the dough from rising during baking.

Bake for a good 30–35 minutes, until the dough looks lightly golden, making sure the underside is also cooked. Remove from the oven, discard the top sheets of paper and dust the pastry generously with icing sugar, covering it completely. Turn your oven to its grill setting. Grill the sugared sheet of cooked pastry, checking very regularly, until the icing sugar has caramelized, 2–5 minutes (this could produce some smoke, so have your fan running). Remove from the oven and leave to cool.

While the pastry is cooling, make the pastry cream. In a medium heavy-based saucepan, combine the milk with the vanilla pod and seeds. Bring to the boil over a medium heat, then remove from the heat.

In a medium heatproof bowl, vigorously whisk the egg yolks and sugar until pale yellow in colour, about 2 minutes. Add the cornflour and pastry cream or custard powder, whisking until smooth.

Remove the vanilla pod from the milk and discard. Then, whisking continuously, slowly pour one-third of the hot milk into the egg and sugar mix to temper it. Slowly pour and whisk in the rest of the milk. Return this custard base to the saucepan. Over a medium heat, return to a simmer, whisking gently but continuously. Remove from the heat, then whisk in the butter until smooth and completely incorporated. Transfer to a storage container and lay clingfilm directly on the surface of the pastry cream to prevent a skin from forming. Refrigerate until completely cold, about 2 hours.

To assemble the mille-feuille, using a long serrated knife, trim the caramelized sheet of puff pastry to a 30 x 24cm (12 x 9½ inch) rectangle, reserving the trimmings. Next, cut the rectangle into three 10 x 24cm (4 x 9½ inch) strips. Crumble the pastry trimmings into flakes of caramelized puff pastry, making your own feuilletine flakes, and reserve. »

Whip the cream to stiff peaks. Using the stand mixer fitted with the paddle attachment, mix the cold pastry cream on low-medium speed to loosen it up. Fold in the whipped cream and transfer to the piping bag.

Place one of the strips of puff pastry on to a small tray, caramelized face up, and pipe 4 lines of pastry cream along the length of the strip, until completely covered in pastry cream. Gently but firmly press the next strip on to the layer of pastry cream, again caramelized face up, and again cover this strip with pastry cream. Lay the final strip of pastry on to the pastry cream, pressing gently. Don't worry about pastry cream oozing out of the sides: using a palette knife, smooth the cream out all along the sides, not being afraid to scrape against the edges of the strips of pastry to create smooth and even sides.

Dab the feuilletine generously along the long edges of the master mille-feuille – using your fingers, a flat spatula or a pastry scraper to apply them to the smoothed pastry cream.

Freeze for 45–60 minutes to firm up before cutting and serving. Do not attempt to cut the pastry from the top through to the bottom. Using a long serrated knife, turn the mille-feuille on to its side before cutting all the way through every 4cm (1½ inches) to make 6 mille-feuilles. Make sure you rinse and dry the blade of your knife between each cut.

Dust with icing sugar (we then add a chocolate disk printed with the Claridge's crest, but this is not essential) and serve.

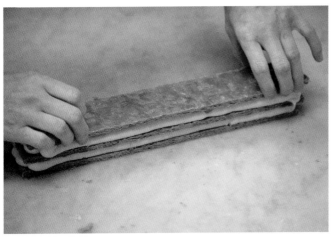

Taïnori
Chocolate Mousse

Taïnori is a chocolate made from rare cocoa beans from the Dominican Republic. The rich dark muscovado sugar paired with the elegant full-flavoured dark chocolate conjures up visions of palm trees waving in the warm Caribbean breeze and rum runners of yore. Again, this dessert, like the entremets on pages 118 and 126, can be prepared over the course of several days to yield a seemingly effortless dessert.

MAKES 12 INDIVIDUAL MOUSSES

YOU WILL NEED:
instant-read digital thermometer
stick blender
2cm (¾ inch) demi-sphere silicone flexi
 mould (with at least 12 indents)
baking sheet, lined with baking paper, or
 silicone baking mat
palette knife
stand mixer fitted with the whisk attachment
two 23 x 33cm (9 x 13 inch) Swiss roll baking
 trays, lined with baking paper
sheet of baking paper
5cm (2 inch) plain pastry cutter
6cm (2½ inch) demi-sphere silicone flexi
 mould (with at least 12 indents)
wire rack fitted over a baking tray with sides
 or a plate
edible bronze lustre spray

FOR THE MUSCOVADO CRÈME BRÛLÉE:
5g (⅛oz) powdered gelatine
2 tbsp cold water
85g (3oz) egg yolks (about 4–5 yolks)
70g (2½oz) soft dark brown sugar
5g (⅛oz) black treacle
170ml (6fl oz) whipping cream
170ml (6fl oz) milk

FOR THE DARK CHOCOLATE GLAZE:
8g (¼oz) leaf gelatine
100g (3½oz) Valrhona Taïnori dark chocolate,
 broken into pieces
90ml (3fl oz) water
90g (3¼oz) caster sugar
60ml (2¼fl oz) liquid glucose
60ml (2¼fl oz) whipping cream
35g (1¼oz) cocoa powder

DAY ONE

For the crème brûlée, sprinkle the gelatine into the measured water. Stir and leave to stand at room temperature for a few minutes. In a small heatproof bowl, combine the egg yolks, brown sugar and treacle. Lightly whisk until combined. In a small to medium saucepan, combine the cream and milk, then bring to the boil. Remove from the heat and slowly add the hot cream to the egg and sugar mixture, whisking constantly to prevent scrambling. Return all mixture to the saucepan and cook, stirring constantly, until the custard reaches 82°C (180°F). Remove from the heat and whisk in the bloomed gelatine. Using the stick blender, blend the custard for 1 minute while still hot to ensure the smoothest, silkiest crème possible. Fill the indents of the smaller flexi mould with the hot crème brulée mixture and freeze completely, for several hours or overnight. (This recipe makes more than you need: any extras can just be eaten or frozen for the next time!)

Next, make the chocolate glaze. Soak the leaf gelatine in cold water for 5 minutes, or until soft and pliable. Place the chocolate into a medium heatproof bowl. In a medium pan, combine the measured water, sugar, glucose, cream and cocoa powder. Bring to the boil over a medium heat, stirring occasionally. Remove from the heat and stir in the soaked and squeezed gelatine until dissolved. Pour the hot cocoa cream mixture over the chocolate. Using a spatula, stir in a circular motion until all the chocolate is melted. Next, transfer to a taller, narrower container and, using the (cleaned) stick blender, blend the glaze for 1–2 minutes until completely smooth. Place clingfilm directly on the surface of the liquid glaze to prevent a skin from forming and refrigerate until firm, at least 4 hours, but overnight or longer is best.

For the grue de cacao tuiles, preheat the oven to 160°C (325°F), Gas Mark 3. In a small saucepan, combine all the ingredients except the grue de cacao, and bring to the boil, stirring constantly with a wooden spoon or spatula. Remove from the heat and stir in the grue de cacao. Pour the mix on to the prepared baking sheet or baking mat. Using a palette knife or the back of a spoon, spread the tuile mixture in a thin layer. Bake for 12–15 minutes, or until the tuile has browned evenly and bubbling begins to subside. Remove from the oven and leave to cool completely. Break into smaller pieces and store in an airtight container.

DAY TWO

To make the sponge, preheat the oven to 200°C (400°F), Gas Mark 6. Using the stand mixer, whisk the egg whites on medium speed until very soft peaks form. (Whisking the egg whites on a slower speed takes longer but it produces a thicker more stable meringue.) While the machine is still running, slowly add the sugar. Continue to whisk the whites until they have formed firm stiff peaks. Remove the bowl from the machine and gently fold the egg yolks into the meringue. Once the yolks are incorporated, very gently fold in the cocoa powder and flour until combined. »

FOR THE GRUE DE CACAO TUILES:

20ml (¾fl oz) milk

60g (2¼oz) caster sugar

20ml (¾fl oz) liquid glucose

50g (1¾oz) unsalted butter

60g (2¼oz) grue de cacao (cacao nibs)

FOR THE CHOCOLATE ROULADE
SPONGE:

135g (4¾oz) egg whites (about 4–5 whites)

110g (4oz) caster sugar, plus extra for
   sprinkling

90g (3¼oz) egg yolks (about 4–5 yolks)

25g (1oz) cocoa powder

20g (¾oz) strong white flour

FOR THE TAÏNORI CHOCOLATE MOUSSE:

220g (8oz) Valrhona Taïnori dark chocolate,
   broken into pieces

4g (⅛oz) leaf gelatine

35g (1¼oz) beaten whole egg (less than 1 egg)

80g (2¾oz) egg yolks (about 4–5 yolks)

60g (2¼oz) caster sugar

40ml (1½fl oz) water

260ml (9¼fl oz) whipping cream

Divide the sponge mixture between the prepared Swiss roll trays. Using a large palette knife, spread it evenly to the edges of the tray. The sponge will be thin! Bake for 10–15 minutes, or until the sponge is soft but dry to the touch in the centre. (It is important to not overcook this sponge or it will be like a crouton, but also if it is undercooked it will never peel off the baking paper!) Working quickly, sprinkle the surface of the sponge with caster sugar and invert the sponge on to a new sheet of baking paper. Then, using a spray bottle or your fingers, spritz the paper that was on the base of the sponge (now facing you) with water. Gently ease the paper off, starting at one end. Cover the sponge with a clean tea towel and leave to cool completely. When the sponge has cooled, cut out 12 discs using the pastry cutter and set aside. Freeze any extra sponge as discs for next time, or spread with whipped cream, roll up and have a snack!

To make the chocolate mousse, melt the chocolate in a heatproof bowl placed over a saucepan of simmering water, or simply in the microwave. Set aside. Soak the gelatine in ice-cold water for 5 minutes, or until soft and pliable. In a heatproof bowl, combine the egg, egg yolks, sugar and measured water. Whisk gently to combine. Set the bowl over a saucepan of simmering water. Whisk frequently but not constantly, just to ensure the egg is not scrambling or sticking on the sides of the bowl. Cook the egg mixture until it reaches 82°C (180°F). Transfer the hot egg mixture to the (cleaned) stand mixer. Whisk on high speed until it has tripled in volume and the bowl is cool to the touch. While the sabayon (egg mixture) is cooling, warm 4 tablespoons of the cream in a small pan or the microwave. Dissolve the soaked and squeezed gelatine in the warm cream. Ensure the gelatine is fully dissolved and there are no lumps on the bottom of the pan or bowl. Whip the remaining cream to soft peaks and set aside. Pour a third of the cooled sabayon into the warm melted chocolate and stir in with a spatula until combined. Add another third of the sabayon and gently fold it into the chocolate mixture. When it is combined, add the remaining sabayon and the warm cream and gelatine mixture and fold in until completely combined. Next, pour half of the whipped cream into the chocolate sabayon and fold in to combine, then fold in the remaining whipped cream completely. Fill the larger dome moulds three-quarters full with the chocolate mousse. There will be a little extra mousse, which you should just pour into a glass to be enjoyed later.

To assemble the mousses, unmould the small domes of frozen crème brûlée. Push 1 frozen insert into each demi-sphere of chocolate mousse, bottom facing up. It should be in the middle of the mousse. Use the palette knife to smooth the mousse flat over the insert. Place 1 disc of sponge, applying gentle pressure to create a seal, on each mousse and freeze for a minimum of 4 hours. (Once the mousses are frozen solid, they can be unmoulded and stored in an airtight container and kept in the freezer for up to 3 months.)

FINISHING TOUCHES/DAY THREE

Warm the chocolate glaze either in the microwave or in a heatproof bowl placed over a saucepan of simmering water. When the glaze is warm enough to be completely melted (about 35–40°C/95–104°F), remove from the heat, and using the stick blender, fully submerge the blender in the glaze so the blade end is touching the bottom of the bowl or pan. Blitz the glaze, not moving the blender to create a centrifugal motion that pulls any air bubbles into the centre and smooths out the glaze. When all the air bubbles are gone, stop the blender and carefully remove it. Take the mousse domes out of the freezer and place them on the wire rack over the baking tray or plate to catch the excess glaze. Now ladle the glaze generously over each dome, allowing the glaze to cascade over the dome, covering it completely. Repeat, as needed, to ensure the domes are completely covered. Slide the palette knife under the dome and gently lift it off the rack. Place each dome directly on the plate it is to be served on. Transfer to the refrigerator and leave to defrost for 2–4 hours.

Just before serving, spray the domes with the edible bronze lustre spray. Snap pieces of tuile and place on the domes to decorate as you like. We also add a flourish of tempered chocolate, but you will enjoy this just fine without.

Lemon Meringue Éclairs

Everyone has a favourite classic pastry; a decision that's often taken very early in life. We see this in the faces of our guests who arrive for afternoon tea and excitedly scour the menu for their favourite afternoon treat. Rum Baba? St Honoré? Mille-feuille? We always try to have one variation on a classic on offer, and this one right here, a tea-sized éclair with the traditional choux paste, a zesty lemon curd and a wave of meringue, packs a punch in terms of textures and flavours.

MAKES 12 MINI ÉCLAIRS

YOU WILL NEED:

stand mixer, with paddle attachment and
    whisk attachment
rolling pin
small tray
instant-read digital thermometer
stick blender
piping bag fitted with 13mm (½ inch) plain
    piping tip
baking sheet, lined with baking paper
wire rack
large piping bag fitted with a 5mm (¼ inch)
    St Honoré piping tip
piping bag fitted with a small plain piping tip
kitchen blowtorch

FOR THE SABLÉ TOPPING:
40g (1½oz) unsalted butter
45g (1½oz) demerara sugar
45g (1½oz) soft white flour
8g (¼oz) ground almonds

FOR THE LEMON CURD (MAKES 500ML/18FL OZ):
140g (5oz) whole eggs (about 3 eggs)
150g (5½oz) caster sugar
zest of 2 lemons
100ml (3½fl oz) lemon juice
200g (7oz) unsalted butter, softened

FOR THE CHOUX:
125ml (4fl oz) milk
65g (2¼oz) unsalted butter
¼ tsp salt
¼ tsp caster sugar
65g (2¼oz) strong white flour, sifted
2 eggs, beaten

Make the sablé topping first. Combine all the ingredients in the stand mixer fitted with the paddle attachment and mix on low speed until well combined. Roll this paste out between 2 large sheets of clingfilm to a thickness of 2mm (1/16 inch). Set on the small tray and freeze for 30 minutes. Remove from the freezer and cut out at least twelve 7 x 3cm (2¾ x 1¼ inch) rectangles and gently transfer them to a small sheet of baking paper. Any remaining sablé dough can be discarded. Return these rectangles to the freezer.

Next, make the lemon curd. In a medium saucepan, combine all the ingredients except the butter. Whisking constantly, bring the mix to the boil over a medium heat initially, then reduce the heat to medium-low as you get closer to a simmer, about 5 minutes. By this time, the lemon mixture will be thick like custard. Once it starts to bubble, remove the pan from the heat and transfer the curd to a clean bowl. Place clingfilm directly on the surface of the curd to prevent a skin from forming. Insert a thermometer probe into the curd and leave to cool until it reaches a temperature of 60°C (140°F). Slowly incorporate the butter into the lemon curd using the stick blender. Continue to blend for 1 minute until the curd is silky smooth. Cover with clingfilm and refrigerate. (You'll be left with extra lemon curd after stuffing the éclairs – it will keep for up to 3 days in the refrigerator.)

Now turn to the choux pastry. In a medium saucepan, bring the milk, butter, salt and sugar to the boil. Remove from the heat and stir in the flour. Mix vigorously until the flour has been absorbed completely – it will look and feel like mashed potatoes. Cook over a low heat, stirring continuously for about 1 minute to cook the flour and remove excess moisture. (Don't worry about any starchy residue on the bottom of the saucepan.) Transfer the dough to the (cleaned) stand mixer fitted with the paddle attachment and mix on low speed for 2 minutes to cool slightly.

Preheat the oven to 190°C (375°F), Gas Mark 5.

Replace the paddle attachment with the whisk attachment, then mix in one-quarter of the beaten eggs at a time, whisking until well incorporated between each addition. The final dough will look shiny, smooth and soft.

Transfer the dough to the piping bag fitted with the 13mm (½ inch) tip. Pipe 12 or more fingers of choux, about 6cm (2½ inches) long, on to the prepared baking sheet. Lay 1 piece of frozen sablé topping directly on top of each éclair.

Bake for 30 minutes, or until the éclair shells are puffed, crisped and evenly browned. The sablé topping will have transformed to look like cracked earth – this is normal. Transfer to a wire rack and, using a sharp paring knife, poke a small hole in each end of the éclairs to release the steam as they cool. (Choux can be made in advance: once cool, these can be stored in an airtight container for 2 to 3 days.)

To make the Italian meringue, using the (cleaned) stand mixer fitted with the whisk attachment, whisk the egg whites on medium speed until foamy, about 1 minute.

Combine the sugar and measured water in a small saucepan. Bring to the boil over a high heat and cook. After about 5 minutes, when the thermometer registers 113°C (235°F), turn

FOR THE ITALIAN MERINGUE:
100g (3½oz) egg whites (about 3–4 whites)
200g (7oz) caster sugar
50ml (2fl oz) water

FOR THE DECORATION:
crystallized lemon peel
(we also add a chocolate disk printed with
the Claridge's crest and a twinkle of silver
leaf, but these are not essential)

the stand mixer back on, at high speed this time, and whisk the egg whites until they form medium-firm peaks, about 2 minutes. When the boiling syrup reaches 121°C (250°F), remove from the heat and let the bubbling subside for a few moments.

Now switch the mixer to a slow-medium speed and slowly pour the hot sugar syrup along the inside edge of the bowl into the egg whites, trying not to get any on the whisk, to avoid lumps. Increase the speed to high and whisk for 2 minutes to cool the meringue quickly, then decrease the speed to medium and continue to whisk until the bowl is lukewarm to the touch, a further 3 minutes. Transfer to the piping bag with the St Honoré tip.

To assemble the éclairs, fill the piping bag with the small plain tip with lemon curd. Insert the nozzle into one of the holes at the end of each éclair and fill with curd. Wipe off any excess curd that may have oozed out.

Next, using a plate or a work surface, practise piping the wave of meringue: you have plenty of extra meringue! When you're feeling ready, pipe a tight wave of meringue on top of each éclair. Using the blowtorch, toast the meringue very slightly, then decorate with a sliver of crystallized lemon peel. If you don't have a blowtorch, you can also flash the éclairs under a preheated grill for 1–2 minutes – just don't take your eyes off of them. These éclairs are best served immediately.

Claridge's Marshmallows

On any given day in our Foyer and Reading Room, you will find ribbons of coconut, passion fruit, blackberry and raspberry marshmallow coiled in glass jars on our sweets trolley. Though destined to be lightly toasted and served alongside our Claridge's Rich Hot Chocolate (see page 146), these are on offer to all of our guests. Marshmallows with a fruit base require invert sugar rather than glucose to set properly. The raspberry purée can be replaced with a fruit purée of your choosing: our favourites are strawberry, blackcurrant, passion fruit and coconut. We only use frozen fruit for our purées for the most consistent flavour. To make a purée at home, blend defrosted frozen fruit and strain this purée through a sieve.

MAKES 88–100

YOU WILL NEED:
fine-mesh sieve
23 x 33cm (9 x 13 inch) baking tray
    (a quarter-sheet with 2.5cm/1 inch
    sides works perfectly)
sugar thermometer or instant-read digital
    thermometer
stand mixer fitted with the whisk attachment
palette knife

FOR THE COATING:
50g (1¾oz) icing sugar
50g (1¾oz) cornflour

FOR THE MARSHMALLOWS:
vegetable oil, for greasing
275ml (9½fl oz) cold water
33g (1¼oz) powdered gelatine
320g (11¼oz) caster sugar
160ml (5¾fl oz) liquid glucose
330g (11½oz) dulce de leche or thick caramel,
    at room temperature
125ml (4fl oz) double cream
sea salt

Salted Caramel Ripple Marshmallows

To make the coating, pass the icing sugar and cornflour through the sieve into a small bowl and set aside. Lightly spray or gently brush the baking tray with oil.

Fill a small saucepan with 220ml (8fl oz) of the measured water, then sprinkle the powdered gelatine over the water, with a quick stir to ensure there are no lumps. Set aside to bloom for 2–3 minutes, or until the water has been absorbed. Over a low heat, warm the water and gelatine mix until the gelatine has dissolved completely. Remove from the heat.

In another small saucepan, bring the caster sugar and remaining water to the boil and cook until the temperature reaches 115°C (239°F), about 5–7 minutes.

While the sugar syrup is cooking, pour the liquid glucose into the bowl of the stand mixer. With the mixer on medium speed, stream the boiling sugar into the glucose. Stop the machine and add in the melted gelatine. Whisk on medium speed until the mixture starts to thicken slightly, like very softly whipped cream, about 3–4 minutes.

Increase the speed to high and whisk until the mixture becomes thick and fluffy, like rich shaving foam, about 3 minutes.

While the marshmallow is whisking, transfer the caramel to a large bowl. Warm the cream in a small saucepan or in the microwave (just until warm, not boiling), then add to the caramel. Combine well, adding sea salt to taste.

When the marshmallow mixture is thick and fluffy but the mixing bowl still feels warm to the touch, transfer half of the marshmallow mixture to the caramel bowl. Mix gently, then fold the caramel mixture back into the plain marshmallow mix and stir gently to create a ripple effect.

Pour the marshmallow mixture into the greased baking tray. Spread evenly using a palette knife or spatula. Dust the top of the marshmallow with a thin layer of the icing sugar and cornflour mix, reserving the rest for the final dusting. Leave the marshmallow to set at room temperature for a minimum of 6 hours.

When the marshmallow is set, turn out on to a chopping board. Dust the now-exposed underside with some of the reserved icing sugar and cornflour mix. Using a large knife, cut into desired shapes (we like 2.5cm/1 inch cubes) and transfer to a large bowl. Toss with the remaining icing sugar and cornflour mix to coat all sides. Tap off the excess sugar and store in a single layer in an airtight container. These will keep for 1 week.

YOU WILL NEED:
fine-mesh sieve
23 x 33cm (9 x 13 inch) baking tray
 (a quarter-sheet with 2.5cm/1 inch
 sides works perfectly)
sugar thermometer or instant-read digital
 thermometer
stand mixer fitted with the whisk attachment
palette knife

FOR THE COATING:
50g (1¾oz) icing sugar
50g (1¾oz) cornflour

FOR THE MARSHMALLOWS:
vegetable oil, for greasing
4 tbsp cold water
28g (1oz) powdered gelatine
300g (10½oz) caster sugar
140g (5oz) raspberry (or any other fruit)
 purée
255ml (9fl oz) liquid invert sugar

Raspberry Marshmallows

To make the coating, pass the icing sugar and cornflour through the sieve into a small bowl and set aside. Lightly spray or gently brush the baking tray with oil.

Pour the measured water into a small saucepan, then sprinkle the powdered gelatine over the water, with a quick stir to ensure there are no lumps. Set aside to bloom for 2–3 minutes, or until the water has been absorbed. Over a low heat, warm the water and gelatine mix until the gelatine has dissolved completely. Remove from the heat.

In a medium saucepan, combine the caster sugar, half of the raspberry purée and 105ml (3¾fl oz) of the invert sugar, stirring to moisten, then cook over a high heat until the temperature reaches 110°C (230°F), about 7 minutes.

While the raspberry sugar syrup is cooking, combine the remaining raspberry purée with the remining liquid invert sugar and the melted gelatine in the bowl of the stand mixer.

Stream the hot fruit sugar syrup into the mixing bowl. Whisk on medium speed until the mixture starts to thicken slightly, like very softly whipped cream, about 3–4 minutes.

Increase the speed to high, whisking until the marshmallow looks thick and fluffy like shaving foam, about 3 minutes. Keep whisking for a few moments longer, until the outside of the bowl feels warm – not hot – to the touch.

Pour the marshmallow mixture into the greased baking tray. Spread evenly using a palette knife or spatula. Dust the top of the marshmallow with a thin layer of the icing sugar and cornflour mix, reserving the rest for the final dusting. Leave the marshmallow to set at room temperature for a minimum of 6 hours.

When the marshmallow is set, turn out on to a chopping board. Dust the now-exposed underside with some of the reserved icing sugar and cornflour mix. Using a large knife, cut into desired shapes (we like 2.5cm/1 inch cubes) and transfer to a large bowl. Toss with the remaining icing sugar and cornflour mix to coat all sides. Tap off the excess sugar and store in a single layer in an airtight container. These will keep for 1 week.

Right: A meringue collective of (top to bottom) strawberry, mango and passion fruit, coconut, raspberry and more coconut.

Claridge's Rich Hot Chocolate

Great hot chocolate is as old as the hills. Well, in fact it dates back to Sir Hans Sloane who brought chocolate back from Jamaica in 1689. The milk was mixed with cocoa and was at the time believed to be a medicine. At Claridge's we still believe this to be true today. Our 70% Valrhona chocolate is blended with hot milk from Nemi Dairy farms, allowing Claridge's to pay their farmers a fair milk price by using their top-quality nutritious milk, rich in selenium. A guardian of the hotel and someone who knows it like the back of her hand is Paula Fitzherbert. Paula has been the director of PR for some 20 years now and guides the hotel and us all as you would your own children. In fact, her actual children have enjoyed this hot chocolate for many years. When we need a critical eye for detail — on all things, not just hot chocolate — Paula is our expert; after all, she was the instigator of The Berkeley's now iconic Prêt-à-Portea afternoon tea. On those days when you have back-to-back meetings, and there are only so many coffees you can consume, this hot chocolate is invaluable.

SERVES 4

200g (7oz) Valrhona Guanaja dark chocolate
(70% cocoa solids), broken into pieces
300ml (10fl oz) whipping cream
1 litre (1¾ pints) hot milk
marshmallows, to decorate

Melt the chocolate in a medium heatproof bowl placed over a saucepan of simmering water, or simply in the microwave.

In a small saucepan, bring the cream to the boil, then immediately remove from the heat.

Pour one-third of the hot cream into the melted chocolate. Using a spatula, stir briskly to incorporate the cream. The chocolate might look grainy and split at this point – don't worry! Repeat twice more, adding another third of the cream at a time. The chocolate should now be smooth and glossy.

This chocolate ganache can be used straight away or refrigerated for up to 5 days and reheated as needed (to reheat, warm gently in the microwave or in a bowl placed over a saucepan of simmering water until the ganache is hot and melted).

We serve our rich hot chocolate as a jug of hot ganache, a jug of frothy steamed milk and an empty mug, so each guest can mix their hot chocolate to their liking. Garnish with marshmallows, as desired.

Cocktails

Cocktails at Claridge's

Arctic Clarity

All Alps and smoke. We infuse our ice cubes with silver needle tea, a nod to Claridge's substantial tea offerings. Warning: this drink is full of flavour but still relatively clear, so the first sip always comes as a surprise.

SERVE IN A ROCKS GLASS

silver needle tea, for the ice cubes
50ml (2fl oz) gin
10ml (¼fl oz) pine liqueur
1 bar spoon (½ tsp) peated Scotch whisky
4 dashes of grapefruit bitters
twist of grapefruit, to garnish

First, brew a pot of silver needle tea. Pour into an ice cube tray and freeze overnight.

Place 4 tea ice cubes in a rocks glass, then pour in all the remaining ingredients. Stir well and finish with the grapefruit twist.

The Flapper

This cocktail was created when Claridge's Bar opened its doors in 1998. We just had to reference these daring 1920s women, forever linked to our Art Deco surroundings: the drink is a feminine blend of strawberry, cassis and Champagne.

SERVE IN A CHAMPAGNE FLUTE

3 strawberries, plus ½ strawberry, to garnish
15ml (½fl oz) crème de cassis
crushed ice
140ml (5fl oz) Champagne

Put the strawberries, cassis and a small scoop of crushed ice into a blender. Blend well and top with the Champagne, before pouring into a flute to serve. Garnish with ½ strawberry on the rim of the glass.

Little Mary

The Little Mary is inspired by the 1920s classic Mary Pickford cocktail: light rum, Maraschino, pineapple and grenadine. That cocktail was devised in Cuba by barkeep Fred Kaufman, while 'America's sweetheart' was on the island filming with Charlie Chaplin and her husband Douglas Fairbanks. Here we infuse Maraschino liqueur with whole star anise and add crushed rose pepper for an exotic twist.

SERVE IN A COCKTAIL GLASS OF YOUR CHOICE

1 tsp rose pepper
50ml (2fl oz) white rum
10ml (¼fl oz) star anise-infused Maraschino liqueur (1 pinch of ground star anise per 250ml/9fl oz) Maraschino liqueur)
1 tsp grenadine syrup
60ml (2fl oz) pineapple juice
3–4 ice cubes
1 dehydrated pineapple wheel, to garnish

Muddle the rose pepper in a cocktail shaker, then add the remaining ingredients with the ice cubes. Shake hard, then single-strain into a cocktail glass. Using a mini peg, attach the pineapple wheel to the rim of the glass and serve.

THE MOST EXPENSIVE MARTINI IN THE WORLD

Ask Lucas in the Fumoir to make you a Martini. Enjoy it. Ask Lucas to make you a second one. Enjoy it again. If you ask Lucas to make you a third Martini, you have no option but to stay at the hotel, thus making it the most expensive Martini in the world. Both the cocktail and the room will be worth it, though — fair warning.

Saffron Sidecar

A Sidecar is a Crusta reincarnated, a drink traditionally made with brandy, citrus, curaçao and finished with a sugar rim. The Fumoir has a long tradition of reinventing timeless classics and this is no exception. This take on the classic Sidecar is made ever more luxurious with the use of saffron-infused curaçao, combined with English pears.

SERVE IN A COUPETTE

¼ fresh pear
50ml (2fl oz) XO Cognac
25ml (1fl oz) lemon juice
25ml (1fl oz) saffron-infused curaçao (1 pinch of saffron per 750ml bottle curaçao)
3–4 ice cubes
1 slice of dehydrated or fresh pear, to garnish

Muddle the ¼ pear in a cocktail shaker. Add the remaining ingredients with the ice and shake hard. Double-strain into a coupette glass and garnish with the pear slice.

Champagne Cobbler

We wanted to create something new for our Champagne cocktail list that would stand out visually, so we arrived at this Cobbler, which is perfect in winter. The Cognac and port evoke log fires and after-dinner festivities, and it's the season for blackberries. The result is a rich, elegant cocktail that feels like mulled wine with a little fizz.

SERVE IN A HIGHBALL GLASS OR JULEP

1 orange wedge, halved
1 lemon wedge, halved
4 blackberries, plus 1 extra to garnish
crushed ice
20ml (¾fl oz) VSOP Cognac
20ml (¾fl oz) ruby port
10ml (¼fl oz) crème de mûre
25ml (1fl oz) Champagne
1 tsp simple syrup
2 dashes of orange bitters
1 cinnamon stick, to garnish

In a cocktail shaker, muddle the fruit, then add a little crushed ice, the Cognac, port and crème de mûre. Double-strain (using a tea strainer as well as a Hawthorne strainer) into a highball or julep glass, then add the Champagne, simple syrup and bitters and stir. Top up with more crushed ice. Garnish with the muddled fruit, a fresh blackberry and a cinnamon stick.

Tropical Morning Glory

In the 1888 edition of The Bartenders' Manual, *Harry Johnson cautions: 'The [Morning Glory Fizz] must be drank as soon as prepared, so as not to lose the effect and flavour. The author respectfully recommends the drink as an excellent one for a morning beverage, which will give a good appetite and quiet the nerves.' Because there's nothing like Scotch and absinthe to quiet the nerves! Our cocktail is a twist on the Morning Glory Fizz.*

SERVE IN A COCKTAIL GLASS OF YOUR CHOICE

45ml (1½fl oz) Irish whiskey
25ml (1fl oz) lime juice
15ml (½fl oz) orgeat syrup
2 drops of absinthe
2–3 ice cubes
1 x quantity Coconut Soda (*see* below)
coconut flakes, to garnish

FOR THE COCONUT SODA:
150ml (5fl oz) coconut water
1 egg white

First, make the coconut soda. Combine the coconut water and egg white in a soda siphon. Charge the siphon with carbon dioxide and shake well. Refrigerate until needed.

In a cocktail shaker, shake the whiskey, lime juice, syrup and absinthe with the ice cubes. Single-strain into a cocktail glass, then top up with the coconut soda. Garnish with coconut flakes.

Pictured overleaf, inside gatefold, from left to right: Claridge's Regal, Bee Pollen Crusta, Champagne Cobbler, Gougères (*see* recipe on page 157), The Bonnie Coll, The Flapper, Arctic Clarity, Coffee Boulevardier, Tropical Morning Glory, Parmesan Bar Snacks (*see* recipe on page 156), Little Mary, Saffron Sidecar.

Bee Pollen Crusta

The Bee Pollen Crusta is a twist on the famous Bee's Knees cocktail – a gin, lemon and honey classic that dates back to Prohibition. Back then, ingredients such as citrus and honey were often added to cover the less-than-ideal smell and taste of bathtub gin. Improving the taste of an inferior gin may have been the goal, but the result was a fantastic concoction that holds its own today. When the Fumoir first opened in 1998 – and there were just 4 tables – it served only Crustas.

SERVE IN A COUPETTE

1 tbsp bee pollen, plus extra for dusting
1 lemon wedge
45ml (1½fl oz) best-quality vodka
25ml (1fl oz) fresh mandarin juice
10ml (¼fl oz) Chestnut Honey Liqueur
    (*see* below)
15ml (½fl oz) lemon juice
15ml (½fl oz) dry vermouth infused with
    Roobois tea
3–4 ice cubes

**FOR THE CHESTNUT HONEY LIQUEUR
(MAKES 450ML/16FL OZ):**
200ml (7fl oz) honey
200ml (7fl oz) water
50ml (2fl oz) chestnut liqueur

To make the liqueur, combine all the ingredients in a jar. It can be kept for up to 1 month.

Place the bee pollen on a saucer. Wet the rim of a vintage coupette glass with the lemon wedge, then slowly run the rim of the glass in the bee pollen.

Combine all the remaining ingredients in a cocktail shaker with the ice, then double-strain into the coupette. Garnish with a dusting of bee pollen.

Coffee Boulevardier

A more sophisticated version of the Espresso Martini.

SERVE IN A COCKTAIL GLASS OF CHOICE (WE SERVE IN LONG-STEMMED RETRO COUPE)

30ml (1fl oz) rye whiskey
30ml (1fl oz) Campari
15ml (½fl oz) sweet vermouth
15ml (½fl oz) Oloroso sherry
1 coffee-infused ice cube

In a cocktail shaker, stir all the ingredients (except the ice cube) well. Single-strain into a vintage coupette glass over the ice.

Claridge's Regal

This cocktail was once declared GQ's cocktail of the month. We loved it so much that it's still being served today in Claridge's Bar

SERVE IN A HIGHBALL GLASS

50ml (2fl oz) blended Scotch whisky
25ml (1fl oz) white vermouth
1 tsp simple syrup
2 lemon wedges
2 orange wedges
5 ice cubes
½ passion fruit and pluck (sprig) of mint,
    to garnish

Combine all the ingredients in a highball glass, muddle gently and stir. Garnish with the passion fruit and mint.

The Bonnie Coll

Coll is Gaelic for 'hazel tree'. Hazels and their nuts have a firm place in Scottish folklore, dating back to the druids, who believed they imparted wisdom. The Bonnie Coll is a warming, sensual cocktail. It is prepared using The Dalmore 18, a veritable winter whisky. The Barolo Chinato, an Italian digestif, brings some very wintry spice flavours, including rhubarb, dates, cloves and five spice. We then add our homemade Port and Hazelnut Soda to the mix. This adds a sweet nuttiness to the cocktail, and we find the chocolatey orange whisky, hazelnut and spices come together to create something extremely wise and quaffable. Sláinte!

SERVE IN A GOBLET OR ROCKS GLASS

40ml (1½fl oz) The Dalmore 18yo Highland
    Single Malt Scotch Whisky
20ml (¾fl oz) Barolo Chinato
½ tsp chocolate bitters
25ml (1fl oz) Port and Hazelnut Soda
    (*see* below)
twist of orange, to garnish

FOR THE PORT AND HAZELNUT SODA:
650ml (23fl oz) port
100ml (3½fl oz) hazelnut liqueur

To make the soda, combine the port and hazelnut liqueur in a soda siphon. Charge the siphon with carbon dioxide and shake well. Refrigerate until needed. (Note: this soda recipe makes enough for 3 drinks.)

Combine the Scotch, Chinato and bitters in a goblet or rocks glass. Stir, then top up with the Port and Hazelnut Soda and garnish with the orange twist.

The

Fumoir

Parmesan Bar Snacks

If you're going to go to the effort of making this savoury puff pastry, you might as well be making a double batch — simply freeze one batch for later use, to enjoy when you have impromptu guests over for a drink. They can be baked from frozen.

MAKES ABOUT 24 PER BATCH

YOU WILL NEED:
equipment listed on page 90
airtight container or small baking sheet, lined
  with baking paper, plus extra paper
baking sheet, lined with baking paper

FOR THE DÉTREMPE (PASTRY LAYER):
60g (2¼oz) cold unsalted butter, cut into
  1cm (½ inch) cubes
230g (8oz) strong white flour, plus extra
  for dusting
8g (¼oz) sea salt
95ml (3¼fl oz) cold water

FOR THE BEURRAGE (BUTTER LAYER):
190g (6¾oz) unsalted butter, cold but
  softening, cut into 1cm (½ inch) cubes
60g (2¼oz) strong white flour
1 tsp freshly ground black pepper
½ tsp cayenne pepper
25g (1oz) Parmesan cheese, finely grated,
  plus extra 20g (¾oz), for sprinkling

mixed seeds of your choice, such as poppy,
  sesame and flaxseed (optional)

The process for making this spiced savoury puff is identical to making traditional puff pastry (*see* page 90), save for the addition of black and cayenne peppers and 25g (1oz) Parmesan in the beurrage. Once the puff pastry has had 5 turns, is rested and chilled, proceed as follows.

On a lightly floured surface, roll out the puff pastry into a rectangle at least 25 x 50 cm (10 x 20 inches) and no more than 2mm (¹⁄₁₆ inch) thick. Trim the edges to create a neat rectangle. Cut the rectangle lengthwise into 2 long strips each 10cm (4 inches) wide. Brush each strip gently with water, then lightly sprinkle the surface with the 20g (¾oz) Parmesan and the mixed seeds, if liked. Now cut each strip into 2cm (¾-inch) wide pieces. You should have about 48 Parmesan strips in total.

To freeze half of these, lay the Parmesan strips on top of the paper in the container, being careful they don't overlap and stick to each other, then lay another sheet of paper on top, and continue filling the container with the Parmesan strips. Alternatively, you can lay them on a small baking sheet, overlapping each layer with baking paper, then wrap the entire tray tightly in multiple layers of clingfilm. These will keep for up to 2 months in the freezer and can be laid out on a larger baking sheet and baked directly from frozen.

Arrange the remaining strips on the prepared baking sheet (they can be placed quite close together), then refrigerate until cold.

Preheat the oven to 190°C (375°F), Gas Mark 5. Bake the Parmesan strips for 24–28 minutes, until deep golden brown. Leave to cool on the baking sheet.

These are best eaten on the same day but will keep in an airtight container at room temperature for up to 3 days.

Gougères

A classic French savoury choux puff, filled with Mornay sauce (a seasoned cheese béchamel), we serve these along with our Parmesan Bar Snacks in the Fumoir at cocktail hour

MAKES 24 (PERFECT FOR 8–12 AT A DINNER PARTY)

YOU WILL NEED:
stand mixer, with paddle attachment and
    whisk attachment
piping bag fitted with a 13mm (½ inch) plain
    piping tip
2 baking trays, lined with baking paper
wire rack
piping bag fitted with a small plain piping tip
1cm (½ inch) plain pastry cutter

FOR THE CHOUX:
125ml (4fl oz) milk
65g (2¼oz) unsalted butter
¼ tsp salt
¼ tsp caster sugar
65g (2¼oz) strong white flour, sifted
2 eggs, beaten

FOR THE FINAL ASSEMBLY:
1 x quantity Mornay Sauce (*see* page 34)
40g (1½oz) Gruyère cheese, thinly sliced and
    cut into 24 x 1cm (½ inch) rounds using
    the pastry cutter

Preheat the oven to 220°C (425°F), Gas Mark 7.

To make the choux, bring the milk, butter, salt and sugar to the boil in a medium saucepan. Remove from the heat and stir in the flour. Mix vigorously until the flour has been absorbed completely – the mixture will look and feel like mashed potatoes. Cook over a low heat, stirring continuously for about 1 minute to cook the flour and remove excess moisture. (Don't worry about any starchy residue on the bottom of the saucepan.) Transfer the dough to the stand mixer fitted with the paddle attachment and mix on low speed for 2 minutes to cool slightly.

Replace the paddle attachment with the whisk attachment, then mix in one-quarter of the beaten eggs at a time, whisking until well incorporated between each addition. The final dough will look shiny, smooth and soft.

Transfer the dough to the piping bag with the large tip. Pipe 2.5cm (1 inch) balls (about the size of a ping-pong ball) 5cm (2 inches) apart on a prepared baking tray.

Bake for 10 minutes, then reduce the heat to 190°C (375°F), Gas Mark 5, and bake for a further 15 minutes, until the choux puffs are crisp and golden brown. Transfer to a wire rack and, using a small knife, poke a small hole in the bottom of each puff to release the steam as they cool. (Choux can be made ahead of time: once cool, these can be stored in an airtight container for 2–3 days.)

Make the Mornay filling (*see* page 34) and transfer warm to the piping bag with the small tip (alternatively, the Mornay can be made ahead of time and reheated to loosen it now).

Preheat the oven to 200°C (400°F), Gas Mark 6.

Pipe some Mornay sauce into each choux puff until you detect a slight bulge, then transfer to the second prepared baking tray. Top each puff with a circle of Gruyère. Bake for 4–5 minutes, just long enough to melt the Gruyère caps and heat the puffs through. These are best served warm.

Dinner

Caviar

Caviar is the prepared roe of sturgeon. For centuries, the eggs from this magnificent deep-sea survivor from the Triassic period has been considered the world's greatest delicacy. We get our caviar from King's, a long-established caviar supplier to Claridge's and very many other hotels and restaurants around the world. Laura King purchased the business from a very dear man, Bob Campbell, in 2003. It was Bob who first introduced me to caviar — I must have been no older than 20 and like most people had never tasted caviar. He was passionate about teaching people about the quality of fine caviar, and would describe what we were tasting with the depth and detail of a wine merchant or cheesemonger. Whatever choice you make for caviar, we suggest making it a sustainable one. In typical Claridge's style we like to serve ours on a cherubic silver stand, a large tin abreast a bed of ice. That said, fish eggs should not be a luxury or saved for the festive season. In fact, we recommend enjoying them on a Tuesday, in bed or for really no reason at all.

PREPARATION IS FOR A 30G (1OZ) TIN, SERVES 2–3

NOTE:
Classically, the garnish was there to mask the taste of poor-quality caviar. However, this is not the case today and, although it looks great as presentation, it adds very little in the way of complementing lovely caviar.

YOU WILL NEED:
25cm (10 inch) nonstick frying pan
5cm (2.5 inch) plain pastry cutter

FOR THE LEMON BLINIS (MAKES 16):
6 tbsp milk
5g (⅛oz) yeast
pinch of salt
75g (2¾oz) strong white flour
50g (1¾oz) yogurt
1 egg, separated
half a lemon, zested
10g (¼oz) finely chopped chives
1 tsp vegetable oil

FOR THE TRADITIONAL GARNISH:
20g (¾oz) sieved hard-boiled egg white
    and yolk
15g (½oz) finely chopped onion
5g (⅛oz) chopped parsley
100g (3½oz) soured cream and chives

Right: At Claridge's, there is no small amount of caviar. Pictured here is 1kg (2lb 4oz) of the finest Oscietra. We also stock Platinum and Beluga.

To make the blinis, place the milk and yeast into a medium saucepan and heat until lukewarm.

Put the salt, flour, yogurt and egg yolk in a bowl. Pour in the warm milk and whisk until you have a smooth batter.

In a separate bowl, whisk the egg white until it forms soft peaks, then gently fold into the batter, being careful not to lose any aeration.

Gently fold the lemon zest and finely chopped chives into the batter.

Place the mixture in a large container, as it can expand to double the size. Cover and set aside for at least 2 hours but no longer than 3 (or place in the refrigerator overnight if preparing your blinis in advance).

Heat the oil in the frying pan, then pour in the mixture (you are aiming for a finished blini about 1cm/½ inch thick). Cook for 3 minutes on each side over a medium heat. You might find it helpful to use a palette knife when flipping the blini.

Slide the cooked blini out of the pan and, using the pastry cutter, cut out 16 rounds.

These blinis will keep, stored in an airtight container in the refrigerator, for up to 2 days and gently warmed before serving but are best served immediately, warm, along with the prepared garnishes – each in its own small bowl.

Duck Terrine

This terrine has been served at Claridge's for as long as I can remember; like all dishes, its popularity has waxed and waned. Though it's had its breaks from the menu, its quality and pure deliciousness keep it coming back. The preparing, cooking and even the slicing of this terrine is a privilege that is handed only to the chefs who have earned it. As you can see from the list of ingredients, it is an expensive item to get wrong. I'm hoping that this recipe and a good preparatory chat with your butcher will give you all that you need.

SERVES 12

NOTE:

We typically serve this recipe with preserved damsons (*see* page 164) and grilled sourdough bread. Damsons are generally available in the UK from August to October. If you're having trouble finding fresh damsons, the terrine would pair just as nicely with damson (or any other plum) jam.

YOU WILL NEED:

ice bath

meat grinder, or grinder attachment for your
    stand mixer with a coarse grinding plate

terrine mould, 24cm (9½ inches) long,
    9cm (3½ inches) wide and 9cm
    (3½ inches) deep

plenty of clingfilm or foil

1 litre (1¾ pint) sterilized jar

roasting tray or oven dish large enough to
    hold the terrine mould

digital thermometer with a probe

piece of cardboard, cut to the size of the
    terrine mould

FOR THE TERRINE:

300g (10½oz) thinly sliced lardo (ask your
    butcher to do it on the meat slicer,
    3mm/⅛ inch thick or less)

1 duck breast, about 400g (14oz)

150g (5½oz) foie gras, deveined (optional)

300g (10½oz) pork chump or neck or
    shoulder, cut into small cubes

200g (7oz) veal rump or loin, cut into small
    cubes

350g (12oz) duck leg meat, cut into small
    cubes

150g (5½oz) flare fat (from the lining of
    the pig's stomach) or back fat, cut into
    small cubes

The key to a successful terrine is to keep all of the meats and fat extremely cold during handling and grinding. I recommend you prepare a large bowl filled with ice and cold water and keep the bowl you're grinding the meat and fat into resting in it. Replenish the ice bath for when you're combining your meats, spices, veal jus, and so on. Also, keep the blade and grinding plate for your grinder in the freezer until you're ready to grind, and the meats and fat in the refrigerator whenever you're not processing them.

Working from one end of the terrine mould to the other, line the mould with overlapping slices of lardo, starting by aligning the end of the lardo strips with the rim on one side but extending the lardo strips about 8–9cm (3¼–3½ inches) over the rim on the other side (this extra lardo will act as a flap to cover the stuffed terrine and become its base). Line the inside ends of the mould with the remaining slices, overlapping these as well. Refrigerate.

Remove the skin from the duck breast. Remove any thick sinew, then cut the breast lengthways into long strips, about 2.5cm (1 inch) wide – you should have 3 or 4. Return to the refrigerator. If you're using the foie gras, cut your piece into smaller 1 x 5cm (½ x 2 inch) pieces, then refrigerate.

Set up the meat grinder. In a medium bowl, combine the cubes of pork, veal and duck leg meat with the diced fat until evenly distributed. Have an empty bowl ready to receive the minced meat resting under the grinder, over an ice bath. Process the meat and fat to a coarse grind. Refrigerate the bowl with the minced meat.

Soak the leaf gelatine in a bowl filled with cold water for 5 minutes, or until soft and pliable. Meanwhile, in a medium saucepan, warm the veal jus to a pourable consistency. Remove from the heat and whisk in the eggs, salt, sugar, spices, the soaked and squeezed gelatine leaves, the flour and alcohols. Cool slightly. Gently stir into the minced meat and fat mixture, then place the bowl over the ice bath.

Remove the lined terrine mould from the refrigerator. Transfer about one-third of the meat mixture to the bottom of the terrine mould and spread out evenly, using your fingers or a spatula.

Lay the duck breast strips down from one end to the other of the mould, trimming them as required, and if using the foie gras, nestle a long line of it between the duck strips. Cover this all with another third of the meat mixture.

Squeeze the water out of the soaking prunes, then line them down the centre of the terrine, placing a line of pistachios on either side.

Carefully cover with a final layer of the meat mixture. It's okay if the terrine mould seems like it's a little overfilled: the meats will condense with cooking.

Fold the extra lardo over to cover the meat mixture completely, trimming any extra length off with scissors and tucking in the lardo at either end of the mould, then wrap the entire terrine »

5 sheets of leaf gelatine

200ml (7fl oz) Veal Jus (*see* page 206)

2 eggs, beaten

12g (½oz) Maldon sea salt flakes

1 tbsp sugar

1 tbsp freshly ground white pepper

1 tsp pâté spice (a blend of ground cinnamon, cloves, nutmeg, ginger and coriander)

5 juniper berries, crushed

25g (1oz) plain flour

55ml (2fl oz) port

40ml (1½fl oz) Madeira

65ml (2¼fl oz) brandy

10–12 pitted prunes, soaked in hot water

20–30 pistachio nuts, shelled

slices of sourdough bread, toasted, to serve

FOR THE PRESERVED DAMSONS:

1kg (2lb 4oz) damsons, washed and stems removed

500ml (18fl oz) water

500g (1lb 2oz) caster sugar

50ml (2fl oz) sloe gin

very tightly in several rounds of clingfilm or foil. Chill for 3 hours – this will help the terrine set nicely.

Meanwhile, bottle the damsons, if you haven't already. Handling the fruit gently, pack the damsons as tightly as you can into the jar. Put a tall pot filled with enough water to submerge the damson jar on to boil. Lay a trivet or folded tea towel into the bottom of the pot.

In a medium saucepan, bring the measured water and the sugar to the boil over a high heat, then cook until the sugar is dissolved, about 2 minutes. Remove from the heat, add the sloe gin, then carefully pour this syrup into the jar, covering the damsons.

Seal the jar and lower into the tall pot of water, making sure it's completely submerged. When the water begins to boil, sterilize for 12 minutes. Remove from the water and leave to cool.

It's now finally time to cook the terrine. Preheat the oven to 160°C (325°F), Gas Mark 3, and put a full kettle on to boil.

Lay the wrapped terrine in the roasting tray or dish and insert the thermometer probe into the centre of the terrine. Place the tray on the middle shelf of the oven and fill with hot water until halfway up the sides of the mould.

Cook until the thermometer registers an internal temperature of 54°C (129°F), about 1½ hours. Remove from the oven and leave to rest – the temperature should continue to rise for the next 10 minutes, to about 65°C (149°F). Leave the terrine to cool for about 10–20 minutes, then transfer to the top shelf of your refrigerator. When the terrine has cooled completely, within 1½ hours or so, place the piece of cardboard on top of the terrine and some cans on top of that to compress it, then return to the refrigerator overnight.

To serve, unwrap and unmould the terrine – run a hot sharp knife along the edges first – and turn on to a wooden board. Trim the end piece off one side of the terrine and proceed to cut and plate 1.5cm (⅝-inch) thick slices.

Count on 3 damsons per person – pit and arrange on each plate. Serve the terrine at room temperature with hot sourdough toast. The terrine will keep, well wrapped, in the refrigerator for up to 2 weeks.

Hand-dived Scallops
English Asparagus, Nantaise Sauce

My executive sous chef Adam Peirson (a great chef and leader who has been with me since 1999) describes it best: 'Picking an icy-cold hand-dived scallop from a delivery crate and edging in a silver table knife, twisting the knife away from you...the freshness of the scallop fighting against your thumb as you reposition your knife and, with a swipe along the top of the inside of the flat shell, the scallop is opened. The sound and the vigour with which the shell tops are being thrown into the bin is an indication to anyone working nearby how proficient and fast a fish cook can work. Some days we might have 600 scallops that need to be prepared in 4 hours' time. That's when the competitive spirit, speed and skill kick in. It is comforting to know that generations of fish chefs have all stood along the long fish sink, looking at the clock, racing against time.'

SERVES 4

YOU WILL NEED:
high-speed blender
ice bath
coffee filter or muslin cloth

FOR THE PARSLEY OIL:
200g (7oz) picked flat-leaf parsley leaves
100ml (3½fl oz) neutral oil, such as
      grapeseed

FOR THE NANTAISE SAUCE:
25g (1oz) finely chopped shallots
100ml (3½fl oz) white wine
70ml (2½fl oz) double cream
250g (9oz) cold best-quality salted cultured
      butter, cut into small cubes
pinch of cayenne pepper
sea salt and freshly ground black pepper

4 spring onions
1 tbsp vegetable oil
12 ramson capers
12 hand-dived scallops
12 cooked sea beet leaves
4 English asparagus spears, barbed
      and blanched (*see* page 176)
      and refreshed in iced water
16 pieces of picked rock
      samphire, blanched and
      refreshed in iced water
4 sea aster leaves
4 nasturtium leaves

First, make the parsley oil. Bring a large pan of water to the boil, then plunge the parsley leaves into the hot water and blanch them for no more than 30 seconds. Drain and shake off any excess water. Combine the leaves with the oil in a high-speed blender and purée well. Set up an ice bath, then transfer the parsley oil to a bowl and rest it in the ice bath –this will set the chlorophyll and ensure the finished oil is a vibrant green. Refrigerate the oil mixture for 4 hours to infuse it, then strain through a coffee filter or muslin cloth into a squeeze bottle or jar. Refrigerate until needed. It can be kept for 1 week or, if frozen, for up to 1 month.

WILD CAPERS

Yun Hider, who forages the Pembrokeshire coast and forests, has had a connection with Claridge's since the late 1990s. He sends us his herbs by post each week, neatly wrapped and chilled. When we worked with Noma in 2012, René's team introduced us to pickled ramson capers, and we've used them since — ingredients you can't just easily buy set a menu apart.

To make the Nantaise sauce, place the shallots and wine in a small saucepan and gently reduce over a medium-low heat to 2 tablespoons of syrup, about 40 minutes. Add the cream and simmer for 5 minutes over a medium heat. Remove the pan from the heat, then whisk in all the butter until incorporated. Season with a pinch of cayenne, salt and pepper, then cover and keep warm until needed.

Moisten the spring onions with a little of the vegetable oil. In a medium frying pan or under a preheated hot grill, char the onions on all sides, then transfer to a container. Add 4 tablespoons of the Nantaise sauce, 2 tablespoons of the parsley oil and the ramson capers, cover with a lid and leave the onions to wilt in the sauce for 15 minutes.

When ready to serve, heat a medium nonstick frying pan over a high heat, add a little of the vegetable oil, then place the scallops into the pan and caramelize on both sides, about 4 minutes in total. Season with salt, then remove from the pan and keep warm. Add the sea beet to the pan to warm.

Place 4 leaves of sea beet in the centre of each warmed plate. Drain the spring onions and place 1 on top of each pile of sea beet. Warm the asparagus in a little seasoned water, then place around the sea beet. Place the seared scallops on top. Dress each plate with Nantaise sauce, 3 capers, 4 samphire pieces, a leaf each of sea aster and nasturtium, plus a few drops of parsley oil.

Claridge's Chicken Pie

Our Chicken Pie has been on the menu forever, but it hasn't always been in fashion. One of my predecessors tried to retire it to make room for something more 'current' and was told by the powers that be, it was him or the pie. The truth is this pie is perfect — so good in fact that getting her hands on the recipe was one of the reasons Meredith wanted to write our book. A couple of years ago we were visited by Alf Parrot, an old friend who worked in the kitchen in the 1930s. He told us how Claridge's had saved his life: when the war came, he was sent to work in the officers' mess hall rather than to the front line. He described how he remembered making the Chicken Pie: the creamy suprême sauce, the mushrooms, the smoked bacon, quail eggs and the mash on the side. We made one for Alf and the joy on his face was a sight to behold. It was exactly as he remembered. This is a dish that links generations, not only in the kitchen but in the dining room as well.

MAKES 4 INDIVIDUAL PIES

NOTES:

We use 500ml (18fl oz) oval ovenproof dishes that are 17 x 11 x 5cm (6½ x 4¼ x 2 inch), to serve this. Adjust your pastry cutting to fit the shape of your dishes, allowing a little extra for overhang. This dish needs to be cooked from perfectly cold, so allow for a 2-hour chilling period before baking.

YOU WILL NEED:

4 ovenproof dishes (or 1 large ovenproof casserole dish)
2cm (¾ inch) plain pastry cutter
5cm (2 inch) fluted pastry cutter
sheets of baking paper and a tray
fine-mesh sieve
baking sheet

FOR THE PIE FILLING AND ASSEMBLY:

120g (4¼oz) pearl onions
plain flour, for dusting
1–1.2kg (2lb 4oz–2lb 12oz) cold Puff Pastry (*see* page 90)
2 egg yolks, beaten, for eggwash
600g (1lb 5oz) chicken breast, cut into 5cm (2 inch) cubes, seasoned with sea salt and freshly ground black pepper
2 tbsp vegetable oil, plus extra if required
120g (4¼oz) streaky bacon, cut into lardons
100g (3½oz) small button mushrooms, quartered
10g (¼oz) flat-leaf parsley, finely chopped
4 quail eggs, hard-boiled (3 minutes in boiling water), shelled

Cook the pearl onions in their skins in a medium saucepan of salted boiling water for 5–7 minutes. Rinse under cold running water to cool, then peel and set aside.

On a lightly floured surface, roll out the puff pastry to a rectangle, about 30 x 60cm (12 x 24 inches) and 2mm (1/16 inch) thick. Starting at the top of the rectangle and with the long edge facing you, use a sharp knife or a pizza wheel to cut out 4 oval lids of 14 x 20cm (5½ x 8 inches). Alternatively, cut out 4 lids of the shape of your chosen vessels, or 1 large lid, as needed – you can place one of the dishes directly on to the pastry to use as a guide, making sure you add on an extra 2cm (¾ inch) all around for overhang. Use the 2cm (¾ inch) pastry cutter to cut out a steam 'chimney' in the centre of each lid. Next, from the bottom of the rectangle, cut away 4 full-length (60cm/24 inch) strips of pastry, each about 2cm (¾ inch) wide – these will form the edges along the rim of each dish to support the pastry lid. Finally, use the larger pastry cutter to cut out 4 rounds of pastry in what is left of the puff pastry rectangle, then cut out a 2cm (¾ inch) hole in the centre of each – these are the decorative rings for each chimney. Now brush a little eggwash around the edge of each of the chimneys and lay 1 decorative ring on top of each chimney, pressing gently to encourage the seal. Stack the 4 lids and the long strips on top of each other, separated by sheets of baking paper, transfer to a tray and refrigerate until assembly time. Discard any leftover pastry.

To make the suprême sauce, heat the oil in a medium frying pan or wide saucepan over a medium heat, add the chicken thighs and lightly cook on all sides for about 4 minutes, until lightly browned. Add the shallots along with the garlic and mushrooms and cook until soft and the onions are translucent, about 5 minutes. Add the white wine, bay leaf, rosemary and thyme and reduce the liquid by half, still over a medium heat, about 6–8 minutes. Add the stock and continue to cook for 15 minutes. Stir and skim occasionally, removing any sediment. Pass through the sieve into a saucepan, then add the cream and bring to the boil over a medium heat. Simmer to reduce until the sauce coats the back of a spoon, about 25 minutes. Meanwhile, in a small pan, melt the butter over a medium heat until frothy, then stir in the flour until you have a smooth paste and cook for 2–3 minutes, stirring continuously, over a low heat. Remove from the heat. When the cream sauce has reduced sufficiently, whisk a little of the cream sauce into the flour mixture until smooth, then return this to the suprême sauce, stirring to incorporate – you should have about 1 litre (1¾ pints) of sauce (don't worry if you're a little short – just adjust with additional stock or cream as desired). Season to taste, then cover and set aside.

Now you're ready to work on the remainder of the pie components. In a large frying pan, sear the diced chicken breast in the vegetable oil over a medium-high heat until it colours »

FOR THE SUPRÊME SAUCE:

2 tbsp vegetable oil

400g (14oz) boneless, skinless chicken
    thighs, cubed

100g (3½oz) shallots, finely chopped

1 garlic clove, peeled and left whole

100g (3½oz) button mushrooms, sliced

300ml (10fl oz) dry white wine

1 bay leaf

1 rosemary sprig

3 thyme sprigs

650ml (23fl oz) Double Chicken Stock (*see*
    page 76), plus extra if required

500ml (18fl oz) double cream, plus extra if
    required

25g (1oz) unsalted butter

25g (1oz) plain flour

sea salt and freshly ground black pepper

slightly, then transfer to the saucepan with the suprême sauce, reserving the frying pan for the bacon and mushrooms. Bring the sauce to the boil, then simmer over a medium heat for 30 minutes, stirring occasionally.

While the chicken is cooking in the sauce, sauté the bacon lardons in the reserved frying pan until crispy. Use a slotted spoon to transfer to a bowl and set aside. Now, still in the same pan, sauté the mushrooms until golden brown, adding a splash more vegetable oil to the pan if needed. Set aside in another bowl.

Using a slotted spoon, portion the pieces of chicken equally into the pie dishes. Then divide the pearl onions, mushrooms, bacon and parsley equally between them. Add one-quarter of the suprême sauce to each dish. The filling should fill each vessel about two-thirds full. Finally, carefully add 1 quail egg to each. Refrigerate for 2 hours or longer, until completely cool.

Preheat the oven to 220°C (425°F), Gas Mark 7.

Brush the rim of each dish with eggwash. Lay a strip of puff pastry all along the edge of each dish, pressing down gently in the centre of the strip to help it adhere to the rim, overlapping the 2 ends and eggwashing them together to form a seal. Next, eggwash the whole strip and carefully drape the puff pastry lids atop each vessel, allowing for a 2cm (¾ inch) overhang all around. Press down gently to form a seal between the rims and the lids. Brush each lid with eggwash.

Place the pies on a baking sheet and bake for 25 minutes, until deep golden brown (a few minutes longer if you're making 1 large chicken pie). Leave to cool for 3 minutes before serving with your favourite mashed potato, green beans and a bottle worthy of your labour.

Line-caught Sea Bass
Tomato Compote, Green Almonds

Wild sea bass is a stunning fish to cook for large numbers, mainly because its oily skin crisps beautifully, while the inside of the thick fillet remains juicy. It's more difficult to overcook than, say, cod or halibut. For this reason it makes an excellent choice for events. I try to pair it with a light clean garnish for summer parties: usually tomato and lemon verbena, macerated gently with buttery, floral Vallée des Baux olive oil, and finished with the squeaky bite of the fresh green almonds.

SERVES 4

FOR THE TOMATO COMPOTE:
65ml (2¼fl oz) olive oil
10g (¼oz) shallots, cut into small dice
4 plum tomatoes, blanched, skinned,
    deseeded and cut into small dice
2 tsp red wine vinegar
5g (⅛oz) black olives, cut into small petals
10g (¼oz) basil leaves, diced
10 lemon verbena leaves
sea salt and freshly ground black pepper
a pinch of sugar

FOR THE POTATOES:
200g (7oz) Jersey Royal potatoes, washed
    very well to remove any excess dirt
5g (⅛oz) mint

FOR THE BEANS AND PEAS:
200ml (7fl oz) water
6g (¼oz) salt
80g (2¾oz) unshelled fresh broad beans
80g (2¾oz) unshelled fresh peas

FOR THE CARROTS AND TURNIPS:
50g (1¾oz) unsalted butter
50ml (2fl oz) water
8 whole baby carrots
8 whole baby turnips

FOR THE FISH:
2 tbsp vegetable oil (note the fish is quite oily,
    so be conservative here)
4 line-caught sea bass fillets, about 160g
    (5¾oz) each, skin on
sea salt and freshly ground black pepper

FOR THE GARNISH:
400g (14oz) spinach leaves, washed and
    sautéed in olive oil
80g (2¾oz) girolle mushrooms, cleaned and
    pan-fried in salted butter
20 fresh green almonds (carefully crack open
    the green nut shells, remove from the
    shell, remove from the outer skin and
    keep in milk until needed)

To make the tomato compote, place a small saucepan over a low heat, add the olive oil and shallots and gently warm. Add the tomatoes, vinegar and a little salt. Leave to warm for 10 minutes. Do not overheat. When ready to use, add the olives, diced basil leaves and verbena leaves, then check the seasoning, adding salt, pepper and sugar to taste.

Place the potatoes and mint in a sauté pan of lightly salted boiling water and gently boil for 8–10 minutes, until cooked through, then leave to cool in the cooking liquid. When cool enough to handle, carefully peel off the light skin that covers them, returning them to the cooking liquid until ready to serve.

Next, cook the beans and peas. Bring the measured water and salt to the boil in a small saucepan. Blanch the broad beans for 30 seconds, then remove with a slotted spoon and peel off the outer skins. Quickly blanch the peas next (small sweet peas are lovely raw; unfortunately most of these end up frozen for the supermarkets, so the quality of fresh peas can vary a great deal, as can their cooking time: the bigger they are, the longer they will take and the less sweet they become). Drain and set aside.

Meanwhile, cook the baby vegetables. In a small saucepan, make an emulsion out of the butter by whisking it with the measured water over a low heat. Pour half of the emulsion into another small saucepan, then cook the carrots and turnips separately until tender, about 5 minutes apiece.

Heat the vegetable oil in a nonstick frying pan over a medium heat. Season the fish well on each side, then gently place skin-side down in the pan. Cook for 8–10 minutes, until you can see the heat creeping up the side of each piece; gently turn over and cook for a further 4 minutes, or until cooked through.

To serve, place the spinach in the centre of each plate, arranging all the other vegetables around the spinach. Spoon the compote around the vegetables, then drain the almonds and place on top. Finally, place a sea bass fillet in the centre of each and serve.

Claridge's Bolognese

Perhaps the ultimate one-pan wonder in our kitchen, this Bolognese really is made in just one frying pan: the same frying pan that I cooked it in when I was a saucier, back when Gran was a girl. The key to a great sauce is to taste, taste, taste, adjusting the seasoning as you go. And yes, near the one-hour mark of cooking the sauce will be a rich, deep chocolatey brown, and yes, that's because we're using a veal jus base here and yes, you're on the right track. We have many guests at Claridge's, families in particular, who place their Bolognese order as soon as they set foot in the Lobby. After their bags have been whisked upstairs, and they've had a chance to check in and unpack, we deliver the warm bowls of ragù straight to their room.

SERVES 4–6

NOTE:
This recipe makes a fairly 'saucy' meat sauce; cook it for longer if you want it to feel even meatier.

50ml (2fl oz) vegetable oil
500g (1lb 2oz) beef rump, minced
1 large onion (about 300g), finely diced
10 button mushrooms, cut into small dice
5 tbsp tomato purée
200ml (7fl oz) dry red wine
400g (14oz) can peeled plum tomatoes, drained and chopped
500ml Veal Jus (*see* page 206), warmed to pourable consistency
1 rosemary sprig
1 generous thyme sprig
2 bay leaves
sea salt and freshly ground black pepper

TO SERVE (OPTIONAL):
500g (1lb 2oz) dried pasta of your choice, cooked
1 loaf of fresh crusty Italian bread

Heat a large frying pan over a high heat. Pour in 1 tablespoon of the oil, then add half the meat, using a spatula or wooden spoon to break it up and help it cook evenly. When the meat is browned, about 4 minutes, transfer to a large bowl. Return the pan to the heat, add another tablespoon of oil and sauté the remaining meat until evenly browned. Transfer to the bowl.

Add 2 teaspoons of the oil to the same pan, add the onion and fry until soft and lightly coloured, about 5 minutes. Transfer to the bowl containing the meat. Add the remaining oil to the pan and sauté the mushrooms, still over a high heat, until they've released their juices and are gently browned, about 5 minutes. Combine the mushrooms with the meat and onion in the bowl.

Next, add the tomato purée to the pan, reduce the heat to low and cook for 5 minutes, stirring occasionally (this caramelizes the sugars in the purée to boost the final flavour of the sauce). Pour in the red wine, increase the heat and bring to a simmer, stirring well. Reduce the heat to low and cook until reduced by half, about 4 minutes.

Add the plum tomatoes and the cooked beef, onion and mushrooms, stirring until well combined. Pour in the veal jus, add the herbs and increase the heat to high. When the sauce is simmering nicely, reduce the heat to low and cook for 1 hour until the beef is tender and the veal jus and tomatoes have been partially absorbed. Be sure to stir the sauce regularly, and always be tasting: add pinches of salt and pepper as you go to shape the seasoning to your liking. Discard the rosemary, thyme and bay leaves before serving.

Serve hot with the pasta of your choice or a side of crusty Italian bread.

Quicke's Cheddar Quiche

A rich savoury custard in a crisp pastry case, cooked ever so gently to set our Burford Brown eggs. The intense tang of the pickled walnuts, a very English delicacy, adds a Ploughman's touch that marries nicely with the cheese. This recipe will likely make you fall in love with quiche all over again.

SERVES 4

YOU WILL NEED:

20cm (8 inch) tart ring or loose-bottomed tart tin, or 4 x 9cm (3½ inch) loose-bottomed square tart tins

baking sheet (lined with baking paper if using a tart ring)

rolling pin

ceramic baking beans

FOR THE PASTRY:

250g (9oz) strong white flour, plus extra for dusting

113g (4oz) cold unsalted butter, cut into 1cm (½ inch) cubes

½ tsp salt

3 tbsp ice-cold water

FOR THE FILLING:

150ml (5fl oz) whipping cream

100ml (3½fl oz) double cream or crème fraîche

2 eggs plus 1 egg yolk

¼ tsp sea salt

⅛ tsp freshly ground black pepper

40g (1½oz) pickled walnuts, drained and chopped (skins discarded)

40g (1½oz) baby spinach leaves, washed, blanched and squeezed dry

60g (2¼oz) Quicke's mature Cheddar (or your favourite mature Cheddar), grated

To make the pastry, place the flour, butter and salt in a mixing bowl. Using your fingertips, rub the butter into the flour until it resembles breadcrumbs. Add the measured water and mix gently until the dough starts to come together. (You can also make the dough in a food processor by pulsing the flour, salt and butter together 7 or 8 times, then adding the water and pulsing 5 or 6 more times.)

Turn the dough out on to your work surface. Gather it up and gently knead 2 or 3 times to create a semi-smooth dough. Pat the dough into a disc shape, wrap tightly in clingfilm and refrigerate for 45 minutes, or until firm. (The dough will happily keep for a couple of days in the refrigerator if you want to make it ahead of time.)

To assemble the quiche(s), place the tart ring on the prepared baking sheet. (If you're using loose-bottomed tart tin/s instead, simply place directly on to the baking sheet.)

On a floured surface, roll out the pastry dough into a 24cm (9½ inch) circle, large enough to fit the tart ring or tin, about 3mm (⅛ inch) thick. Or, if you're using the individual square tins, roll the dough into a 26cm (10½ inch) square, then cut into 4 x 13cm (5 inch) squares.

Lay the dough inside the tart ring or tin(s). Gently press the dough to the sides of the ring or tin(s), making sure the sides stand straight and the bottom lies completely flush on the baking paper or tin base. Using a sharp paring knife, trim any excess dough hanging over the tart ring or tin(s). Refrigerate or freeze for 20–30 minutes until firm.

Preheat the oven to 200°C (400°F), Gas Mark 6.

Line the pastry case(s) with baking paper and baking beans. Bake for 10 minutes, then remove the beans and discard the paper. Return to the oven and bake for a further 5 minutes until the pastry looks dry and light golden brown. Set aside. Reduce the oven temperature to 160°C (325°F), Gas Mark 3.

Meanwhile, in a medium bowl, whisk together the creams, eggs, egg yolk and salt and pepper until well combined.

When the pastry is cool to the touch, after about 10 minutes, arrange the walnuts, spinach and cheese evenly in the case(s). Pour in the egg and cream mixture. Bake for 22–27 minutes until the custard looks about set and lightly golden. Leave to stand for 5 minutes before serving warm.

Tournedos of Aberdeen Angus Beef
Truffle, English Asparagus & Madeira

The starting point for this beef dish was a meeting on a cold October day with a bride-to-be about a garden-themed summer wedding the following June. Starting with a blank page in my notebook, I start adding words as the conversation develops; often the first few points I write down give me a sense of someone's personality and an idea of the style they're looking for. With this dish it was simply, 'the groom loves steak', so I knew Aberdeen Angus right away, but was it a fillet or côte de boeuf? We often have to think creatively in the 'off' season, but a garden in June immediately has the pen scribbling: broad beans, fresh peas, English asparagus, young vegetables, herbs, green purée…Side notes on the page read: particular, detailed, very neat! So the picture starts to build in my head as we speak of what the dish is going to look like. But what would make this luxurious or elevate it to a great wedding dish? Of course, truffle! Peas and truffle are the perfect pair! I describe my vision of a very neat garnish, sitting tightly under the tournedos beef, a vivid pea purée, a generous shaving of earthy fragrant truffle. There are smiles around the table as the decision is made. I knew that the success of this dish would be its simplicity, its freshness and the detail in its execution.

SERVES 4

YOU WILL NEED:
mandoline slicer
ice bath
blender

FOR THE PEA PURÉE:
300g (10½oz) shelled fresh peas
sea salt and freshly ground black pepper

FOR THE VEGETABLES:
8 English asparagus spears
20g (¾oz) shelled peas
20g (¾oz) shelled broad beans
4 baby carrots
4 baby turnips
20g (¾oz) girolles, cleaned
1 tsp unsalted butter
10g (¼oz) green courgette, sliced into very thin ribbons
10g (¼oz) yellow courgette, sliced into very thin ribbons
1 tsp grapeseed oil with a squeeze of lemon

FOR THE MEAT:
4 beef tournedos, about 160g (5¾oz) each
45g (1½oz) salted butter
120ml (4fl oz) Madeira Sauce (*see* page 207)

FOR THE GARNISH:
10g (¼oz) white summer truffle
12 red veined sorrel leaves

To make the pea purée, blanch the peas in salted boiling water (3g/⅛oz salt for every 100ml/3½fl oz water), then refresh in iced water. Drain, place in a blender and blend to a smooth purée, working quickly as the heat from the machine will discolour the purée. Season to taste and place in an airtight container in the refrigerator until needed.

Taking the asparagus, remove the barbs from around the top end, not the very top. This is 3 or 4 barbs around the tip of the asparagus. Peel the stalk of the asparagus two-thirds of the way up the spear from the base. Cook in salted boiling water for 3 minutes, then refresh in iced water and drain. Remove the tips from the asparagus right above the peeled part, cut the removed stalks into discs but only use the tender part as the base can sometimes be very woody.

In a large pan of boiling water, blanch the 20g (¾oz) peas. Remove with a slotted spoon and set aside. Blanch the broad beans next, about 30 seconds, and set aside. Keep warm.

In a small saucepan, gently cook the baby carrots in a little simmering water with a pinch of salt until tender, about 6 minutes. Drain and chill.

Repeat this for the baby turnips, cooking for 8 minutes.

In a small saucepan, quickly poach the girolles in simmering water with a pinch of salt and the butter. Remove from the pan with a slotted spoon and chill until needed.

Place the courgette ribbons into a bowl, lightly salt and add the lemon juice-flavoured oil to marinate.

Preheat the oven to 200°C (400°F), Gas Mark 6.

In a hot frying pan, seal each piece of beef on every side using 30g (1oz) butter at first, then adding the rest of the butter as necessary and basting until nicely sealed. Transfer the beef to a roasting tin and place in the oven for 8 minutes.

Heat the Madeira sauce in a small saucepan and reheat all the vegetables.

Reheat the pea purée, then place a spoonful in the centre of each plate and use the spoon to push the purée out from the centre to form a well. Arrange the vegetables atop the purée. Place the tournedos in the centre, brush with a little Madeira sauce and garnish with freshly sliced truffle and the sorrel leaves

Roast Rack of Kentish Lamb
Jersey Royals & Wild Garlic

Kentish lamb with mushrooms, wild garlic and Jersey Royals epitomizes (to me at least) spring in London. This dish is all about the produce. Though it may seem overkill to some, we love the kick of sweetbreads and find it makes the whole dish moreish, but you can of course omit them if you wish.

SERVES 4

YOU WILL NEED:
foil
blender
roasting tray

FOR THE SWEETBREADS (OPTIONAL):
40g (1½oz) lamb sweetbreads
200ml (7fl oz) milk
40g (1½oz) strong white flour, mixed with
     a pinch of sea salt and freshly ground
     black pepper
1 egg, beaten
60g (2¼oz) fresh white breadcrumbs
100g (3½oz) goats' butter

FOR THE VEGETABLES:
1 purple carrot, peeled
30g (1oz) salted butter, plus extra for greasing
12 small Jersey Royal potatoes, washed
1 mint sprig
1 orange carrot, peeled
100ml (3½fl oz) orange juice
½ star anise
200g (7oz) large-leaf spinach, washed, stalks
     removed and drained
20ml (¾fl oz) vegetable oil
20g (¾oz) wild garlic leaves, picked and washed
small pinch of nutmeg
sea salt and freshly ground black pepper

**FOR THE JERUSALEM ARTICHOKE
PURÉE (OPTIONAL):**
200g (7oz) Jerusalem artichokes, peeled and
     cut into 5mm (¼ inch) pieces
30g (1oz) salted butter

FOR THE MEAT:
2 tsp vegetable oil
2 racks of new-season Kent lamb

TO SERVE:
40g (1½oz) fresh morels, cleaned, cut into
     equal pieces and pan-fried in goats' butter
160ml (5½fl oz) Red Wine Jus (*see* page 207)

If using, trim the sweetbreads, then soak them in the milk for 2 hours. Remove from the milk and then blanch quickly in a pan of salted boiling water. Drain well. Cut into nugget-sized pieces and then roll in the seasoned flour, tapping off any excess. Next, dip them in the beaten egg, again tapping off any excess. Finally, roll in the breadcrumbs. Chill for 1 hour.

Meanwhile, preheat the oven to 180°C (350°F), Gas Mark 4. Wrap the purple carrot in buttered foil and bake for 40 minutes, until cooked through.

Carefully pick over the potatoes, removing any eyes; never peel them, the flavour is in the skin. Place them in a pan of cold water, with a little salt and the mint sprig, then bring to the boil and cook until a small pointed knife slides out easily. Leave to cool in the water. When ready to serve, gently bring back to the boil, drain and glaze with a little salted butter.

Meanwhile, in a small pan, cook the orange carrot with the orange juice, star anise and a pinch of salt until tender, about 8 minutes. Set aside in the cooking liquid to keep warm.

To make the Jerusalem artichoke purée, if using, boil them gently with the butter in a small saucepan of water. Drain, then tip into a blender and blend to a smooth purée. Transfer to a clean pan and keep warm.

Remove the purple carrot from the oven and leave to cool slightly, then cut into slices across the centre and on an angle. Transfer to a clean small pan and keep warm.

Next, cook the meat. Heat the oil in a large frying pan. Season the lamb racks, place fat-side down in the pan and seal, rendering the fat slowly, until crisp and golden. Turn over and quickly seal the meat at the bottom of the rack. Transfer to a roasting tray and roast for 9 minutes, until firm to the touch. Leave to rest for 10 minutes. Reduce the oven temperature to 140°C (275°F), Gas Mark 1.

Sauté the spinach in the oil, then add the wild garlic and cook for 30 seconds until gently wilted. Season with salt, pepper and a small pinch of nutmeg. Keep warm.

To cook the sweetbreads, heat the goats' butter in a small pan until foaming, add the crumbed sweetbreads and cook until golden, about 5 minutes. Drain on kitchen paper and place in the oven to keep warm.

Remove the orange carrot from its cooking liquid and slice as you did the purple carrot.

To serve, if using, place a good spoonful of the artichoke purée in the centre of each plate, spreading it out using the back of the spoon. Spoon over the spinach and garlic leaves, arrange the carrots and potatoes around the spinach and then scatter over the morels. Carve the racks of lamb into 6 cutlets per rack and arrange on the spinach. Finish by adding the crispy sweetbread nuggets , if using, and serve with a little Red Wine Jus.

Lobster Thermidor

Lobster Thermidor is taken right from the pages of Louis Saulnier's Le Répertoire de la Cuisine, *a reference to Escoffier's: a cooked lobster is halved, topped with a glazed sauce made from a reduction of lobster bisque with brandy and tarragon, a little béchamel and mustard, and then finished with a spoonful of whipped cream and an egg yolk. Spooned over the lobster, this sauce quickly turns golden when placed under a hot salamander. This style of sauce is now almost a lost technique, but still an integral part of a Claridge's chef's education.*

SERVES 4

YOU WILL NEED:
heavy knife or crackers to crack the shell
fine-mesh sieve
1 baking tray

4 whole cooked lobsters
1 x quantity Mornay Sauce (*see* page 34)
2 tarragon sprigs, finely chopped
40g (1½oz) salted butter, softened

FOR THE LOBSTER BISQUE:
100g (3½oz) salted butter
400g (14oz) lobster shells (from the claws
    and knuckles)
300ml (10fl oz) brandy
60g (2¼oz) peeled chopped carrot
60g (2¼oz) peeled chopped fennel
60g (2¼oz) peeled chopped onion
25g (1oz) tomato purée
100ml (3½fl oz) white wine
25g (1oz) plain flour
1 litre (1¾ pints) hot Double Chicken Stock
    (*see* page 76)
3 unpeeled garlic cloves, crushed
3 star anise
1 chopped lemon grass stalk
4 tarragon sprigs

FOR THE GARNISH:
sea salt
pea shoots

Cut each lobster in half; this is a two-stepped process. Insert the point of the knife into the centre of the head (you will see the natural point), then take the knife through the front of the head. Turn the lobster and cut in the other direction towards the tail. Trim away the thin spiny legs. Remove the knuckles and claws. Clean the cavity of the front shell. Carefully lift out the tail, turn over on to a chopping board and cut through 4 times. Crack the claws and remove the shell, then do the same with the knuckles. Keep the lobster meat refrigerated until needed.

To make the bisque, add half of the butter to a heavy-based saucepan and place over a high heat. Add the claw and knuckle shells and gently caramelize. Add half of the brandy, flame and leave to reduce for 2 minutes. Add the remaining butter and brandy. Reduce the heat to medium, add the carrot, fennel and onion and sweat for 4 minutes.

Stir in the tomato purée and cook for 3 minutes. Add the white wine and reduce for 2 minutes. Stir in the flour, then add the hot stock. Mix well. Add the garlic, star anise and lemon grass. Bring to the boil, skim and cook for 40 minutes. Remove from the heat and add the tarragon sprigs. Leave to stand for 5 minutes before passing through the sieve. Over a medium heat, reduce the lobster bisque by half, to about 160ml (5½fl oz), 8 minutes or so. Leave to cool.

Preheat the oven to 180°C (350°F), Gas Mark 4.

In a small bowl, mix together 100g (3½oz) of the Mornay sauce, about three-quarters of the reduced bisque and the finely chopped tarragon.

Place the empty lobster shells on the baking trays. Carefully place the cut lobster tails presentation side up (meaning the opposite tail in the opposite shell, red side up, into the tail shell) and the claw and knuckle meat into the empty front cavity shell. Brush all the lobsters with the soft butter. Cover with foil and reheat gently in the oven for 4 minutes.

Remove the foil from the lobster heads only. Fill this shell and cover the lobster meat with the lobster Mornay glaze. Brown under a hot preheated grill, remove the remaining foil and serve garnished with the sea salt and pea shoots.

Claridge's Cheeseburger

What can you expect from a cheeseburger at Claridge's? We ask ourselves this question (and many more) on a weekly basis. Our cheeseburger only arrived on the menu in 2000 (though, of course, you could request one long before then). The meat is best-quality sirloin mixed with onion, parsley and seasoning, and shaped as a thick patty. The burgers are cooked on our Big Green Egg charcoal grills. The bun is brioche, made in-house, as are the mayonnaise and smoked tomato chutney. A burger order at Claridge's is treated à la minute and is in many ways more labour-intensive than many of our other dishes. It might not be the most on-trend burger, but it could be the most cared for.

MAKES 4 X 260G (9¼OZ) CHEESEBURGERS

NOTES:
This is how we serve the burger at Claridge's. Of course, you may (as our guests do) modify it. The smoked tomato sauce is our ketchup and the mayonnaise is mixed with tomato chutney.

BURGER COOKING
Internal temperature of the meat:
Rare: 38°C (100°F)
Medium-rare: 45°C (113°F)
Medium: 48°C (118°F)
Medium-well: 52°C (126°F)
Well done: 60°C (140°F)
Rest for 3 minutes before serving.

YOU WILL NEED:
baking tray
old roasting tin or cast-iron pan, a handful each of wood chips and hay and an old rack (for smoking; *see* page 194)
4 x 1kg (2lb 4oz) sterilized jars
meat grinder, or grinder attachment for your stand mixer with a coarse grinding plate
4 x 10cm (4 inch) ring moulds
baking sheet lined with baking paper
digital thermometer with a probe

FOR THE SMOKED TOMATO CHUTNEY:
2kg (4lb 8oz) plum tomatoes
2kg (4lb 8oz) onions, chopped
4 heaped tbsp sea salt
1.5 litres (2¾ pints) malt vinegar, plus a little extra
2 tbsp mustard powder
2 tbsp curry powder
3 heaped tbsp cornflour
1kg (2lb 4oz) soft light brown sugar

FOR THE SMOKED TOMATO MAYONNAISE:
100g (3½oz) Claridge's Mayonnaise (*see* page 108)
25g (1oz) Smoked Tomato Chutney (*see* left)
sea salt and freshly ground black pepper

FOR THE SMOKED TOMATO SAUCE:
100g (3½oz) tomato ketchup
20ml (¾fl oz) Worcestershire sauce
1 tsp chipotle Tabasco sauce
15g (½oz) diced sweet dill pickle

FOR THE BURGERS:
400g (14oz) sirloin, fat and sinew removed
320g (11oz) diced onion, sautéed
60g (2¼oz) chopped parsley
325g (11½oz) minced sirloin beef fat
sea salt and freshly ground black pepper

FOR THE FINAL ASSEMBLY:
4 slices of Gruyère cheese
4 sesame seed brioche buns
2 sweet dill pickles, thinly sliced
1 beefsteak tomato, sliced
1 head of round lettuce leaves, cleaned and torn

First, make the smoked tomato chutney. Skin and remove the stalk part of the tomatoes, then chop. Place on the baking tray and smoke over wood chips for 45 minutes. Mix the tomatoes and onions with the salt and leave to stand overnight. Drain and rinse the tomatoes and onions, then put in a large pan and three-quarters cover with the malt vinegar. Boil for 10 minutes, then reduce the heat to a simmer. Mix the mustard powder, curry powder and cornflour to a paste with some malt vinegar and add to the pan together with the sugar. Simmer for 1 hour until very thick. Bottle in jars (*see* page 164 for the bottling process). Store in a cool, dark place for 3 months before opening. The chutney will keep for up to 3 months.

For the mayonnaise, mix the mayonnaise with the chutney. Season to taste with salt and pepper and set aside.

For the smoked tomato sauce, mix the ketchup, Worcestershire and Tabasco sauces together, then add the dill pickle.

To make the burgers, mince the meat and then gently mix all of the burger ingredients with your hands until well incorporated. Season to taste, then press into the ring moulds on the prepared sheet and refrigerate until ready for cooking, at which point you can remove the moulds.

In a frying pan or over a barbecue, cook the patties, turning from time to time to ensure they cook evenly. For medium-rare, seal the burgers for 2 minutes. Using a spatula, flip over and cook on the other side for 1½ minutes. Repeat this flipping over 3 times, for 1½ minutes on each side. On the last turn, top with the cheese and melt for 30 seconds.

We trust you can handle the assembly and topping aspect. You could even crown your burger with an onion ring, as we do. Claridge's flag optional.

Sole Meunière

If turbot is the king of fish, then sole is the queen. When a guest orders sole during a busy service, we still feel a certain exclusive excitement: this dish requires your undivided focus and care, and it's something we enjoy cooking as much as our guests enjoy eating. Indeed, the pleasure of turning over a perfectly coloured Dover sole and basting it with foaming beurre noisette never leaves you. For cooks at home, frying sole is a simple but still technical process. Your goal is to keep the sole cooking without ever letting the butter burn. Please note that cooking one sole takes about 12 minutes.

SERVES 1

NOTE:
When buying the fish, ask your fishmonger to prepare it for 'meunière' – scaled, top skin removed and trimmed.

YOU WILL NEED:
carving fork or fish slice
sieve

1 whole Dover sole, about 500g (1lb 2oz)
1 lemon
handful of parsley leaves, finely chopped
50g (1¾oz) plain flour
2–3 tbsp vegetable oil
225g (8oz) unsalted butter, cubed
sea salt and freshly ground black pepper

Rinse the fish thoroughly (but gently) under cold running water. Pat dry.

Prepare your garnish: halve the lemon, reserving one half for juice. On the other half, remove all zest and pith using a sharp knife, then cut into 3–4 thin slices. Dip a side of each slice into the chopped parsley and set aside.

In a large bowl or platter, season the flour generously with salt and pepper, then dredge the sole on both sides, shaking off any excess flour.

Heat a frying pan large enough for the sole over a medium-high heat, coating the base with the vegetable oil. Carefully place the sole into the pan skin-side down and cook until golden in colour, about 4–5 minutes.

Using a carving fork or a fish slice, carefully lift the fish by the spine and turn it over gently in the pan.

Wait for about 30 seconds, then add half of the butter to the pan. Reduce the heat to medium and let the butter foam around the fish. Using a large spoon, start to baste the sole with the butter continuously, aiming for an even golden colour all over. You may need to tilt your pan slightly to collect the butter for basting. This will take about 6 minutes over a low-medium heat.

Carefully slide the fish out of the pan, and place, skin-side down, on to a warm plate to rest for 5 minutes, keeping the butter in the pan. Garnish with the slices of parsley lemon.

While the fish is resting, bring the butter back up to a foam over a medium heat, then add the remaining butter to the pan as well as a big squeeze of the remaining lemon half to finish making your beurre noisette. Strain this sauce and serve in a sauceboat on the side.

**A NOTE
ON DEBONING**

Dover sole is a flat fish and its spine runs through its centre. To fillet it, place a sharp knife atop the end of the spine but under the top fillets, and slide it gently and flatly along the spine from one end of the fish to the other. Set aside the top fillets. The spine can then be lifted up to separate it from the bottom fillets (it may need a little encouragement from the point of your knife to begin).

Game of the Season

By definition, game is any meat or poultry that comes from birds and animals that have been hunted, rather than raised on a farm. Years ago, game and wildfowl featured much more freely in people's diets, particularly those living within easy reach of the countryside. Although it fell out of favour for a while, game is now experiencing a revival as an increasing number of people become disillusioned with modern farming methods and look for a quality meat. Game has always featured in the gastronomic history of Claridge's, and we keep a close eye on the culinary calendar: in August, guests eagerly anticipate the arrival, late into the night of the 12th, of the first grouse of the shooting season.

Now, stories of guests sitting in the restaurant on 'The Glorious Twelfth' for their first taste of grouse have a certain English charm about them. How nice the grouse would have been is questionable, as it really needs to hang for a few days to relax, become more tender and develop its flavour. It was really ceremony over culinary reason and is less likely to happen these days, but of course, if it was requested, we would endeavour to prepare the birds.

Red grouse are native to Britain. The first recorded grouse shoot was in 1853, started by the Victorians when newly constructed railways made it easier to get to the moors. Shooting parties were held on private estates; gamekeepers would be responsible for the management of the land and the beaters, who would walk and flush the birds from the cover of the heather; a gentleman would be accompanied by his dog, who would retrieve the birds without damaging them. The large country house hosting these parties would have been staffed with butlers, footmen, chefs and gardeners. These experiences created standards and expectations, which in turn became traditions to which people became accustomed, so when in London they expected no less. This way of life was really the acorn from which luxury hotels have evolved and grown.

Traditionally roasted hot for a short time, to ensure it was served pink, the bird was presented whole on a silver platter with game chips, bread sauce, watercress, foie gras croutons and game jus. In recent years, we have sealed the grouse in plenty of butter and then roasted it very gently at 65°C (149°F) to a probed temperature of 54°C (129°F), which results in a very evenly cooked, tender bird. As the 12 August is still really summer, and earlier than you associate with eating game dishes, our Yorkshire Grouse recipe (*see* page 192) is inspired by the August hedgerow, blackberries and damsons. The watercress adds freshness and summer greenery, and paired with the bread sauce infusion is a nod to the classic, but remains a light dish.

Note: woodcock and snipe are often eaten straight away as they tend to be cooked with the entrails left in them and are also most often trussed using their unique long beaks.

The game season

Grouse: 12 August – 10 December
Duck, Goose and Common Snipe:
　1 September – 31 January
Partridge: 1 September – 1 February
Woodcock: 1 October – 31 January
Pheasant: 1 October – 1 February
Venison: 1 August – 30 April (Sika Stag);
　1 November – 31 March (Sika Hinds)

Hanging times

Differences of opinion about how long game should hang are rife, but it really just depends on your taste. Cooked soon after being shot, the meat will likely be tight and lacking in flavour; left to hang in a cool place – a cold room, the refrigerator or your locked garden shed – the meat will relax and deepen in flavour. The important thing is to be mindful of the outside temperature, whether the game is outside or inside: if it's 7°C (45°F) and below the game is in a good place; below zero (32°F) it could freeze; and at about 8°C (46°F) and above it will ruin. If the temperature is too warm, game will need to mature in a cooler space (the refrigerator) for a few days.

Duck and Goose: 1–2 days
Partridge: 3–4 days
Grouse: 3–7 days
Pheasant: 5–7 days
Woodcock and Common Snipe:
　up to 6 days
Venison: 3 days – 2 weeks depending on
　the age of the animal

Game Pie

Each year as Game Pie Season begins — as the pâté en croûte moulds are being dusted off and lined up in the Claridge's kitchen — the chefs who mastered this classic the previous year are feeling nostalgic and wanting to pitch their skills against those larder chefs who are embarking on their Game Pie debut. The pie requires a very hot oven to bake the pastry — will it burn? The jelly is poured into the pie as it cools — will it hold? Then the time comes for nervously plucking the pins from the hinges in the mould, removing the sides. . .to reveal golden, cooked pastry. Chefs always share that first slice — ostensibly to confirm the seasoning but really to mark this rite of passage. This pie is featured on our menu du jour throughout autumn; by December, it's not unusual to find game pies lined up in our refrigerator with guests' names on luggage tags, ready for collection for Christmas.

SERVES 12–16

YOU WILL NEED:
rolling pin
30 x 7 x 8cm (12 x 2¾ x 3¼ inch) pâté
    en croute mould (available from
    Continental Chef Supplies)
baking paper
pastry brush
2.5cm (1 inch) plain pastry cutter
5cm (2 inch) plain pastry cutter
baking sheet
digital thermometer with a probe
small funnel

FOR THE HOT-WATER CRUST:
150ml (5fl oz) water
150ml (5fl oz) milk
175g (6oz) lard
670g (1lb 8oz) plain flour
1 tsp salt
1 egg, beaten, for the eggwash

FOR THE FILLING:
1.4kg (3lb) game meat (8 partridge breasts,
    8 grouse breasts, 3 pheasant breasts,
    2 duck breasts), sinews and any shot
    removed
a splash of port and brandy
400g (14oz) streaky bacon rashers
6 sheets of leaf gelatine
300g (10½oz) girolles, sautéed and cooled
300g (10½oz) foie gras, deveined, cut into
    batons

First, make the dough for the hot-water crust. In a large saucepan, heat the measured water, milk and lard to a simmer (not to a rolling boil), whisking gently until combined. Using a spatula, mix in the flour and salt and combine until smooth. Knead a little to bring together. Depending on how confident you are with the warm paste, there are two options here:

Option 1: Refrigerate the dough, wrapped in clingfilm, until firm, about 6 hours, or overnight. It can be easier to work with, but will need to be worked slightly when removing from the refrigerator to make it pliable again. Proceed as Option 2 below.

Place all the game breasts on a tray, sprinkle with a splash of port and brandy and leave to marinate for 30 minutes or so.

Option 2: Proceed with the warm paste. Roll out the dough to a thickness of about 4mm (⅛ inch) – you should have a rectangle of about 48 x 54cm (19 x 21¼ inches). Cut a 32 x 52cm (12½ x 20½ inch) rectangle for the mould, then cut a separate 16 x 52cm (6¼ x 20½ inch) rectangle of pastry from the leftover pastry for the lid.

Gently drape the larger rectangle of dough into the mould, keeping the pastry loose at the top while ensuring it reaches nicely into all the corners. It's okay for some of the excess pastry to overlap inside the side edges. You should have about a 4cm (1½ inch) overhang of pastry all around.

To assemble the pie, on a large piece of baking paper, overlap the bacon rashers to create a large 38cm (15 inch) square. Flip the paper over, bacon-side down, into the pastry-lined mould, making sure you have a 4cm (1½ inch) bacon overhang on either long side of the mould. Place the unbloomed gelatine in the base – it will feel wrong to use the gelatine leaves crisp and whole. Trust us, it's the right thing to do: the steam that builds up inside the pie will do the necessary melting.

Layer in the game meats: partridge, followed by half the mushrooms, then grouse, the foie gras, the remaining mushrooms, and finally the pheasant and the duck.

When the pie is built up above the top of the mould, fold the overhanging bacon up over the top of the game. Brush the pastry resting on the edges of the mould with eggwash.

Using the smaller pastry cutter, cut away 2 holes (for steam vents) towards either end of the dough lid, about 12cm (4½ inches) apart. Lay the pastry lid overtop the bacon, pressing gently along the edges to create a seal between the pastry in the mould and this lid. Trim away any excess dough with a sharp knife, reserving the trimmings. »

10 sheets of leaf gelatine

400ml (14fl oz) Chicken Consommé (*see* page 74) or Double Chicken Stock (*see* page 76)

Crimp the edges of the dough by hand or using a fork. From the trimmings, cut out 2 x 5cm (2 inch) rounds, then cut out a 2.5cm (1 inch) hole in the centre of each. Eggwash the lid completely, then lay these rings around each steam vent, and eggwash them. Once the pie is cooked, you will use these vents to fill the pie with jelly. You can also add any decorative dough touches (such as leaves or birds) to the top of the pie now, making sure to eggwash. Refrigerate for at least 1 hour before baking.

Preheat the oven to 250°C, or as high as your oven will go. Brush the pie with one final coat of eggwash and place on a baking sheet. Insert the thermometer probe into one of the vents. Bake for 8–10 minutes until beginning to colour, then reduce the oven temperature to 200°C (400°F), Gas Mark 6, cover the pie with foil and continue to cook until the thermometer registers an internal temperature of 54°C (129°F), about 35 minutes. (You want to cook the filling and melt the lard, but not overcook the pastry.) Remove from the oven to a cool place and leave to rest.

For the jelly: once the pie has cooled slightly, soften the sheets of gelatine in just enough cool water to cover for 5 minutes, or until soft and pliable. In a small saucepan, heat the consommé and stir in the softened and squeezed gelatine until completely dissolved. Leave to cool slightly. Then, using a funnel, and working gradually, fill the pie with the liquid jelly, allowing it to drop down as it settles into the pie, before adding more. Keep going until the liquid fills the pie to the top. The jelly is an ancient preservation method: the jelly sets, trapping the meat inside and removing any oxygen, thereby preserving the contents; this, combined with refrigeration, increases the shelf life of the pie. The cool jelly also adds moisture to the pie as it cools. Leave to cool for at least 20 minutes before refrigerating, preferably overnight.

When ready to serve, remove the pie from the refrigerator and carefully unmould. Slide off the bottom base, then remove the corner pins to release the sides. Leave to cool slightly (10 minutes), then serve with Cumberland Sauce (*see* below) and tremendous pride.

Cumberland Sauce

MAKES 180G (6½OZ)

YOU WILL NEED:
ice bath

2 oranges
1 lemon
20g (¾oz) fresh root ginger, peeled and finely chopped
100ml (3½fl oz) ruby port
200g (7oz) redcurrant jelly

Using a potato peeler, remove thin strips of zest from the oranges and lemon, avoiding the pith as much as possible. Cut the zest into very thin strips, then blanch 3 times to remove bitterness: drop into a small pan of boiling water for 30 seconds, then remove with a slotted spoon and transfer to an ice bath to cool. Repeat 2 more times. Drain and set aside.

Next, place the ginger in a saucepan with the citrus zest and the port. Over a low heat, reduce slowly to a light syrup consistency, about 10 minutes – you should be left with 20ml (¾fl oz) of liquid. Whisk in the redcurrant jelly while the syrup is still warm.

Leave to cool for 30 minutes before serving. Kept in a sterilized jar, this sauce will keep for a few weeks, like jam.

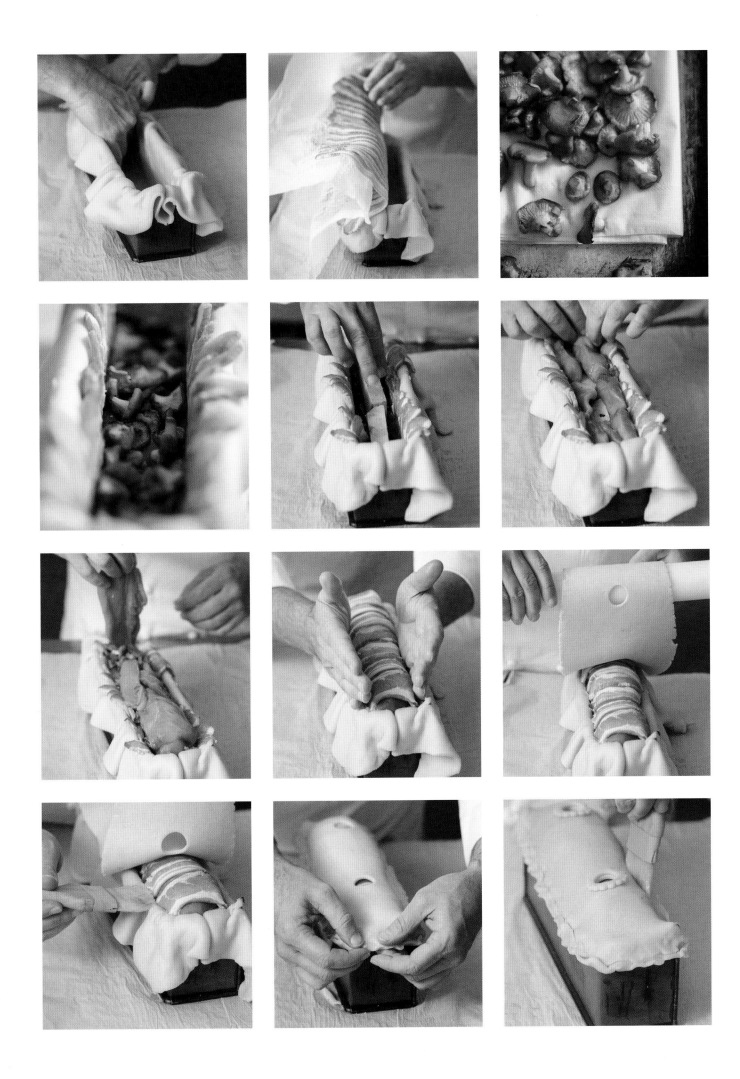

Yorkshire Grouse
Cauliflower, Bread Sauce, Damsons

This is a plated game dish: grouse breast with a reduction of grouse leg, cauliflower roasted in goats' butter, and a bread sauce to coat the greens and for texture. And damsons, for that hit of sweet and sour that all game needs. A rewarding lunch after a morning of walking in the country, or perhaps just around Mayfair.

SERVES 4

NOTE:
Bread sauce has a lowly beginning: bread crusts were placed under roasting meats to collect the juices. House staff were, of course, not privileged enough to enjoy the meat, but they could enjoy the most delicious bread baked and caramelized in the roasting juices.

YOU WILL NEED:
cast-iron ovenproof frying pan or roasting tray
digital thermometer with a probe
sieve

FOR THE GROUSE:
4 young grouse, legs removed for the sauce
8 juniper berries
bunch of fresh thyme
100g (3½oz) salted butter
2 streaky bacon rashers
sea salt and freshly ground pepper

FOR THE GROUSE SAUCE:
100g (3½oz) chicken trimmings
8 grouse legs, boned and diced (*see above*)
1 tbsp vegetable oil
20g (¾oz) shallots, roughly chopped
20g (¾oz) mushrooms, roughly chopped
1 back bacon rasher, chopped
1 thyme sprig
20g (¾oz) plain flour
200ml (7fl oz) red wine
200ml (7fl oz) Double Chicken Stock (*see page 76*)

FOR THE VEGETABLES:
200g (7oz) goats' butter
500g (1lb 2oz) cauliflower, trimmed into florets
2 tbsp vegetable oil
120g (4¼oz) Cavolo Nero kale, stalks removed, leaves cut into 4cm (4½ inch) strips

FOR THE BREAD SAUCE:
400ml (14fl oz) milk, plus extra if needed

1 whole white onion, peeled and studded with a bay leaf and 2 cloves
good pinch of nutmeg
4 slices of white bread, chopped into coarse crumbs
60g (2¼oz) unsalted butter

FOR THE GARNISH:
4 blackberries
8 preserved damsons (*see page 164*), pitted
bunch of fresh watercress

Begin with the grouse sauce: in a medium saucepan, caramelize the chicken trimmings and grouse leg meat in a little vegetable oil, then add the shallots, mushrooms, back bacon and thyme. Leave to soften and gently caramelize until lightly coloured, about 5 minutes. Add the flour, mix well and cook for a further 5 minutes, stirring occasionally. Add the wine and reduce by half. Pour in the stock and gently simmer for 40 minutes, occasionally stirring and skimming to remove fat and impurities as it cooks.

While the sauce is cooking, place the goats' butter in a heavy-based pan over a medium-high heat and add the cauliflower. Bring the butter to a foam and cover with a lid, reducing the heat and leaving the cauliflower to slowly caramelize and almost cook through, about 25–30 minutes. Leave to stand for a further 10 minutes, as the heat of the butter will finish cooking the cauliflower. Transfer the cauliflower to kitchen paper and set aside.

Remove the grouse sauce from the heat and set aside.

For the bread sauce, bring the milk to the boil with the studded onion and nutmeg, then turn off the heat and infuse for 20 minutes. Remove the onion and mix in the breadcrumbs and 50g (1¾oz) of the butter, then cook over a low heat for 2 minutes just to combine. Adjust the seasoning and finish with a little more

butter. The sauce needs to be of a loose, dropping consistency and may need a little more hot milk if it becomes too thick. Soften the remaining butter and brush a little over the top to prevent a skin from forming. Set aside and keep warm.

Preheat the oven to 200°C (400°F), Gas Mark 6.

For the grouse, lightly season each legless bird. Press 2 juniper berries and a small sprig of thyme inside each cavity.

Heat a heavy-based, preferably cast-iron, pan over medium heat. Melt the butter, add the grouse and seal gently on each side for about 2 minutes each. At this point, add the streaky bacon and allow to crisp with the grouse. Nestle all 4 birds and the bacon into a roasting tray (if your current pan is not ovenproof) and bake in the oven for 12 minutes, or until the grouse reaches a core temperature of 38°C (100°F). Remove and rest for 10 minutes.

While the grouse is baking, cook the kale. Place the oil in a large heavy-based pan over a high heat. Add the kale and sear quickly and at a high temperature. Drain on to kitchen paper and keep warm, ready for use.

Back to the grouse: pour any juices from the roasting tin into the grouse sauce, strain through the sieve and adjust the seasoning as required, then keep warm.

Carefully remove the grouse breasts from the bone and keep warm. Finely dice the streaky bacon and add to the sautéed kale, then adjust the seasoning.

To serve, place the kale and bacon in the centre of each plate. Arrange the breasts on top, along with the cauliflower. Garnish with the blackberry, damsons and watercress, placed down the centre of the breasts. Glaze with 2 dessertspoons of the grouse sauce. Whisk the bread sauce lightly and spoon it around the edge of the kale.

Hay-smoked Venison Loin

One of the high points of the Noma pop-up menu at Claridge's was the lamb neck: as each plate made its way upstairs, the bed of hay the lamb was resting on would be set on fire, releasing a rich, tea-like, smoky, meadow-flower aroma throughout the dining room — somehow transporting diners to Copenhagen, and into one of the great restaurants of the world. Here, we've adapted the recipe to venison, which we serve with 'scalloped' turnips and a beetroot salad. The pungent horseradish is perfect for a game pairing (in fact, these turnips would be great with any of our game recipes, starting on page 188). Don't be put off by the home-smoking: it really can be done quickly and easily in your kitchen without setting off your smoke alarm.

SERVES 4

NOTE:
Getting your hands on hay is easier than you think: try a pet shop, or ask anyone you know with a rabbit or gerbil for a pet; it can also be ordered online. Make sure you get Timothy hay or feeding hay.

YOU WILL NEED:
foil
baking tray
pestle and mortar, or small electric coffee
    grinder
mandoline slicer
old roasting tin or cast-iron pan
a handful each of wood chips and hay
rack (for smoking)
oven thermometer with a meat probe, or
    instant-read digital thermometer

FOR THE BEETROOT SALAD:
2 beetroot
1 tbsp vegetable oil
50ml (2fl oz) ruby port
100ml (3½fl oz) beetroot juice
1 tsp sugar
pinch of Winter Spice (*see* page 196)
1 tsp cornflour, mixed with a splash of water
1 tbsp balsamic glaze
1 tsp red wine vinegar
sea salt and freshly ground black pepper

Right: Pictured here is how this dish was served during the Noma Olympics pop-up. We have adapted the recipe so you don't have to set fire to hay in your living room and can enjoy a more substantial plate.

Start with the beetroot. Preheat the oven to 200°C (400°F), Gas Mark 6. Splash the beetroot with a little vegetable oil and sprinkle with salt, then wrap each up tightly in foil and place on the baking tray. Roast for 1½ hours, or until a sharp paring knife can slide into the beetroot with little resistance. Leave to cool.

While the beetroot is roasting, make the winter spice: lightly toast the spices in a frying pan over a medium heat until fragrant, then crush in the mortar with a pestle, or use a coffee grinder. Set aside.

Next, make the rye crumbs. In a large frying pan, heat the butter over a medium-high heat, then add the chopped breadcrumbs, stirring to coat. Add a good pinch of the winter spice and fry until crisp, about 5 minutes. Transfer to kitchen paper and then into a container. Set aside.

Salt the turnip slices very generously and leave to sit in a bowl for 10 minutes. Once wilted and soft, wash the turnips in plenty of cold running water to remove the majority of the salt (taste them as you go), then squeeze them dry and, in a small bowl, combine with the crème fraîche and horseradish to taste. Set aside.

Now make the beetroot dressing. In a small pan, reduce the port by half over a medium-high heat, about 2–3 minutes. Stir in the beetroot juice, sugar and winter spice, and reduce for a few minutes. Add a few drops of the cornflour paste to help thicken to a light syrup consistency, then remove from the heat and add the balsamic glaze and vinegar, then season to taste.

Peel the cooled beetroot and cut into small dice. Combine with the beetroot dressing in the small saucepan. Keep warm over the lowest heat.

Now, the exciting part: smoking the venison loin. First, reduce the oven temperature to 180°C (350°F), Gas Mark 4.

Cover the bottom of an old roasting tin or cast-iron pan with foil. Lay a handful of wood chips on to the foil, then place the hay on top. Next, lay a well-oiled rack atop the hay. Place the tin or pan over a high heat. Have the meat and more foil ready next to the hob, as well as a container of water to eventually stop the smoking. The wood chips will self-ignite within 8–10 minutes and set the hay smoking as well. When the smoking starts to really happen, lay the meat on the rack and cover the tin or pan tightly with foil. Now is the time to turn on your kitchen fan and maybe crack open a window for good measure. Keep the meat covered and the pan going over a high heat for 5 minutes. »

FOR THE WINTER SPICE:
1 tsp coriander seeds
1 tsp caraway seeds
8 juniper berries

FOR THE RYE CRUMBS:
25g (1oz) salted butter
2 slices of rye bread, chopped into coarse
    crumbs
pinch of Winter Spice (*see* above)

FOR THE TURNIPS:
1 turnip, peeled and sliced paper-thin on
    a mandoline slicer
1 tsp sea salt
1 tbsp crème fraîche
horseradish root, peeled and finely grated,
    to taste (or use horseradish sauce)

FOR THE MEAT:
vegetable oil, for oiling and frying
350g (12oz) venison loin
200ml (7fl oz) Red Wine Jus (*see* page 207)
splash of red wine vinegar
1 slice of garlic
splash of walnut oil
handful of parsley leaves, to garnish
    (optional)

Remove from the heat. Remove the top layer of foil, then transfer the meat to a plate. Put out the smoking chips and hay by dousing with water.

In a flameproof sauté pan coated with a generous splash of oil, sear the venison quickly on all sides over a medium-high heat. Transfer the whole pan to the oven and roast the meat until the internal temperature registers 48°C (118°F), likely no more than 5 minutes. Remove from the oven, transfer the meat to a wooden board and leave to rest for 15 minutes, or until the thermometer registers 55°C (131°F).

Make the sauce for the venison while the meat is resting. In the same frying pan, over a medium heat, combine the red wine jus with the venison's drippings. Add the vinegar, garlic and walnut oil, then remove from the heat.

Carve the meat into thick slices, ideally 3 slices per person.

To serve, place a large spoonful of the beetroot salad in the centre of each plate. Add a small mound of the creamy turnip to each, then the venison slices. Garnish generously with rye crumbs, a few spoonfuls of the pan sauce and the parsley leaves, if liked.

Venison Wellington
Celeriac Purée

This is an absolute classic and typifies the type of cuisine you would expect to find in a grand hotel — during the festive season, we send out close to 400 Wellingtons a week. When I first arrived at Claridge's this dish was served from a trolley and only ever on Friday nights. Today, we find making a larger one en croûte still yields that 'wow' factor, when we carve and serve this to guests as a fillet. Our venison meat comes from Sika deer via Finclass, our London-based butchers, but it's been raised on the Yattendon estate in West Berkshire, or in the Scottish Highlands. The suppliers we use work with the Forestry Commission and certain stalkers to obtain the highest-quality venison possible. We like Sika because it's a smaller animal, with a smaller loin perfect for this dish. Although beef is what people associate the most with the Wellington treatment, venison is lean and marries perfectly to buttery puff pastry and the creamy chicken and chestnut mousse. You can serve this with Madeira Sauce (see page 207), Braised Red Cabbage (see page 98), celeriac purée and kale. Because the meat is cooked en croûte, we recommend having a meat thermometer on hand so you can check for doneness. We promise it won't take away from the excitement of gallantly cutting into it and seeing that you've achieved that perfect cuisson.

SERVES 4–6 (DEPENDING ON HOW HUNGRY OR GENEROUS YOU ARE)

NOTES:
The Wellington needs to be chilled in the refrigerator for a minimum of 2 hours before baking. You can, if you choose, make it, chill it and wrap it in the morning and bake it that evening. Important: the Wellington needs to rest for 4–5 minutes when removed from the oven. Any longer, and the pastry will become soft. Any less, and the juices will bleed when you cut into it. Like a soufflé, timing is everything here. So, at home, hand the conversation to your partner and tend to that Wellington.

YOU WILL NEED:
rolling pin
lattice pastry cutter
2 baking trays, lined with baking paper
ice bath
food processor
pastry brush
stick blender
digital thermometer with a probe

strong white flour, for dusting
400g (14oz) + 200g (7oz) cold Puff Pastry (*see* page 90)
8–10 large spinach leaves
600g (1lb 5oz) venison loin, free of sinew and trimmed

First things first: on a lightly floured surface, roll out both pieces of puff pastry to about 2mm (1/16 inch) thick: you should have a 30cm (12 inch) square to wrap the venison in, and a 20 x 15cm (8 x 6 inch) rectangle for the lattice. Cut the lattice pattern into the dough now. Don't fret about the smaller dimensions: the lattice will stretch nicely when you lay it over the wrapped Wellington. Transfer the pieces to a lined tray and refrigerate until needed, at least 2 hours.

In the meantime, if you haven't already, complete your mise en place: blanch the spinach leaves in a pan of salted boiling water, then transfer to an ice bath to cool. Squeeze dry, and reserve.

To make the chicken mousse, place your food processor bowl and blade in the freezer for 20 minutes, then blitz the chicken and egg white in a food processor for 1 minute until it forms a thick paste. Transfer to a bowl and, using a spatula, incorporate the cream. In a frying pan, over a medium-high heat, sauté the cèpes in a splash of oil until lightly browned, about 3 minutes. Pat the mushrooms between 2 pieces of kitchen paper to remove any excess oil. Leave to cool. Add the chopped chestnuts, the sautéed mushrooms, cèpe powder and salt and pepper to the chicken mixture. Refrigerate.

Meanwhile, make the celeriac purée. In a saucepan, over a medium-high heat, bring the milk to the boil. Add the celeriac and seasoning and simmer over a low heat for 20–25 minutes, testing with a small knife, as you would potatoes, to see if the celeriac is cooked. Drain thoroughly, return the celeriac to the saucepan, add the butter and blend to a fine purée. Keep warm until ready to serve. (This purée will also keep, chilled in the refrigerator, for up to 2 days).

Season the venison liberally with salt and pepper. In a frying pan over a high heat, sear the meat for 30 seconds on all sides, until it's browned all over. Transfer to a plate and refrigerate for 1 hour to cool completely.

It's now time to begin assembling the Wellington. Lay a large rectangle of clingfilm on your work surface. Overlap the spring-roll pastry squares to form a 25cm (10 inch) square, brushing their edges with eggwash to create a seam, then arrange the spinach to cover the spring-roll pastry completely. Place the venison in the centre of the square and spoon ❯❯

4 spring-roll pastry sheets, about 20cm (8 inches) square (check the freezer section at any Asian grocer)
2 egg yolks, beaten, for the eggwash
sea salt and freshly ground black pepper

FOR THE CHICKEN MOUSSE:
125g (4½oz) chicken breast, cut into small cubes and chilled
½ egg white
100ml (3½fl oz) double cream
25g (1oz) cèpes mushrooms, finely chopped (or 5g/⅛oz dried cèpes or porcini, rehydrated, or 25g/1oz frozen cèpes)
1 tbsp vegetable oil
20g (¾oz) chestnuts, finely chopped
½ tsp cèpe powder (make your own by blitzing dried cèpes in a spice grinder)
pinch of salt
pinch of freshly ground white pepper

FOR THE CELERIAC PURÉE:
500ml (18fl oz) milk
200g (7oz) celeriac, peeled and diced
½ tsp salt and freshly ground black pepper
30g (1oz) unsalted butter

TO SERVE:
400ml (14fl oz) Madeira Sauce (see page 207)
Braised Red Cabbage (see page 98)
kale (see page 192)

the chicken mousse along the length of the venison. Using the clingfilm or a clean tea towel for support, carefully roll up the spring-roll pastry and spinach over the meat and mousse to form a tight roll. Wrap tightly and refrigerate to set, about 1 hour.

Lay out the square of cold puff pastry on a lightly floured surface. Remove the clingfilm or towel from the venison log, then place in the centre of the square of puff pastry. Wrap the venison log in the pastry. Using a sharp knife, trim any excess pastry from each end of the log and discard. Brush all over with eggwash, paying particular attention to sealing the seams. Next, gently pick up and stretch open the lattice dough to cover the first layer of dough, trimming the lattice of any excess dough. Transfer to the prepared small baking tray and refrigerate for at least 2 hours.

Preheat the oven to 220°C (425°F), Gas Mark 7. Brush the dough with eggwash. (For extra browning, you can return the Wellington to the refrigerator for 10 minutes, then eggwash a second time.) Insert the thermometer into the venison section of the Wellington (you'll know you're in the right place by the resistance you encounter). Transfer to the oven and cook for 7 minutes, then reduce the oven temperature to 190°C (375°F), Gas Mark 5. Roast for about a further 25 minutes, or until the probe or digital thermometer registers an internal temperature of 36°C (97°F). Transfer the Wellington to a board and leave to rest for 4–5 minutes until the thermometer registers 52°C (126°F).

Cut and serve with warmed Madeira sauce and the vegetable sides of your choice.

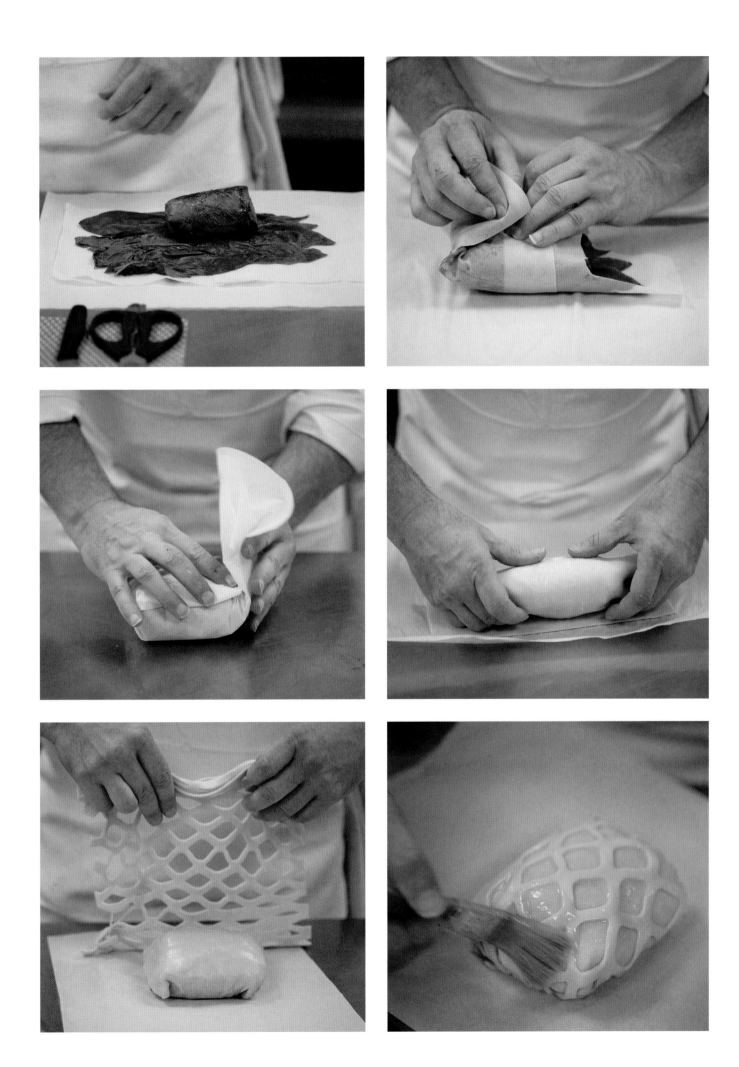

Lobster Wellington

For the 2016 Claridge's Christmas Tree Party – an annual tradition since 2009 – we substituted the venison (as used for the recipe on page 198) with lobster tail. A decadent alternative, fitting for such a festive affair. This Wellington is smaller in size and more delicate than the venison version. The mousseline is prawn here, and the method is similar to the chicken mousse in the Venison Wellington (see page 198). For this Wellington variation you will need all the equipment and ingredients listed on pages 198 and 200, omitting the spinach, venison and chicken mousse, plus the ingredients listed below.

90g (3¼oz) raw peeled prawns (about 5)

18g (¾oz) egg white (less than 1 white)

50ml (2fl oz) double cream

pinch of salt

pinch of freshly ground white pepper

2 tbsp reduced Lobster Bisque (*see* page 180)

2 tbsp Béarnaise Sauce (*see* page 207)

90g (3¼oz) cooked lobster tail

In a blender, purée the prawns and the egg white together. Add the double cream, salt and white pepper. This is the prawn mousseline. Transfer to a bowl and chill.

In a separate bowl, mix together the lobster bisque and béarnaise sauce. Roughly chop the lobster tail meat and mix with the bisque and béarnaise, being sure to coat the lobster well. Set aside to chill.

Follow the pastry and assembly instructions for the Wellington on page 198. When it's time to work on the filling, pipe the mousseline along the centre of the spring-roll pastry square. Place the lobster mixture down the centre, then continue to fold in the ends and roll up to form a long parcel following the instructions on pages 198 and 200. Transfer to the prepared small baking tray and refrigerate for at least 2 hours.

Preheat the oven to 200°C (400°F), Gas Mark 6 as you continue to prepare the Wellington.

Wrap the lobster roll in an 18 x 21cm (7 x 8¼ inch) rectangle of puff pastry, followed by the lattice pastry, then brush with the eggwash. Bake for 8 minutes, then reduce the oven temperature to 180°C (350°F), Gas Mark 4, and cook for a further 5 minutes.

Slice into 2cm (¾ inch) fingers and serve.

Pot-roasted Breast of Partridge
Truffle Sauce & Celeriac

A classic Claridge's combination: a princely game bird that appears on the menu only for a few months of the year, coupled with intensely earthy but creamy celeriac roasted in goats' butter, which elevates it from its lowly root-vegetable status, and finished with decadent fresh Périgord truffle.

SERVES 4

FOR THE CELERIAC:
1 celeriac, about 500g (1lb 2oz), scrubbed
200g (7oz) goats' butter

FOR THE TRUFFLED MADEIRA SAUCE:
20g (¾oz) fresh black truffle, finely chopped
25g (1oz) salted butter
50ml (2fl oz) ruby port
50ml (2fl oz) Malmsey Madeira
120ml (4fl oz) Madeira Sauce (*see* page 207)
sea salt and freshly ground black pepper

FOR THE PARTRIDGE:
200g (7oz) salted butter
4 oven-ready partridges (gutted and tied)
sea salt

FOR THE VEGETABLES:
150g (5½oz) kale leaves
25ml (1fl oz) vegetable oil
8g (¼oz) pine nuts
200g (7oz) salsify, peeled and cut into 9cm
　　(3½ inch) batons
50g (1¾oz) goats' butter

TO SERVE (OPTIONAL):
8 Chantenay carrots, peeled and cooked in a
　　butter and water emulsion for 8 minutes
1 golden and 1 purple beetroot, peeled, baked
　　in foil with salted butter and thyme, then
　　cut into eighths

Cook the celeriac first as this large orb will need a good 30 minutes to cook to the texture and taste we want. Place the celeriac in a heavy-based saucepan over a medium heat and add the goats' butter. Heat until the butter is foaming, then cover with a tight-fitting lid and reduce the heat. Turn occasionally to ensure even colouring. Test for doneness with a knife, as you would potatoes. Set aside.

Preheat the oven to 220°C (425°F), Gas Mark 7.

Next, make the truffled sauce. Over a medium-low heat, sweat the truffle in the butter for 4 minutes. Add the port and Madeira. Reduce slowly to half the amount, about 10 minutes. Meanwhile, warm the Madeira sauce in a separate saucepan. Transfer the truffle sauce to the Madeira sauce and bring to the boil. Reduce the heat and simmer very gently for 20 minutes, skimming occasionally. Season to taste, then remove from the heat.

To cook the partridges, foam the butter over a medium-high heat in a heavy-based frying pan. Add the partridges and baste the birds generously, season with salt. Transfer to the oven and roast for about 6–8 minutes, until the birds appear golden brown.

While the birds are cooking, sauté the kale very quickly in a pan with a little vegetable oil. Add the pine nuts. In a separate pan, caramelize the salsify in the goats' butter until tender, about 15 minutes, then drain on kitchen paper and set aside.

Remove the birds from the oven and leave to rest for 10 minutes. While the birds are resting, check the temperature of your vegetables and sauce and reheat as needed. Cut the celeriac into wedges.

To serve, remove the breasts from the bone and carefully remove the skin. Place the kale in the centre of each plate together with 2 batons of salsify, 2 carrots, 2 wedges each of purple and golden beetroots, and 2 wedges of celeriac. Arrange the partridge breasts on top and finish with about 2 dessertspoonfuls of the truffled Madeira sauce over the breasts.

Our Favourite Sauces

We make our veal stock from scratch, in 300 litre (66 gallon) batches, using 100kg (220lb) of veal bones and a substantial pressure boiler; to this stock, we add 6kg (13lb) of veal, 3kg (6lb 8oz) of shallots and 3kg (6lb 8oz) of button mushrooms to extract 80 litres (140 pints) of veal jus – which we do, day in day out, every day except Christmas Day. To make the Madeira sauce or the red wine jus, you'll first need to make the veal jus and proceed from there. The recipe below yields 500ml (18fl oz) veal jus (the amount needed for both sauces), but you'd be smart to double or even quadruple the recipe, and to freeze the jus in 500ml (18fl oz) amounts until needed. Both the veal jus and two sauces will keep in the refrigerator for 5 days in a sealed container and also freeze very well. Any leftover sauce can be used to add texture and richness to a stew, gravy or a Bolognese (see page 174).

YOU WILL NEED:
stockpot or large saucepan
fine-mesh sieve

Veal Jus

MAKES 500ML/18FL OZ

50ml (2fl oz) vegetable oil
200g (7oz) veal (ask your butcher for trimmings and/or veal shoulder)
40g (1½oz) shallots, chopped
40g (1½oz) mushrooms, sliced
1 tbsp tomato purée
30g (1oz) strong white flour
600ml (20fl oz) veal stock (available from your butcher)
sea salt and freshly ground black pepper

In a wide, heavy-based saucepan, heat the oil over a high heat. When the oil is hot, add the veal trimmings and cook, stirring occasionally, until nicely browned all over, about 5–7 minutes. Add the shallots and mushrooms, stirring to coat, and reduce the heat to medium. When the shallots are translucent, add the tomato purée and cook for 3 minutes over a medium-low heat.

Add the flour, one-third at a time, stirring after each addition, and, reducing the heat to low, cook for 5 minutes. Gradually stir in the veal stock, using a spatula to scrape any starch and caramelized meat particles off the bottom of the pan.

Transfer the jus base to a stockpot or large saucepan and bring to the boil over a high heat. Reduce the heat to low and simmer for 2 hours, skimming it regularly.

Lightly season the jus, then strain it through a fine-mesh sieve. Refrigerate or freeze until ready to use, or proceed with making the Madeira Sauce or Red Wine Jus now.

Madeira Sauce

MAKES 400ML/14FL OZ

30g (1oz) salted butter
50g (1¾oz) shallots, chopped
50g (1¾oz) mushrooms, sliced
350ml (12fl oz) Malmsey Madeira
3 white peppercorns
½ bay leaf
1 thyme sprig
500ml (18fl oz) Veal Jus (*see* left)
sea salt and freshly ground black pepper

Heat a medium saucepan over a medium heat. Add the butter, then the shallots and mushrooms. Sweat until the mushrooms have released their liquid and the shallots are softened and starting to lightly colour, about 5 minutes. Add the Madeira, peppercorns, bay leaf and thyme and bring to the boil. Reduce by half over a medium-low heat, about 10 minutes.

Stir in the veal jus and simmer for 40 minutes, or until the sauce coats the back of a spoon (when you run a finger along the back of the sauced spoon, exposing the metal, the sauce should not re-cover your finger's trail). Check and adjust the seasoning to taste. Pass through a fine-mesh sieve and keep warm until ready to use.

Red Wine Jus

MAKES 400ML/14FL OZ

30g (1oz) salted butter
50g (1¾oz) shallots, chopped
50g (1¾oz) button mushrooms, chopped
1 garlic clove, sliced
50g (1¾oz) smoked bacon or pancetta, chopped
350ml (12fl oz) red wine
3 white peppercorns
½ bay leaf
1 thyme sprig
500ml (18fl oz) Veal Jus (*see* far left)
sea salt and freshly ground black pepper

Heat a medium pan over a medium heat. Add the butter, then the shallots, mushrooms, garlic and bacon. Sweat until the mushrooms have released their liquid and the shallots are softened and starting to lightly colour, about 5 minutes. Add the red wine, peppercorns, bay leaf and thyme and bring to the boil. Reduce by half over a medium-low heat, about 10 minutes.

Stir in the veal jus and simmer for 40 minutes, or until the jus coats the back of a spoon (when you run a finger along the back of the sauced spoon, exposing the metal, the sauce should not re-cover your finger's trail). Check and adjust the seasoning to taste. Pass through a fine-mesh sieve and keep warm until ready to use.

Béarnaise Sauce

MAKES 320G (11¼OZ)

50g (1¾oz) egg yolks (about 2–3 yolks)
250g (9oz) clarified butter, warmed
4 tarragon sprigs, leaves stripped and finely chopped
sea salt and freshly ground black pepper

FOR THE VINEGAR REDUCTION:
62ml (2¼fl oz) good-quality white wine vinegar
10g (¼oz) finely chopped shallots
2 white peppercorns
4 tarragon sprigs

To make the vinegar reduction, place all the ingredients in a small saucepan and gently reduce by half to 2 tablespoons. Leave to cool and then strain.

Whisk the egg yolks in a heatproof bowl placed over a saucepan of simmering water until they start to thicken slightly and become frothy. Gradually add a little of the warm clarified butter, then continue to slowly add the remaining butter, occasionally adding about 1 teaspoon of hot water to the mixture as necessary (it will thicken as the butter is added and may need to be loosened in order to take more butter).

Finally, add the cooled vinegar reduction and chopped tarragon to taste, then season and keep warm until ready to use.

Our Favourite Sides

Beetroot & Eel Gratin

Beetroot is truly an amazing ingredient. How can a simple root vegetable have such a strange, moody colour, an earthy and sweet flavour? This side dish is a great accompaniment to the main event when it's a smoky, horseradish-loving item such as beef, salmon, mackerel, herring, duck or even a decadent burger.

SERVES 4

YOU WILL NEED:
foil
6 x 8cm (2½ x 3¼ inch) baking dish

1 purple beetroot, peeled
1 golden beetroot, peeled
30g (1oz) salted butter, softened
80g (2¾oz) crème fraîche
40g (1½oz) Parmesan cheese, grated
40g (1½oz) Gruyère cheese, grated
80g (2¾oz) smoked eel, skinned, fat
    trimmed, any bones removed and cut
    into 1cm (½ inch) cubes
1 tsp sea salt
½ tsp freshly ground white pepper

Preheat the oven to 190°C (375°F), Gas Mark 5.

Roll the beetroots in the butter, then wrap in foil and bake for 1½ hours, or until cooked but still toothsome. Leave to cool in the foil.

Reduce the oven temperature to 150°C (300°F), Gas Mark 2.

Unwrap the beetroot and cut into 1cm (½ inch) thick slices. Place in a bowl and mix with the crème fraiche, half the Parmesan and Gruyère and the salt and pepper.

Arrange half the beetroot mixture into the baking dish, add the eel, then cover with the remaining beetroot. Sprinkle with the remaining cheese. Bake for 15 minutes, then brown briefly under a hot grill.

Kale, Peanut & Ginger Salad

This salad is a tremendous side to accompany a sirloin, veal or even sushi (homemade or takeaway). It's packed with vitamins A and C and is a supreme digestive for the healthy or the hungover.

SERVES 4

250g (9oz) smooth peanut butter
zest and juice of 4 limes
20ml (¾fl oz) ginger juice
1 shallot, finely diced
300g (10½oz) kale, washed, stalks removed
    and hand-shredded
handful of dry-roasted salted peanuts, halved

In a large bowl, whisk together the peanut butter, lime juice and zest, ginger juice and shallot. You want a creamy consistency. If it's still a bit thick, add water to thin out.

Toss the kale generously with the peanut dressing, adding more or less to your liking.

Divide into 4 bowls and top each portion with a sprinkling of peanuts. Any leftover dressing will keep in the refrigerator for up to 1 week.

Truffled Macaroni Gratin

Though we do love a good Mac 'n' Cheese, it seemed a bit too pedestrian for our sides menu and so we decided to up the ante with creamy suprême sauce, Parmesan, a good helping of wild mushrooms and Périgord truffles. Though it most certainly won't win any healthy meal awards, it's versatile enough to accompany any main dish.

SERVES 4

YOU WILL NEED:
coffee grinder
large baking sheet

2 litres (3½ pints) water
24g (1oz) sea salt
100ml (3½fl oz) vegetable oil
260g (9¼oz) macaroni pasta
2 tbsp olive oil
130g (4½oz) wild mushrooms, cleaned and
    trimmed
15g (½oz) unsalted butter
½ x quantity Suprême Sauce (*see* pages
    168–70)
1 tsp dried cèpes, blended to a powder in a
    coffee grinder
¾ tsp truffle oil
150g (5½oz) Parmesan cheese, grated
2 tbsp Truffled Madeira Sauce (*see* page 204)
sea salt and freshly ground black pepper

Bring the measured water to a rapid boil, then add the salt and vegetable oil. Add the macaroni and cook for 5 minutes, then drain and spread out on to a large baking sheet to cool. Mix in the olive oil to stop the pasta from sticking together.

Sauté the wild mushrooms in the butter, season lightly, then drain on kitchen paper.

In a medium ovenproof pan, combine the suprême sauce, cèpe powder and truffle oil. Bring to the boil over a medium-high heat, then add the macaroni, mushrooms and Parmesan and return to the boil, stirring well. Spoon over the truffle sauce and then glaze under a hot grill for 3 minutes. Adjust the seasoning and serve.

Les Pommes Chateau

Classical pommes chateau date back to when French cuisine ruled the world. Potatoes are deliberately trimmed or 'turned' into 6.5cm (2½-inch) long neat barrel shapes, then browned in butter and braised in the oven until tender. Because of their shape, they cook evenly and are quite pleasing to the eye. Nothing makes me feel older than when a new kitchen recruit replies, 'Turning, what's that?' when asked to make these. These potatoes are known as chateau because they were the traditional accompaniment to a Chateaubriand steak.

SERVES 4

YOU WILL NEED:
10 x 30cm (4 x 12 inch) baking dish

6 large Maris Piper potatoes
60g (2¼oz) salted butter
500ml (18fl oz) Double Chicken Stock (*see* page 76)
½ bay leaf
1 thyme sprig
pinch of sea salt

Preheat the oven to 160°C (325°F), Gas Mark 3.

First, cut the potatoes into 8cm (3¼-inch) long and 5cm (2-inch) wide pieces. Next, 'turn' each potato piece with a sharp paring knife into a 7-sided barrel, about 6.5cm (2½ inches) long and 4cm (1½ inches) wide: trim along the length of the potato, then turn the potato slightly to continue trimming the next facet of the 'barrel', and so on. Working in long smooth motions will yield the best results. And, of course, practice – lots of it – makes perfect! You should end up with 12 turned potatoes.

In a sauté pan, seal the potatoes in the butter until golden brown. Transfer to the baking dish and half-cover with stock. Add the bay leaf, thyme and salt.

Braise in the oven for 25 minutes, or until a small knife can be released easily when placed in the thickest part of the potatoes. Drain before serving.

Game Chips

Game chips are classically served with game and are really just fancy crisps with tiny holes in them, also known as 'waffle chips' in North America.

SERVES 4

YOU WILL NEED:
mandoline slicer fitted with a rippled/zigzag blade
table-top deep-fryer or large, deep, heavy-based pan (*see* Note on page 56)
deep-frying thermometer
bowl lined with kitchen paper

400g (14oz) Maris Piper potatoes, peeled
1 litre (1¾ pints) vegetable oil, for deep-frying
pinch of sea salt

Carefully slide a potato down the mandoline; this will put teeth marks in the potato. Rotate the potato 90 degrees, then slide down the mandoline again. This will make a slice. Do a few sample slices to check that the thickness is correct, about 3mm (⅛ inch), then repeat with all the potatoes.

Once all the potatoes are sliced, transfer them to a colander and wash once in cold water, to remove excess starch. Drain very well and lay out on kitchen paper to dry for 15 minutes.

Heat the oil to 180°C (350°F). Working in batches, carefully scatter the potato slices in the oil and cook until light golden and crisp, about 3 minutes. Remove using a slotted spoon and transfer to the prepared bowl. Season lightly with salt and enjoy.

How to Host
Dinner for 100 (or more)

What is it that makes a great dinner party? The flowers? The flowing Champagne? The guest list? The décor? Arguably it's all of these, at Claridge's we take our parties very seriously indeed. But for us in the kitchen it's obviously the food.

Now when I say the food, I mean two things: first there must be a coherence to the menu. A côte de boeuf with sauce béarnaise and pommes frites, for example, should not be followed by a tiramisu, it simply doesn't work. The menu needs to flow from course to course. Secondly, there is the issue of execution. Each individual dish must sing on its own. Which is to say it must taste like it was created for one, even if in reality that number is closer to 240. To create a great event is to walk a fine balance between the art and style of details and the science of timing and preparation.

At Claridge's the number of diners can be dizzying. Most nights of the week there are events taking place in both the Drawing Room (holds 92) and the Ballroom (holds 240). We have had the privilege to host state dinners, weddings, awards dinners, birthdays, diplomatic events, make-or-break deals... and parties for no reason at all. Guests place their trust in us to think of everything from menu cards

to place settings. We like to think that an invitation from Claridge's is an invitation well received.

Our event planning starts with a meeting, where we listen and learn about the host's perfect vision. On many occasions events remind us of a dish and we will then introduce it to our du jour menu. The Roast Duck Breast (*see* page 98) for example, was a dish that we created for the Whisky Club of London where we had to come up with a dish that would pair with peaty whisky.

Some of the most legendary parties in London have happened in the Claridge's Ballroom. Audrey Hepburn cut her welcome home cake at Claridge's during the *Roman Holiday* wrap party and for the Diane von Furstenberg party the theme was a Deco Jazz Supper Club for which we served one of Diane's favourites, the Lobster Risotto (*see* page 80). For the Royal Academy of Culinary Arts Dinner we served roast loin of rosé

veal and for dessert a lemon and vanilla soufflé. The idea here was to showcase French technical cookery in the tradition of the Royal Academy. Often the case is that if the party upstairs is content, then so are the chefs below.

BEHIND THE SCENES

Events are as dramatic behind the scenes as they are in front: waiting staff are poised at the stairs, orchestrated, theatrical, only a few moments to deliver 2 or 3 days' work. When it's time to serve, we've done the work, we just need to deliver it. Coming off the pass, the silver weighs more than some of the staff and the heat alone could sear a misplaced elbow. We can send 250 covers in about 11 minutes. The plates leave the banquet kitchen in waves of 40 at a time. We wait, charged for the 10-minute countdown on the sea bass course. The head waiter gives the signal and it's 'mains away', as the service team files uniformly up on the staircase. Where the restaurant service is controlled like an orchestra, the banquet kitchen needs control with military nerve, knowing when to hold back and when to strike. Start plating too early and the food will not stay hot, leave it too late and the service will take too long. And so the chef de cuisine stands with courage and says to wait, knowing from experience that diners will be seated a couple of moments late and the ducks can be crisped a few seconds longer, so the cuisson is indeed medium rare. With two minutes left on the clock, the garnish is being plated, the final sounds of duck skin crisping in the oven can be heard. Sous chefs glance towards the head waiter to be ready for the command to 'pick up', the first sea bass is placed and the plates are passed to the waiting teams like clockwork; the chefs pick up their pace, dressing the garnish, then after hours of preparation it's over in minutes.

CLARIDGE'S EVENT RULES

*Listen to the guest. If they want a 20-course meal in 1 hour we believe them, which leads to the second rule...

*We never commit to something we can't achieve.

*The meal has to come together in a complete way, from start to finish. Review the menu well.

* Execution: We have to be able to make a dish for 240 as well as we would for 1. The expectation that people have when they come to Claridge's is they're the only one. And we like that. We want them to feel that. It is en masse but it's not en masse. Every event to us is unique and individual.

Dessert

Soufflés

The great Pierre Hermé says you should never show a soufflé your fear. He's right. Soufflés are not about expensive ingredients, but rather all about timing and care: if you're having people over, you can have the soufflé base sitting in ramekins ahead of dinner, so that when the time comes for dessert, you only have to bake them. A properly mixed soufflé base can stay stable for a good hour in the refrigerator before cooking. However, once cooked, a soufflé waits for no one, so make sure you're about ready for dessert when you put these in the oven. The three variations we're including all take this Vanilla Soufflé, below, as their starting point and also make 6 soufflés each.

MAKES 6 INDIVIDUAL SOUFFLÉS

YOU WILL NEED:
6 x 10cm (4 inch) ramekins, each with a
    capacity of 240ml (8½fl oz)
pastry brush
fine-mesh sieve
stand mixer fitted with the whisk attachment
small baking sheet

FOR THE RAMEKINS:
unsalted butter, softened
caster sugar

FOR THE SOUFFLÉ BASE:
250ml (9fl oz) milk
½ vanilla pod, split lengthways and seeds
    scraped
37.5g (1¼oz) unsalted butter
30g (1oz) strong white flour
100g (3½oz) egg yolks (about 5–6 yolks)
50g (1¾oz) icing sugar, plus extra for dusting
13g (½oz) cornflour
200g (7oz) egg whites (about 6–7 whites),
    at room temperature
13g (½oz) caster sugar

Vanilla Soufflé

Begin by buttering the bottom and sides of the ramekins with a pastry brush, using vertical strokes along the wall of the ramekins, then sprinkle with caster sugar to coat, shaking off any excess. Those upward strokes of butter and the sugar will provide the soufflé mix something to hold on to when rising (a few deliberate gestures make a soufflé!). Refrigerate the ramekins until ready to fill.

In a small saucepan, combine the milk and vanilla pod and seeds, then bring to the boil. Remove from the heat, discarding the vanilla pod.

In a separate medium saucepan, melt the butter. Next, whisk in the flour to make a paste. Slowly add the hot milk, whisking constantly to remove any lumps. Bring to the boil, then remove from the heat.

Whisk in the egg yolks until well combined. Transfer to a large mixing bowl and lay clingfilm on the surface of the custard base to prevent a skin from forming. Leave to cool.

Sift the icing sugar and cornflour into a bowl. Set aside.

Using the stand mixer, beat the egg whites on medium speed until they reach soft peaks. With the machine running, gradually add the caster sugar and beat until the egg whites become glossy and just start to form stiff peaks. (Whites whisked on medium speed rather than high speed will hold their structure better and longer; over-whisked whites will result in surface cracks in your soufflé!). Reduce the speed to low and whisk in the icing sugar and cornflour mixture.

To ensure soufflé lightness, vigorously stir one-quarter of the egg whites into the vanilla custard base to lighten it – it's okay if you deflate this portion of the whites – before gently folding in the remainder of the egg whites.

If you plan on baking the soufflés now, preheat the oven to 220°C (425°F), Gas Mark 7.

Place the ramekins on the baking sheet. Gently divide the mixture among the ramekins, leaving 2cm (¾ inch) free at the top for the rise. If you're working ahead, you can now refrigerate these soufflés for up to 1 hour, remembering to preheat your oven beforehand.

Transfer to the oven. Immediately reduce the oven temperature to 190°C (375°F), Gas Mark 5, and bake for 17–20 minutes. The soufflé is ready when it has risen fully, probably some 3–4cm (1¼–1½ inches) above the rims of the ramekins.

Dust liberally with icing sugar and serve immediately.

Chocolate Soufflé

1 x quantity Vanilla Soufflé base (*see* page 218)

50g (1¾oz) dark chocolate, broken into pieces

35g (1¼oz) cocoa powder

Make the soufflé following the Vanilla Soufflé recipe on page 218. When the egg yolks have been added to the custard base, stir in the chocolate pieces until melted and well combined. Sift the cocoa powder with the icing sugar and cornflour into a bowl, then continue following the Vanilla Soufflé recipe.

Harlequin Soufflé

YOU WILL ALSO NEED:

2 piping bags, each fitted with a large plain piping tip

10cm (4 inch) round piece of cardboard

1 x quantity Vanilla Soufflé base (*see* page 218)

50g (1¾oz) dark chocolate, broken into small pieces

To make these half-vanilla, half-chocolate soufflés, follow the Vanilla Soufflé recipe on page 218.

After whisking in the egg yolks, divide the mixture equally into 2 bowls. Stir the dark chocolate pieces into one bowl until melted and combined. Cover the surface of both custards with clingfilm and set aside. Continue with the Vanilla Soufflé recipe.

Divide the stiff egg white mixture in half, then stir one-quarter of the egg whites into each custard base to lighten it, before gently folding in the remainder of the egg whites.

Fill each piping bag with one of the mixes. Hold (or ask someone to hold) the cardboard divider vertically in the middle of a ramekin. Pipe each mix on either side of the divider, then gently lift it out, wipe and repeat with the remaining ramekins. Your ramekins are ready to be refrigerated or baked now.

Soufflé Rothschild

30g (1oz) glacé cherries, finely chopped

30g (1oz) mixed peel, finely chopped

75ml (2½fl oz) Grand Marnier

100ml (3½fl oz) water

100g (3½oz) caster sugar

1 x quantity Vanilla Soufflé base (*see* page 218)

zest of 1 orange

6 sponge fingers, halved

A few hours ahead of time, combine the cherries, mixed peel and 25ml (1fl oz) of the Grand Marnier in a small bowl. Leave to soak.

In a small saucepan, boil the measured water and sugar together until dissolved. Remove from the heat and add a further 25ml (1fl oz) of the Grand Marnier. Leave to cool.

Make the soufflé following the Vanilla Soufflé recipe on page 218. When the egg yolks have been whisked into the custard base, also stir in the orange zest and remaining Grand Marnier. Continue with the Vanilla Soufflé recipe.

When the egg whites have been folded into the custard base, very gently mix the soaked fruits into the soufflé mixture.

Before filling the ramekins, quickly dip the sponge fingers in the Grand Marnier syrup and place 2 halves in the base of each ramekin, then fill with the soufflé base. Your ramekins are ready to be refrigerated or baked now.

Praline
Bombe Glacée

This is a frozen ice cream mousse served with a warm chocolate sauce; it was popularized by Escoffier, who also gave the world the Peach Melba and Poire Belle-Hélène. For something that can be put together fairly quickly on the day-of, this dessert looks wildly impressive and tastes completely decadent.

**MAKES 6 INDIVIDUAL BOMBES
OR 1 LARGE BOMBE**

YOU WILL NEED:
baking paper
instant-read digital thermometer or sugar
    thermometer
stand mixer fitted with the whisk attachment
6cm (2½ inch) demi-sphere silicone flexi
    mould (with at least 12 indents), or a
    600ml (1 pint) pudding basin (we use
    Mason Cash's S30), lined with a double
    layer of clingfilm
stick blender

FOR THE PECAN PRALINE:
75g (2¾oz) caster sugar
125g (4½oz) pecan nuts

FOR THE BOMBE:
1 vanilla pod, split lengthways and seeds
    scraped
250ml (9fl oz) whipping cream
100g (3½oz) caster sugar
2 tbsp water
75g (2¾oz) egg yolks (about 4 yolks)
125g (4½oz) Pecan Praline (*see* above),
    roughly chopped

FOR THE CHOCOLATE SAUCE:
170g (6oz) dark chocolate (55% cocoa solids
    or more), roughly chopped
25g (1oz) caster sugar
250ml (9fl oz) milk
50ml (1¾fl oz) liquid glucose

Start by making the caramel for the praline. Place a medium saucepan over a medium heat. Leave to warm for 3–4 minutes, then sprinkle 1 tablespoon of the sugar evenly over the bottom. This should melt very quickly. When the sugar is melted and clear, sprinkle another tablespoon of sugar into the pan. Repeat this until all the sugar has been added to the pan and is liquid. If part of the sugar starts to caramelize more than other parts, slowly and gently swirl the pan to achieve an even caramel, or add a few drops of water to help it along. When a deep amber colour is achieved, immediately stir in the pecans using a heatproof spatula. When all the nuts are evenly coated in the caramel, quickly pour out on to a piece of baking paper and spread the nuts into a single layer as much as possible. Leave to cool completely, then roughly chop. The praline will keep, stored in an airtight container, for 1–2 weeks.

To make the bombe, combine the vanilla seeds with the cream in a medium bowl, then whip to soft peaks. Set aside. In a small saucepan over a high heat, bring the sugar and measured water to the boil, then reduce the heat to medium-low. Continue cooking until the thermometer reads 121°C (250°F), about 7 minutes. While the sugar syrup is cooking, in the stand mixer, whisk the egg yolks on medium-high speed until thick, foamy and pale yellow, about 5 minutes. When the sugar syrup reaches temperature, remove from the heat and let the bubbling subside slightly. With the mixer running at medium-low speed, slowly add the syrup to the egg yolks, pouring down the inside of the bowl and avoiding the whisk, to prevent lumps. Increase the speed to medium-high and continue whisking until the exterior of the bowl feels cool to the touch and the egg yolks are pale, thick and fluffy like shaving foam, 3–4 minutes. Remove the bowl from the mixer. Using a spatula, gently fold the whipped cream into the egg foam (known as pâte à bombe), then fold in 125g (4½oz) of the chopped pecan praline, reserving the leftovers for decoration.

Divide the mixture between 12 demi-spheres indents and freeze for 4–6 hours or overnight. If you are using the pudding basin instead, pour in the pâte à bombe, wrap the top and freeze for 6–8 hours or overnight. (These can be kept, tightly wrapped, for up to 2 months in the freezer but really are best served soon after making – the sugar around the caramelized pecans starts to dissolve and loses some of its crunch – but the bombe will still taste great.)

To make the warm chocolate sauce, place the chocolate in a heatproof bowl. In a medium saucepan, combine the sugar, milk and glucose, then bring to the boil over a medium heat. Pour over the chocolate and leave to stand for a few minutes. Stir with a whisk until smooth, then switch to the stick blender to blitz any lumps and emulsify the milk, sugar and chocolate. Transfer to a jug to serve immediately while still hot, or reserve and reheat as needed (in the microwave or a small saucepan).

To serve, chill your bowls or serving plate prior to serving. If using the demi-spheres, unmould and press 2 domes together to create a ball, working quickly to ensure there are as few fingerprints as possible. Run your hand over the ball to smooth it as needed. Place a ball in each bowl. Scatter the reserved praline over the top of each. Serve with a jug of warm chocolate sauce for people to pour over their bombe. If you used the pudding basin instead, leave to stand at room temperature for a minute or so, then pull on the clingfilm to get it out of the basin. Peel off the wrap, place on a chilled plate or serving platter and scatter with the reserved praline. Slice with a hot knife and serve with the hot chocolate sauce as above.

Salted Caramel Peanut Bars

This is essentially the most luxe, crispy, rich and chocolatey bar going. We serve these for elevenses topped with gold leaf and accompanied with honeycomb, peanuts, chocolate streusel, caramel sauce and vanilla ice cream. Enjoying a bar at home with a cup of tea will prove quite indulgent.

MAKES 24

NOTE:
This can be made and served on the same day, or made one day and then, the following day, simply glazed and cut.

YOU WILL NEED:
stand mixer fitted with the whisk attachment
fine-mesh sieve
23 x 33 x 4.5cm (9 x 13 x 1¾ inch) cake tin, lined with baking paper
palette knife
stick blender

FOR THE CHOCOLATE SPONGE:
2 eggs, separated
40g (1½oz) caster sugar
40g (1½oz) strong white flour
5g (⅛oz) cocoa powder

FOR THE CRISPY PEANUT LAYER:
70g (2½oz) Valrhona Jivara milk chocolate, broken into pieces
25g (1oz) unsalted butter
250g (9oz) unsweetened natural peanut butter (chunky or smooth as you prefer)
35g (1¼oz) toasted unsalted peanuts, roughly chopped
60g (2¼oz) puffed rice cereal

FOR THE SALTED CARAMEL GANACHE:
80g (2¾oz) caster sugar
11ml (¼fl oz) liquid glucose
180g (6½oz) unsalted butter, softened
250ml (9fl oz) double cream
40g (1½oz) honey
1 tsp vanilla extract
470g (1lb 1oz) Valrhona Jivara milk chocolate, broken into pieces
generous pinch of sea salt

FOR THE CHOCOLATE TOPPING:
200g (7oz) dark chocolate, broken into pieces
1 tbsp vegetable oil

Preheat the oven to 160°C (325°F), Gas Mark 3.

First, make the sponge. Using the stand mixer, whisk the egg whites on medium-high speed until soft peaks form. While the machine is still running, slowly add the sugar. Continue to whisk until a stiff, glossy meringue has formed, about 2 minutes. Remove the bowl from the mixer and gently fold in the egg yolks until just combined. Sift the flour and cocoa powder into the meringue mixture, then fold in gently until fully combined. Spread the sponge mixture into the prepared cake tin. Bake for 8–12 minutes, or until the sponge is dry on top and springs back when gently pressed in the centre. Leave to cool in the tin.

Next, make the crispy peanut layer. Melt the chocolate and butter in a heatproof bowl placed over a saucepan of simmering water or in the microwave. When the mixture is warm and completely melted, remove the bowl from the heat and, using a spatula, stir in the peanut butter. Add the chopped peanuts and puffed rice and mix until completely combined but without crushing the puffed rice. Tip the puffed rice mixture on to the cooled sponge (it's okay if the sponge is still slightly warm). Using a palette knife, level the top and then refrigerate for 20 minutes, until set.

Meanwhile, make the ganache. Put the sugar and glucose into a medium saucepan and cook over a medium heat, stirring occasionally with a wooden spoon until the sugar has liquefied and turned a dark amber colour, about 5–8 minutes. When caramelized, carefully add 65g

(2¼oz) of the butter and stir until melted and fully incorporated into the caramel. Add the cream, honey and vanilla extract and bring the sauce to the boil, stirring to ensure there are no lumps of hard sugar. When it boils, remove the pan from the heat and set aside while you melt the chocolate.

Melt the chocolate in a heatproof bowl placed over a saucepan of simmering water or in the microwave. When melted, remove the bowl from the heat and add the hot caramel sauce, one-third at a time, stirring it in well with a spatula after each addition. When all of the sauce is added, using the stick blender, slowly incorporate the remaining butter, then add the salt. Blend the ganache until it is completely smooth, then pour on to the crispy layer. Refrigerate until semi-firm, about 1 hour.

To make the chocolate topping, melt the chocolate with the oil in a heatproof bowl placed over a saucepan of simmering water until smooth and liquid, then pour over the semi-set ganache layer. Spread evenly with a palette knife. Return the tin to the refrigerator and chill until the salted caramel ganache layer is firm enough to cut, about 4 hours or overnight.

To serve, run a sharp knife under hot water, then dry. Rest the hot, dry knife on the top of the chocolate as though you are going to cut it into bars. Allow the heat of the knife to melt through the chocolate topping before slicing through to the base. (The process of letting the hot knife melt the chocolate is a bit slow but will ensure your chocolate topping doesn't shatter.) Cut into 24 bars, each 2.5 x 9cm (1 x 3½ inches).

Serve the bars chilled. These will keep in a sealed airtight container in the refrigerator for up to 5 days.

Rice Pudding

Arsenal versus Chelsea, Labour versus Conservative, hob versus in-the-oven rice pudding: these are the major conundrums of our day. Those in favour of the hob will argue there is more control over consistency. Those for oven baking will attest that in the oven the milk almost caramelizes to a sumptuous brown, which adds a next-level dimension with every spoonful. We have been known to spruce up our rice pudding with seasonal favourites, such as stewed berries, baby pink rhubarb and mint (pictured). Rice pudding may not be the star of our menu, but it will always be there for you. It is, simply put, a great comfort.

SERVES 6

1 litre (1¾ pints) milk
1 vanilla pod, split lengthways and seeds
    scraped
110g (4oz) caster sugar
125g (4½oz) Arborio rice
75g (2¾oz) egg yolks (about 4 yolks)

Pour the milk into a medium heavy-based saucepan, then add the vanilla pod and seeds. Add half of the sugar and bring to the boil. Stir in the rice and reduce the heat to medium while still maintaining a simmer. Gently cook the rice until the milk has thickened slightly and the rice is tender, about 25 minutes, stirring regularly to ensure the rice doesn't stick to the bottom and the milk doesn't burn.

When the rice is cooked, stir in the remaining sugar. Remove from the heat and discard the vanilla pod. Quickly stir in the egg yolks.

Transfer the rice pudding to a clean bowl. Cover with clingfilm and leave to cool for 1 hour. Serve either warm or cold.

This will keep refrigerated for 3 days.

Baked Alaska

Alaska the dessert, much like the place, has a big impact. We've served this classic for New Year's Dinner many years in a row. Fresh summer raspberries made into sorbet are mellowed with velvety vanilla parfait, topped off with a duvet of silky toasted meringue. This really does make a stunning end to any meal. We serve it in 300 individual portions, getting them the right colour on time, then individually lit with a sparkler and out the door before the clock strikes midnight.

SERVES 4–6

NOTES:

We have included a raspberry sorbet recipe. It's not easy. There are beautiful sorbet options out there available to you if you decide to go the store-bought route, in which case you will need 250g (9oz) ready-made raspberry sorbet. If you plan on enjoying the Alaska for dinner, you will need to make it in the morning as there is a minimum chilling time of 6–8 hours. If you are making the raspberry sorbet, start a day earlier.

YOU WILL NEED:
stand mixer fitted with the whisk attachment
fine-mesh sieve
20cm (8 inch) round cake tin, lined with
    baking paper
1 litre (1¾ pint) pudding basin (we use Mason
    Cash's S30)
instant-read digital thermometer, or sugar
    thermometer
pastry brush
palette knife
kitchen blowtorch

IF YOU ARE MAKING YOUR OWN SORBET, YOU WILL ALSO NEED:
high-speed blender
ice cream maker

Right: For an even more theatrical dessert, very gently warm 25ml (1fl oz) each of brandy and kirsch in a small pan with a handle. Carefully light, then gently pour over the Alaska. Note: as the brandy and kirsch warm, the alcohol is released into the air and it is quite flammable, so stand back a little when you light it and do not leave the alcohol near a flame.

If you are making your own raspberry sorbet, place all the sorbet ingredients in the blender. Blend on high speed for 1–2 minutes, or until completely smooth except for the seeds. Strain the mixture through a fine-mesh sieve into a medium saucepan, discarding the seeds, and bring to the boil over a medium heat, stirring frequently. Remove from the heat, transfer the purée to a clean bowl or storage container, cover and leave to cool completely or overnight in the refrigerator.

To make the sponge, preheat the oven to 160°C (325°F), Gas Mark 3. Using the stand mixer, whisk the egg whites on medium-high speed until soft peaks form. While the machine is still running, slowly add the sugar. Continue to whisk until a stiff, glossy meringue has formed, about 2 minutes. Remove the bowl from the mixer and gently fold in the egg yolks until just combined. Sift the flour into the meringue mixture, then fold in gently until fully combined. Pour the sponge mixture into the prepared cake tin. Bake for 12–15 minutes, or until the sponge is dry on top and springs back when gently pressed in the centre. Leave to cool completely in the tin.

Pour the cold raspberry sorbet mixture into the ice cream maker and churn following the manufacturer's instructions.

Meanwhile, remove the cooled sponge from the tin and cut it in half horizontally through the middle. Using the upturned pudding basin as a guide, cut out a sponge disc from one of the sponge halves and set aside. Save the remaining sponge half for later use, or discard. Line the pudding basin with clingfilm.

Next, make the syrup. In a small pan, combine the measured water and sugar, then bring to the boil. Remove from the heat and add your alcohol of choice.

Scoop the churned sorbet (or ready-made sorbet) into the prepared pudding basin. Press it evenly and flat in the bottom of the basin, then freeze while you make the vanilla parfait.

To make the parfait, combine the vanilla seeds with the cream in a bowl and whip to soft peaks. Set aside. In a small saucepan, bring the sugar and measured water to the boil over a high heat, then reduce the heat to medium-low. Continue cooking until the thermometer registers 121°C (250°F), about 7 minutes.

Meanwhile, whisk the egg yolks in the (cleaned) stand mixer until thick, foamy and pale yellow, about 5 minutes.

When the sugar syrup reaches the required temperature, remove from the heat and let the bubbling subside slightly. With the mixer running at medium-low speed, slowly add the hot sugar syrup to the egg yolks, pouring down the inside of the bowl and trying not to get any on the whisk, to avoid lumps. Increase the speed to high and continue whisking until the exterior of the bowl feels cool to the touch and the egg yolks are pale, thick and fluffy like shaving foam, 3–4 minutes. Remove the bowl from the mixer. Using a spatula, fold the whipped cream, in thirds, into the egg foam. »

FOR HOMEMADE RASPBERRY SORBET (OPTIONAL):

115ml (4fl oz) water
10ml (¼fl oz) liquid invert sugar
70g (2½oz) caster sugar
2.5g (1⁄16oz) sorbet stabilizer
25g (1oz) atomized glucose or 60ml (2¼fl oz) liquid glucose
225g (8oz) raspberry purée (*see* page 142)

FOR THE GENOISE SPONGE:

2 eggs, separated
40g (1½oz) caster sugar
45g (1½oz) strong white flour

FOR THE SYRUP:

50ml (2fl oz) water
50g (1¾oz) caster sugar
50ml (2fl oz) Grand Marnier, brandy or kirsch

FOR THE VANILLA PARFAIT:

1 vanilla pod, split lengthways and seeds scraped
250ml (9fl oz) whipping cream
100g (3½oz) caster sugar
2 tbsp water
75g (2¾oz) egg yolks (about 4 yolks)

FOR THE ITALIAN MERINGUE:

50g (1¾oz) egg whites (about 1–2 whites)
100g (3½oz) caster sugar
2 tbsp water

Pour the vanilla parfait on to the frozen raspberry sorbet in the pudding basin (it should be soft enough to level itself). Place the reserved sponge disc on top, then brush the sponge all over with the reserved flavoured syrup. Cover tightly with clingfilm and freeze for at least 4 hours, or until the parfait is completely frozen.

When ready to serve, make the Italian meringue. Using the (cleaned) stand mixer, whisk the egg whites on medium speed until foamy, about 1 minute. Combine the sugar and measured water in a small pan. Bring to the boil over a high heat and cook. After about 5 minutes, when the thermometer registers 113°C (235°F), turn the stand mixer back on, at high speed this time, and whisk the egg whites until they form medium-firm peaks, about 2 minutes. When the boiling syrup reaches 121°C (250°F), remove from the heat and let the bubbling subside for a few moments.

Now switch the mixer to a slow-medium speed and slowly pour the hot sugar syrup along the inside edge of the bowl into the egg whites, trying not to get any on the whisk, to avoid lumps. Increase the speed to high and whisk for 2 minutes to cool the meringue quickly, then decrease the speed to medium and continue to whisk until the bowl is lukewarm to the touch, a further 3 minutes.

Remove the Alaska from the freezer. Very carefully turn it upside down and wedge the bombe out on to a serving plate removing the clingfilm. Using a palette knife, spread the Italian meringue over the bombe, leaving no gaps. Channelling your inner pastry chef, create nice tips and waves. Using a blowtorch, toast until golden. Serve soon after with pride.

Right: Pastry chef Kimberly Lin. (Also pictured with Martyn Nail on page 57.)

Chocolate Fondants
with Raspberry Ripple Ice Cream

This versatile fondant is a staple of the Claridge's pastry section and makes appearances on both the events menu and our dessert menu. We make ripple ice cream using many variations on the same principle: layers of vanilla ice cream alternating with a sorbet of some kind. We make our bases and churn them in-house, so it is easy for us to switch up. . .not to mention our large freezers and cold-storage space. If you wish to save time and buy a good-quality vanilla ice cream and fruit sorbet of your choice, you have our blessing. Ignore the ice cream recipes herein and skip straight to the layering method for the ripple.

MAKES 6 INDIVIDUAL FONDANTS

NOTE:
The ice cream and sorbet stabilizers may seem superfluous, but they do noticeably improve the texture of the final product. You can order these speciality ingredients and the mousse moulds from suppliers such as MSK Ingredients and Amazon.

YOU WILL NEED:
instant-read digital thermometer
fine-mesh sieve over a large mixing bowl set
    over ice
ice cream maker, with (ideally) an extra
    freezer bowl
900g (2lb) loaf tin (23 x 13cm/9 x 5 inches)
stand mixer, with whisk attachment and
    paddle attachment
6 x 6cm (2½ inch) mousse rings
baking tray, lined with baking paper
six 10 x 20cm (4 x 8 inch) strips of baking
    paper
disposable piping bag (no tip needed, just cut
    the bag)

FOR THE VANILLA ICE CREAM:
500ml (18fl oz) milk
150ml (5fl oz) whipping cream
1 vanilla pod, split lengthways and seeds
    scraped
30g (1oz) glucose powder
15g (½oz) skimmed milk powder
¾ tsp ice cream stabilizer
140g (5oz) caster sugar
pinch of sea salt
95g (3¼oz) egg yolks (about 5–6 yolks)

You can start this recipe way in advance as the ice cream will keep frozen for up to 2 months.

First, make the vanilla ice cream. In a medium or large saucepan, combine the milk, cream and vanilla pod and seeds, then bring to the boil. Meanwhile, mix together the glucose powder, milk powder, ice cream stabilizer, sugar and salt in a heatproof bowl, then whisk in the egg yolks. If the mix is too dry, add a ladle of the milk mixture to loosen the yolk mix. Mix well until there are no remaining dry ingredients and it is lump-free. When the milk has come to the boil, remove from the heat and pour one-third into the egg yolk mixture, whisking constantly. Return the pan of milk to a medium heat and add the yolk mixture. Cook the ice cream base, stirring constantly with a spatula, until it reaches 84°C (183°F), about 5–7 minutes. Pour the mixture through the sieve into a bowl set over ice. Cool completely or overnight in the refrigerator. Pour into an ice cream maker and churn, following the manufacturer's instructions.

To make the raspberry sorbet, mix the glucose powder, sugar and super neutrose together. Pour the measured water into a medium pan, then whisk in the dry ingredients and bring to the boil, stirring often. Remove from the heat and pour into the raspberry purée in a heatproof bowl. Whisk well. Cool completely or overnight in the refrigerator. Pour into an ice cream maker and churn, following the manufacturer's instructions.

If you were able to churn both the vanilla and the raspberry mixtures simultaneously, you can start layering now, to prepare for the ripple effect. Spread one-quarter of the freshly churned (and not yet frozen) vanilla ice cream in the bottom of the loaf tin and freeze for 20 minutes. Store the remaining vanilla ice cream and raspberry sorbet in the refrigerator during this time. Next, spread one-third of the freshly churned raspberry sorbet on top of the vanilla ice cream. Freeze for 20 minutes. Repeat this layering twice more. Top the final raspberry layer with the rest of the vanilla ice cream. Freeze until needed. (If you don't have 2 freezer bowls for your ice cream maker, make the vanilla ice cream, then spread one-quarter of it into the loaf tin. Freeze the loaf tin, the remaining ice cream and the (cleaned) ice cream bowl for a few hours, before churning the sorbet. As the sorbet is churning, remove the ice cream from the freezer to soften, and proceed as outlined above.)

Now make the chocolate fondants. In the stand mixer fitted with the whisk attachment, mix the egg yolks, whole eggs and sugar at medium speed until tripled in volume, about 6 minutes (you may want to increase the speed to high in the last 2 minutes).

Meanwhile, melt the chocolate and butter in a heatproof bowl placed over a saucepan of simmering water or in the microwave.

When the egg mixture is thick, pale and very fluffy, remove from the mixer. By hand, slowly stir in the warm melted chocolate. When all the chocolate is incorporated, gently fold in the flour. Transfer the chocolate mixture to a clean bowl and chill until firm, about 2 hours. **»**

30g (1oz) glucose powder

120g (4¼oz) caster sugar

¾ tsp super neutrose or sorbet stabilizer

250ml (9fl oz) water

500g (1lb 2oz) raspberry purée (*see* page
142)

FOR THE CHOCOLATE FONDANTS:

80g (2¾oz) egg yolk (about 4 yolks)

180g (6½oz) whole eggs (about 3 eggs, plus
1 egg yolk)

90g (3¼oz) caster sugar

180g (6½oz) dark chocolate (55% cocoa
solids), broken into pieces

180g (6½oz) unsalted butter

50g (1¾oz) plain flour

icing sugar, for dusting

berries of your choice, to decorate

Preheat the oven to 190°C (375°F), Gas Mark 5.

Transfer the fondant base to the (cleaned) stand mixer fitted with the paddle attachment. Paddle the mix just a couple of turns to soften the mixture but not rewhisk. Place the rings on the prepared baking tray, then line each ring with a strip of baking paper. Fill the piping bag with the softened fondant mixture and pipe equally into each ring (the rings should be about three-quarters full). Bake immediately or refrigerate until you are about ready for dessert (these will keep, refrigerated, for up to 3 days).

Bake for 17–20 minutes, until the edges are pale and set and the middle still wobbly.

While the fondants are baking, remove the ice cream from the freezer to soften.

Remove the fondants from the oven. Leave to stand for 2–3 minutes before removing the rings and unwrapping the paper strips. Dust liberally with icing sugar.

To serve, scoop the ripple ice cream on to each plate. Transfer the fondants to the plates, decorate with berries and serve immediately. During service, we plate our ripple ice cream onto a crumb base (*pictured* on page 233) to prevent it from sliding around the plate during service – an unnecessary precaution when serving at home.

Passion Fruit Posset with Rum Baba

It's a short trip from Paris to London, and an even shorter trip from King's Cross to Claridge's. Just to know we have easy access to such a food rich city as our French neighbour fills us with inspiration. Here we take the quintessentially British posset and pair it with the sturdy baba and a flamboyant rum and pineapple syrup. Delicious and diplomatic in equal parts.

SERVES 8

NOTES:

The posset can be made up to 2 days ahead. Keep covered with clingfilm in the refrigerator and assemble just before serving. Make sure you use the juice and pulp from fresh passion fruits, not commercial passion fruit juice or concentrate. We use a savarin mould instead of the traditional dariole shape for the baba because it is an accompaniment for the posset rather than a standalone dessert. If you need to prepare the Tropical Compote in advance, it's best to cut the fruit up and keep separately until you need them; this helps to retain their individual flavours and stop their natural fruit acids working against each other. Because the fruit is cut into a fine dice, this reduces its shelf life to 1 day.

YOU WILL NEED:

8 dessert glasses
stand mixer fitted with the dough hook
mini savarin silicone mould (with at least 8 indents)
disposable piping bag (no tip needed, just cut the bag)
fine-mesh sieve
wire rack
baking tray with sides

FOR THE PASSION FRUIT POSSET:

500ml (18fl oz) double cream
225g (8oz) caster sugar
200ml (7fl oz) strained fresh passion fruit juice (about 12–15 passion fruit)

FOR THE BABAS:

250g (9oz) strong white flour
25g (1oz) caster sugar
5g (⅛oz) sea salt
140g (5oz) whole eggs (about 3 eggs), beaten
100ml (3½fl oz) milk

10g (¼oz) fresh yeast, crumbled, or 4g (⅛oz) instant yeast
60g (2¼oz) unsalted butter, melted

FOR THE BABA SOAKING SYRUP:

500ml (18fl oz) water
250g (9oz) caster sugar
peel of 1 lemon in strips
peel of 1 orange in strips
50ml (2fl oz) pineapple juice
1 vanilla pod (it's okay here to use a leftover pod that's been scraped free of seeds)
100ml (3½fl oz) dark rum, plus 120ml (4fl oz), to serve

FOR THE TROPICAL COMPOTE:

1 mango, peeled and finely diced
1 papaya, peeled and finely diced
½ pineapple, peeled and finely diced
2 kiwi, peeled and finely diced
baby mint leaves, to serve

First, make the posset. Bring the cream to the boil in a medium saucepan. Reduce the heat to medium and whisk in the sugar. Return to the boil, then add the fruit juice. Boil for 1–2 minutes, whisking constantly. Divide the mixture between the dessert glasses. Refrigerate to set, about 3 hours. When cool, cover with clingfilm.

For the babas, combine all the ingredients except the butter in the stand mixer. Mix on medium speed until the dough looks smooth, glossy and elastic. This can take up to 10–15 minutes. Stop the mixer and remove the bowl. Pour the melted butter on top of the dough. Cover with clingfilm and leave to stand in a warm area until the dough has doubled in size, about 45 minutes.

Preheat the oven to 200°C (400°F), Gas Mark 6.

Once the dough has doubled in volume, return to the stand mixer and knead with the dough hook until smooth again. Pipe the dough into the 8 cavities of the savarin mould, allowing a small amount of room for them to rise. Bake for 5 minutes, then reduce the oven temperature to 180°C (350°F), Gas Mark 4, and bake for a further 10 minutes, or until deep golden and dry-looking. Remove and transfer to a wire rack to cool completely.

For the baba syrup, combine all the ingredients except the rum in a medium saucepan and bring to the boil. Once the syrup has boiled for a minute or so and the sugar is completely dissolved, remove from the heat and add the 100ml (3½fl oz) rum. Pass through the sieve to remove the peels and vanilla pod. Leave to cool until warm, or chill completely and rewarm as needed.

When ready to serve, make the compote by mixing the fruits together.

Soak the babas in the warm syrup, turning over a couple of times to ensure they are completely saturated. Be gentle: as the babas absorb the syrup they become more fragile. With a large spoon, transfer the babas to the wire rack with the baking tray underneath to allow the excess syrup to drip down.

To serve, carefully spoon some compote on top of a posset, completely covering the surface with a thin layer of fruit. Place 1 soaked baba in the middle, spoon over 1 tablespoon of the extra rum and garnish with baby mint leaves. Repeat with the remaining possets. As an added layer of interest and detail, we fill a tiny pipette with a little rum syrup and press it into the baba for the guest to squeeze over the top of their dessert.

Petits Fours & Mignardises

The perfect finish to a meal; the small bit of sugar with coffee at the end of a good meal; dark chocolates. Years ago, as with so many things, it was presentation over flavour, and quantity over quality; in our Ballroom we wanted a scene of a silver tray filled with lines of chequerboard biscuits, fondant-dipped cape gooseberries, pâtes de fruit, sugar-dipped grapes, shaped marzipans. . .I'm pleased to say that these are still possible but we've updated our offerings to be as enticing on the palate as they are on the eyes.

Caramel Truffles

MAKES 30

NOTE:
The ganache needs to be made 12 hours ahead of filling the truffle shells.

YOU WILL NEED:
stick blender
disposable piping bag (no tip needed, just cut the bag)
tray lined with baking paper
a partner to help you coat the truffles
pair of latex gloves
fine-mesh sieve placed over a bowl

FOR THE CARAMEL GANACHE HEART:
125g (4½oz) Valrhona Caramélia milk chocolate, broken into pieces
75ml (2½fl oz) whipping cream
pinch of sea salt
20g (¾oz) unsalted butter

FOR THE TRUFFLES:
30 dark or milk chocolate truffle shells
200g (7oz) dark or milk chocolate, broken into pieces
200g (7oz) cocoa powder

Make the ganache. Melt the chocolate in a medium heatproof bowl placed over a saucepan of simmering water, or simply in the microwave. In a small saucepan, over a medium heat, bring the cream to the boil, then remove from the heat. Pour one-third of the hot cream into the melted chocolate. Using a spatula, stir briskly to incorporate the cream. The chocolate might look grainy and split at this point – don't worry. Repeat twice more, adding another third of the cream at a time. Add the salt and butter, and combine using the stick blender placed directly on the bottom of the bowl. Do not move the blender back and forth or agitate the chocolate – you're trying to avoid whipping air into the ganache. (Depending on the size of your bowl, you might need to tip the bowl to one side and position the blender in the centre of the chocolate puddle.)

Using a spatula, clean the sides of the bowl, scraping any errant ganache back into the mix. Place a sheet of clingfilm directly on to the surface of the ganache. Leave to crystallize and set at room temperature for 12 hours.

Transfer the ganache to the piping bag. Fill the hollow truffle shells until just full. You'll notice that the ganache will settle into the shell and sink a little, releasing some air bubbles. Place on the prepared tray and freeze for 20 minutes or so while you prepare your dipping set-up for the truffles.

Melt the dark or milk chocolate in the microwave or in a heatproof bowl over a saucepan of simmering water. Pour the cocoa powder into a separate bowl.

It's now time to glove up! Working quickly to avoid melting the shells, the person with the gloves dips and rolls the stuffed truffle shells in the melted chocolate, making sure the hole in the shell is no longer visible, then drops them into the bowl of cocoa powder. The second person moves the bowl around to roll and coat the truffles in the powder. Transfer the powder-coated truffles to the sieve placed over a bowl.

When all the truffles have been rolled and dusted, gently tap on the side of the sieve to remove any excess cocoa powder.

Stored in an airtight container, these truffles will keep for 3 days at room temperature or 1 week in the refrigerator.

Palmier Sticks

MAKES 24–30

YOU WILL NEED:
tray lined with baking paper
pastry brush
baking sheet lined with baking paper

strong white flour, for dusting
300g (10½oz) cold Puff Pastry (*see* page 90)
1 egg, beaten, for the eggwash
demerara sugar, for sprinkling

On a lightly floured surface, roll out the puff pastry into a 36cm x 20cm (14 x 8 inch) rectangle, about 2.5mm (⅟₁₆ inch) thick. Trim the edges to create a neat rectangle. Cut the rectangle into 2 long strips 9cm (3½ inches) in width. Transfer to the prepared tray. Brush each strip gently with the eggwash, then lightly sprinkle the whole surface with sugar, covering them completely. Freeze for 2 hours.

Preheat the oven to 190°C (375°F), Gas Mark 5.

Cut each puff pastry strip into sticks about 2.5–3cm (1–1¼ inches) wide. You should have about 24–30 palmier sticks in total. Arrange on the prepared baking sheet (they can be placed quite close together).

Bake for 22–26 minutes, until deep golden brown.

These are best eaten on the same day but will keep in an airtight container at room temperature for 3 days.

Mandarin Pâte de Fruit

MAKES 55 PIECES

NOTE:
You can use any number of fruit juices to make different flavours of pâtes de fruit. This recipe includes apple juice, so any fruit you use will set with the pectin. However, if you're using a sweeter type of fruit, reduce the sugar content slightly. By the same token, very acidic fruit might require an increase in the amount of sugar.

YOU WILL NEED:
23 x 33cm (9 x 13 inch) baking tray, lined with baking paper
high-speed blender
instant-read digital thermometer

neutral spray oil, for greasing
12 mandarins, juiced
60ml (2¼fl oz) liquid glucose
320g (11¼oz) caster sugar
6g (¼oz) yellow pectin (or classic pectin) powder
4½ tsp apple juice
7.5g (¼oz) tartaric acid
granulated sugar, for dusting

Line the baking tray with baking paper, using a spray of oil on the tray to prevent the paper from curling up. Set aside. Put a side plate in the freezer.

Over a medium heat, heat the mandarin juice in a saucepan. When the temperature registers about 45°C (113°F), stir in the glucose and 290g (10¼oz) of the caster sugar. Bring to the boil.

Meanwhile, combine the pectin powder and remaining caster sugar. When the mandarin juice starts to boil, pour in the apple juice and add the pectin and sugar blend.

Cook, stirring constantly and checking the temperature at very regular intervals. When the temperature registers 105°C (221°F), about 15 minutes, remove the pan from the heat and stir in the tartaric acid, which adds a little zing to the final flavour and helps set the pâte mixture. Return to the heat and bring back to the boil for a moment.

Remove the side plate from the freezer and spoon a little dollop of the pâte de fruit mixture on to the plate. If it becomes very firm in a couple of seconds, the pâte is ready. If it doesn't perform conclusively, return the saucepan to the heat and cook until the thermometer registers 106°C (223°F) instead of 105°C (221°F). Repeat the test, increasing the cooking temperature by 1°C (2°F) as needed.

Pour the pâte into the prepared baking tray and leave to cool and set at room temperature, about 1 hour.

When the pâte de fruit is set, dust the top generously with granulated sugar, then gently turn out on to a chopping board, with the sugared side directly on the board. Remove and discard the paper. Dust the now-exposed underside with granulated sugar. Then, using a large knife, cut into desired shapes (we like 2.5cm/1 inch cubes). Gently roll the cubes in the excess granulated sugar to coat on all sides.

Store in a single layer in an airtight container. These will keep for up to 2 weeks.

Nougat

NOTES:

Be very careful when handling the hot sugar syrups. This recipe can be doubled, if you're making nougat as a gift.

YOU WILL NEED:
2 baking trays
clean tea towel
sugar thermometer
stand mixer fitted with the whisk attachment
sheet of baking paper, cut to 20 x 30cm
**   (8 x 12 inches)**
rolling pin

100g (3½oz) blanched almonds
100g (3½oz) shelled pistachio nuts
100g (3½oz) hazelnuts
413g (14½oz) caster sugar
115ml (4fl oz) liquid glucose
125ml (4fl oz) water
60g (2¼oz) egg whites (about 2 whites)
113g (4oz) honey
100g (3½oz) crystallized orange peel,
        chopped
50g (1¾oz) icing sugar, for dusting

Preheat the oven to 200°C (400°F), Gas Mark 6. Spread the almonds and pistachios on one baking tray, and the hazelnuts on the other. Toast the nuts until golden, about 8–10 minutes, then set aside in a warm place (you'll want them still warm when you add them to the meringue). To peel the hazelnuts, lay them on the tea towel, then rub them together in the towel to release the skins.

Combine 400g (14oz) of the caster sugar, the glucose and measured water in a medium saucepan. Boil over a high heat until the thermometer registers 156°C (313°F), about 10–15 minutes.

Meanwhile, using the stand mixer, whisk the egg whites with the remaining sugar on medium speed until soft peaks form, about 2–3 minutes. Stop whisking.

In a small saucepan over a high heat, bring the honey to the boil, then reduce the heat to medium-low. Continue cooking until it reaches 135°C (275°F), about 10 minutes.

Resume whisking the egg whites on low-medium speed and slowly pour the hot honey into the egg whites, in the space between the whisk attachment and the wall of the bowl. Avoid pouring it on the whisk, to prevent lumps.

When the sugar and glucose syrup mixture reaches 156°C (313°F), add it to the meringue in the same way as the honey, slowly pouring it down the inside of the bowl, with the machine running at low-medium speed. Increase the speed to medium-high and continue whisking the meringue until the exterior of the bowl feels cooler to the touch but not cold.

Check that the reserved nuts are still warm to the touch – if not, flash them in the oven for a minute or so.

Stop the mixer, and, using a spatula, stir in the toasted nuts and crystallized orange peel until evenly distributed.

Dust the sheet of baking paper with some of the icing sugar, and, using a spatula or a dough scraper, spread the meringue on to the paper into a rectangle shape. Dust the top heavily with icing sugar and pass over with a rolling pin to achieve a flat uniform surface and an even thickness of 2cm (¾ inch) or so throughout. Dust with more icing sugar as needed so the rolling pin doesn't stick. Leave to cool at room temperature.

When cool, trim the nougat edges to make a nice rectangle, then, using a long serrated knife, cut the rectangle into strips 2cm (¾ inch) in width, then each strip into 2cm (¾ inch) cubes. Make sure you clean and dry the knife between each cut, if the nougat is sticking to it.

This nougat will keep for several weeks – at least 4 in our kitchen – wrapped tightly in clingfilm and stored in a cool and dry place.

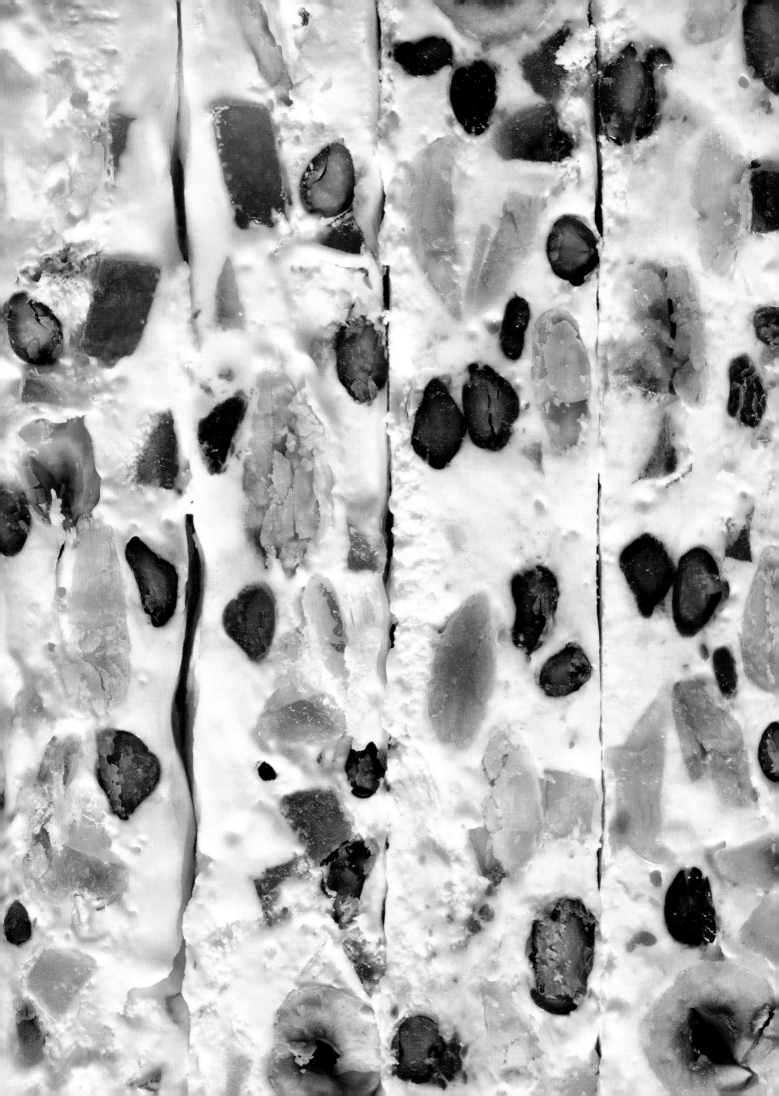

Claridge's Christmas Pudding

Are we cooking a Christmas pudding or are we cooking a dream? The secret to this century-old recipe has been kept in the vault until now. Each autumn, our pastry team prepares our Christmas pudding mix for the festive season. Originally, this recipe was heavy on molasses, Cognac and dark rum, typical of the fruit cakes of yore. Recently, the recipe has been lightened and subtly updated: we now use lighter sugars, fruit-based liqueurs and fresh brioche crumbs, giving the pudding a more nuanced, sophisticated, but still deeply rich flavour. As a finishing ritual, the whole pastry team gather around a giant basin to stir the mix by hand and make wishes of good fortune and goodwill to all. Once cooked, each Claridge's crest-engraved china bowl is wrapped in white muslin cloth, packaged in our signature eau-de-nil box and wrapped in a thick satin ribbon.

MAKES 2 LARGE PUDDINGS: ONE FOR YOU AND ONE TO GIVE TO A FRIEND. EACH PUDDING SERVES 4–6

NOTES:
The initial marinated fruit should be made 1 week ahead, before the recipe can be completed. Following the age-old tradition, you might want to slip a silver sixpence in the pudding before packing the basin – for wealth and good luck in the year to come. The pudding will keep for at least a year in a cool, dark place.

YOU WILL NEED:
2 litre (3½ pint) jar or container with a lid, for the marinated fruit
food processor
2 x 1 litre (1¾ pint) pudding basins (we use Mason Cash's S30)
kitchen scissors
8 x 30cm (12 inch) squares of baking paper
4 x 30cm (12 inch) squares of foil
4 x 1m (3ft) lengths of kitchen string
2 steamers with lids, large enough to accommodate each pudding bowl
palette knife

FOR THE MARINATED FRUIT:
227g (8oz) currants
227g (8oz) sultanas
227g (8oz) golden raisins

Right: Between them, Roman Proboziak (*left*) and Michael Lynch (*right*) have been welcoming guests – and Christmas – to Claridge's for more than 80 years.

In a large bowl, mix together all the marinated fruit ingredients. Transfer to the jar or container and seal, then leave to mature for 1 week in a dry, dark place.

A week later, transfer the marinated fruit to a large bowl.

In the food processor, pulse the fresh brioche until reduced to crumbs. Next, mix those crumbs, in a medium bowl, with the flour and ground almonds.

In a separate bowl, stir the golden syrup, eggs, milk and suet until loosely combined.

In a fourth bowl, combine the prunes, carrot and apple.

Proceeding in batches, stir the crumb and flour mixture into the matured dried fruit, alternating with the milk and eggs mixture. Stir well. Finally, stir in the prunes, apple and carrot.

Lightly grease the pudding basins, then transfer the mixture to the basins, packing the fruit in tightly. Next, cover each pudding with 2 squares of baking paper, followed by 1 square of foil. Wrap 1 length of string tightly around (and under) the rim of each pudding basin to ensure the paper and foil cover is taut across the top, making a double knot to secure the string. Drape the additional length of string across the top, tying it to the other side to fashion a handle. Cut away any excess paper and tuck the foil under itself.

Place each pudding in a steamer set over a saucepan filled with simmering water and steam, covered, for 6 hours (if you only have one steamer or no steamer at all, you can also place the pudding in a large saucepan filled with water to halfway up the basin). Be sure to keep an eye on the water level – you'll probably need to refill at the 3–4-hour mark (using boiling water from the kettle).

When the puddings have finished steaming, remove from the saucepans and leave to cool completely at room temperature. When cool, remove the baking paper, foil and string and replace with the remaining squares of paper and foil, and tie with a fresh piece of string as above. Store in a cool, dry place until ready to eat.

When you are ready to serve your Christmas Pudding, place in a steamer, or pan of simmering water. Steam or boil for at least 2¼ hours. Check the internal temperature of the pudding is piping hot before serving.

Slide a palette knife all around the edges of the pudding and turn it out on to a warmed plate.

At the hotel, puddings are flamed with brandy at the table and served with brandy sauce. Brandy butter is optional and available on request. But why not serve yours with both? »

227g (8oz) raisins
114g (4oz) dried cranberries
114g (4oz) dried sour cherries
114g (4oz) mixed peel
zest of 2 oranges
zest of 3 lemons
170g (6oz) light brown sugar
1 tsp mixed spice
2 tsp ground cinnamon
pinch each of ground cloves, ground nutmeg
	and salt
120ml (4fl oz) India Pale Ale
120ml (4fl oz) Grand Marnier

TO COMPLETE THE PUDDING:
170g (6oz) fresh brioche, torn into medium
	pieces
114g (4oz) plain flour
35g (1¼oz) ground almonds
70ml (2½fl oz) golden syrup
2 eggs, beaten
4 tbsp milk
185g (6½oz) shredded vegetable suet
90g (3¼oz) prunes, pitted and minced
85g (3oz) carrot, peeled and grated
114g (4oz) apple, peeled and grated
unsalted butter, for greasing

FOR THE BRANDY BUTTER
(MAKES 8 GENEROUS DOLLOPS,
APPROXIMATELY 200G/7OZ)

YOU WILL NEED:
stand mixer fitted with the paddle
	attachment

125g (4½oz) unsalted butter, softened
125g (4½oz) icing sugar
50ml (2fl oz) good-quality brandy

FOR THE BRANDY SAUCE
(MAKES ENOUGH FOR 6–8 SERVINGS,
APPROXIMATELY 600ML/1 PINT):

YOU WILL NEED:
instant-read digital thermometer
stick blender

80g (2¾oz) caster sugar
5g (⅛oz) cornflour
60g (2¼oz) egg yolks (about 2–3 yolks)
500ml (18fl oz) milk
25g (1oz) unsalted butter, softened
50ml (2fl oz) brandy (or more if you like)

Brandy Butter

Using the stand mixer, cream the butter and icing sugar until very pale, light and fluffy, about 5 minutes.

Stop the machine and, using a spatula, scrape down the sides and the bottom of the bowl. Add the brandy and mix slowly until it is fully incorporated.

Transfer the brandy butter to a serving dish. Keep at room temperature until serving, if using the same day. Alternatively, the butter will keep in the refrigerator for up to 2 weeks, but allow it to come to room temperature and rewhip until nice and fluffy before serving.

Brandy Sauce

In a small bowl whisk together the caster sugar, cornflour and egg yolks. Set aside.

In a medium saucepan bring the milk to the boil. Pour one-quarter of the hot milk over the egg yolk mix, whisking to combine.

Return the milk pan to a medium heat and pour in the now-warmed egg yolk mix. Cook the brandy sauce, stirring gently and constantly with a spatula, until it reaches 82°C (179°F).

Remove the sauce from the heat and pour into a clean bowl. Add the butter to the sauce and, using the stick blender, blitz for a minute or so to ensure the sauce is silky smooth and the butter is completely emulsified.

Stir in the brandy. Serve immediately or within the hour.

We never refrigerate brandy sauce; we always make it fresh as needed. However, if you really must make yours in advance, chill it thoroughly (it will keep refrigerated for up to 2 days) and then, prior to serving, reheat it very gently in a saucepan over a low heat, stirring constantly.

Mince Pies

If you visit us between November and January, you will be greeted with a little glass cloche of mince pies and clementines upon arrival. And yes, now that we've put this in print, we realize we've cemented expectations. During the festive season, it will start to feel like we've been making mince pies forever, especially in the pastry department where in the past there could be a mise en place request for 5,000 pies to be made overnight. We typically make an average of 1,000 a week during this season.

MAKES 24

NOTES: The mincemeat needs at least a week to mature, so start this well ahead of time. This recipe will yield enough mincemeat for 36 pies in total and a large batch of Eccles Cakes (*see* page 248). It can also easily be doubled but please don't be tempted to reduce the recipe, as mincemeat keeps for a very long time in the refrigerator and mince pies are quick to disappear.

YOU WILL NEED:
blender
1 litre (1¾ pint) glass jar or airtight container
rolling pin
7cm (2¾ inch) plain pastry cutter
2 x 12-hole mince pie baking trays (with 6cm x 2cm/2½ x ¾ inch shallow cups)
6cm (2½ inch) plain, or star-shaped, pastry cutter
small tray, lined with baking paper, and a few sheets cut to the size of the tray
pastry brush
wire rack

FOR THE MINCEMEAT:
1 orange
2 Granny Smith apples
25g (1oz) raisins
250g (9oz) currants
75g (2¾oz) mixed peel
25ml (1fl oz) brandy
25ml (1fl oz) rum
15ml (½fl oz) Grand Marnier
300g (10½oz) light brown sugar
50g (1¾oz) shredded suet (or vegetable suet if you're making vegetarian mincemeat)
1 tsp ground nutmeg
1 tsp mixed spice
1 tsp ground ginger
1 tsp ground cloves
2 tsp ground cinnamon
50g (1¾oz) unsalted butter, cut into small cubes and frozen

FOR THE PASTRY:
350g (12oz) plain flour, plus extra for dusting
220g (8oz) cold unsalted butter, cut into 1cm (½ inch) pieces
1 tsp salt
120g (4oz) ice-cold water
½ tsp white wine vinegar
1 egg yolk, mixed with a splash of cream, for the eggwash
caster sugar, for dusting

First, make the mincemeat: start by zesting and juicing the orange and reserve both juice and zest. Cut what's left of the orange into small pieces, then place in a small saucepan and fill with enough water to cover. Bring to the boil, then simmer over a low heat until completely soft, about 1 hour, checking at regular intervals and adding more water as needed to keep covered.

Meanwhile, in a large bowl, grate the apples. Add all of the remaining ingredients, except for the butter, and mix well.

When the orange is soft, drain it well, then combine it with the reserved juice and zest in the blender and purée until smooth. Stir the orange purée into the mincemeat mixture. Transfer to the jar or airtight container and refrigerate for at least 1 week.

To make the pastry, place the flour, butter and salt in a mixing bowl. Using your fingertips, rub the butter into the flour until it resembles pea-sized pieces. Add the measured water and vinegar and mix gently until the dough starts to come together. (You can also make the dough in a food processor by pulsing the flour, salt and butter together 5 or 6 times, then adding the water and vinegar and pulsing 3 or 4 more times.)

Turn the dough out on to your work surface. Gather it up and gently knead 2 or 3 times to create a semi-smooth dough with some

small lumps of butter still visible. Pat the dough into a disc shape, wrap tightly in clingfilm and refrigerate for 45 minutes, or until firm. (The dough will keep for a couple of days in the refrigerator.)

To assemble the mince pies, on a lightly floured surface roll out the dough into a large circle about 1–2mm (⅟₁₆ inch) thick. Cut out a 7cm (2¾ inch) round in the edge of the dough and double-check that it fits nicely into a cup in your mince pie tray before you cut out a further 23 circles – change the size of your pastry cutter as needed. Lay the rounds directly into your mince pie trays. Next, cut out 24 smaller rounds, or stars, for the pie lids and stack those neatly on the prepared tray, separating them with the layers of baking paper as needed. You may need to gather up the scraps of dough and roll them into a ball, kneading it a few times until smooth, then roll it out to obtain your last few pie lids. Refrigerate all the pastry dough for 15–20 minutes to chill.

Preheat the oven to 200°C (400°F), Gas Mark 6. In a medium bowl, mix the mincemeat with the frozen butter cubes. Remove your mince pie trays from the refrigerator and spoon no more than 1 tablespoon of the mincemeat mixture into each case. Do not be tempted to add just a little more mincemeat – if you do, the filling will expand and burst through the seams! Place the smaller rounds on top of each pie and gently press to create a seal. Brush with the eggwash.

Bake the pies for 20 minutes, or until the pastry is golden. As soon as the pies come out of the oven, dust heavily with caster sugar. Transfer to a wire rack to cool.

These can be stored in an airtight container for up to 1 week, but are best served warm.

Cheddar & Pear Eccles Cakes

We serve a smaller version of these Cheddar Eccles cakes as a savoury for festive afternoon tea. During this phenomenally busy period, we produce over 10,000 of these bites in just 6 weeks (that's approximately 30kg/66lb of Cheddar and 50kg/110lb of mincemeat just for this item). Because the production is so large and time-consuming, this is one of the few jobs, like Christmas puddings, that will involve the whole pastry team. So, every second day of the festive season, at the end of the day, we set up a production line and everyone has a role, from filling to wrapping, to dipping in the topping to packing them away in our storage baskets. We have really mastered this task and can produce 750 cakes in under an hour. Don't worry: you only have to make 16 and they are sturdier in size than the ones we produce.

MAKES 16

NOTE:
To make Cheddar Eccles does require a bit of forward thinking: you'll need matured mincemeat and puff pastry. But these are well worth the effort for the festive season.

YOU WILL NEED:
small jar
rolling pin
baking tray, lined with baking paper
pastry brush

plain flour, for dusting
400g (14oz) cold Puff Pastry (*see* page 90)
1 egg, beaten, for the eggwash

FOR THE SPICY TOPPING:
50g (1¾oz) pumpkin seeds
15g (½oz) flaxseeds
15g (½oz) crushed Maldon sea salt flakes
15g (½oz) poppy seeds
7g (¼oz) black pepper, very coarsely ground
35g (1¼oz) demerara sugar
1 tsp cayenne pepper

FOR THE ECCLES FILLING:
400g (14oz) Mincemeat (*see* page 246)
60g (2¼oz) walnuts, toasted and chopped
250g (9oz) pears, peeled and cut into small dice
250g (9oz) good-quality Cheddar cheese, cut into small dice
250g (9oz) ground almonds, very finely ground in a food processor
90g (3¼oz) pickled walnuts, drained and crushed (skins discarded)

To make the spicy topping, combine all the ingredients in a small bowl and transfer to a small jar for later use.

In a large bowl, combine all the ingredients for the filling. Using a spatula or wooden spoon, mix until evenly combined and set aside.

On a lightly floured surface, roll out the puff pastry into a large 40cm (16 inch) square, about 2mm (¹⁄₁₆ inch) thick. Using a sharp knife or a pizza wheel, cut the dough into 16 x 10cm (4 inch) squares.

Working with one square of dough at a time, spoon about 70g (2½oz) of the filling into the middle. Gather the corners of the dough into the centre, pinching them together tightly to seal (make sure the filling is in fact completely sealed in) and twisting off any excess pastry. Lay this parcel seam-side down on the prepared baking tray. Repeat with the remaining squares.

Pour the spicy topping into a shallow bowl.

Brush the top of the parcels lightly with the eggwash, then dip each top into the topping, returning the cakes to the baking tray. Refrigerate until the dough is cold again, about 20 minutes. (You can also freeze them now for later use – just defrost in the refrigerator before baking.)

Preheat the oven to 200°C (400°F), Gas Mark 6.

Using a sharp paring knife, cut 3 x 1cm (½ inch) slits in the top of each Eccles cake and brush lightly with eggwash.

Bake for 25–30 minutes, until a deep golden brown. Leave to cool slightly before serving.

These are best served warm and on the day they were made.

Christmas
at Claridge's

Our favourite time of year, when Claridge's becomes just that bit more magical...

Christmas, for most of us, is a special time spent with family and friends. At Claridge's, it is a time of tradition and celebration when many of our guests and their families choose to come and stay with us. Our preparations start months earlier with passionate discussions and careful thought on such critical subjects as: who will design our tree; what will be the theme of our decorations and, most importantly, what will we put in our Christmas stockings?

While we honour the time-old and treasured traditions of Christmas, we are always determined to add some extra layers of Claridge's magic, whether it be the introduction of Christmas Pudding choc ices or design-your-own gingerbread houses.

Over generations, we have been truly privileged that Claridge's has become the beacon of celebration in London for so many; from an extravagant Christmas party in our Ballroom to toasting the season with close friends and family in the Fumoir.

Deep in the kitchen it's traditionally a time to prepare rich, luxurious and typically festive ingredients: oysters; smoked salmon; chestnuts; goose; an extraordinary amount of Mince Pies (*see* page 246) and Cheddar Eccles cakes (*see* page 248).

As Christmas Eve approaches, the pace quickens and the excitement mounts – guests arrive laden with presents, and children's whoops of delight fill the Lobby as they get their first glimpse of The Claridge's Christmas Tree. At bedtime, guests leave carrots for the reindeers, milk and ginger cookies for Father Christmas and the final touch is a stocking on each door handle ready for the Christmas elves.

Dawn breaks on Christmas morning and the kitchen brigade are already in full force stuffing turkeys, peeling chestnuts and turning potatoes (*see* page 211); the most important meal of the year is about to be served to more than 500 of our very special guests.

It's at this point that we remember to acknowledge the team who are with us during this time of year. Once the last Christmas Pudding (*see* page 242) has been lit, we take a moment to raise a glass to them, thank them for their contribution and, even more importantly, thank their families for sparing them on this special day.

TREES OF
CHRISTMAS PAST

The Claridge's Christmas Tree has become a legendary landmark in the capital and its annual unveiling marks for many the arrival of the festive season in London. The combination of Christmas afternoon teas, open fires and an angelic children's choir makes Claridge's a magical festive destination.

Since 2009, Claridge's has invited a favourite notable guest to design The Claridge's Christmas Tree. In the past we have been honoured to work with some of the most distinguished names in fashion and design (clockwise from top left, opposite): Domenico Dolce and Stefano Gabbana, 2013; Christopher Bailey for Burberry, 2015; Sir Jony Ive and Marc Newson, 2016; John Galliano for Dior, 2009.

Index

page numbers in italic type refer to photographs and captions

In the pastry kitchen, for the sake of efficiency and time, we weigh all of our ingredients, wet or dry, on a digital scale. A scale will also always yield a more precise measurement than any measuring jug. We strongly recommend that you use a digital scale to weigh all of your ingredients. If doing so, for liquid measures that are given in ml (fl oz), keep the quantity the same but weigh instead in g (oz).

All fl oz measures are imperial not US.

Standard level spoon measurements are used in all recipes:
1 tablespoon = one 15ml spoon
1 teaspoon = one 5ml spoon

Imperial and metric measurements have been given in all recipes. Use one set of measurements and not a mixture of both.

Eggs should be medium (US large) unless otherwise stated. The Department of Health advises that eggs should not be consumed raw. This book contains dishes made with raw or lightly cooked eggs. It is prudent for more vulnerable people such as pregnant and nursing mothers, invalids, the elderly, babies and young children to avoid uncooked or lightly cooked dishes made with eggs. Once prepared, these dishes should be kept refrigerated and used promptly.

Milk should be full fat (whole) unless otherwise stated.

Fresh herbs should be used unless otherwise stated.

Unwaxed citrus fruits should be used for any recipe that calls for zest or peel.

Ovens should be preheated to the specific temperature – if using a fan-assisted (convection) oven, follow manufacturer's instructions for adjusting the time and the temperature.

This book includes dishes made with nuts and nut derivatives. It is advisable for customers with known allergic reactions to nuts and nut derivatives and those who may be potentially vulnerable to these allergies, such as pregnant and nursing mothers, invalids, the elderly, babies and children, to avoid dishes made with nuts and nut oils. It is also prudent to check the labels of pre-prepared ingredients for the possible inclusion of nut derivatives.

Acknowledgements

Meredith Erickson would like to thank:
First and foremost, to Martyn Nail. Four years later, here we are. Thank you for your generosity of time and spirit. These projects take an immense amount of focus and you always delivered and made it happen; a major feat considering the kitchen you run daily. As I've said from the start: there is nothing more badass than running a kitchen week after week for 30 years+. I think it's important to document that, and I'm so proud of how we did it. Of all the things to come from this, your friendship, Martyn, is the most important. Thank you for sharing this book with me.

To Paula Fitzherbert, thank you for entrusting us with such a legendary brand. Thank you for your support as a mentor of all things Claridge's. You're a legend in London and beyond, and I hope you know that. To Orla Hickey for being such a supportive force though thick or thin.

To Paul Jackson for allowing us to continue a real labour of love. You were judicious and thoughtful. Thank you for allowing all doors of the hotel to be open. Thank you to Paddy McKillen for allowing us the opportunity in the first place, and for being supportive of this book since day one.

A very, very big thank you to John Carey for the stunning photography. There is a very large new contingency of people who are falling in love with Claridge's, and that's because of you.

A giant thank you to Kendra McKnight, our official recipe tester. You 'my friend' not only make recipes possible, you make them a pleasure. Your work here was tremendous. So, thank you.

To my Claridge's kitchen co-patriots, Kimberly Lin and Adam Peirson: you two didn't need to work alongside me as much as you did. You are both complete professionals and this couldn't have happened without you. I'm in awe of your work ethic. Here's to dining together in the future!

Thank you to Ioannis Papaostolou for keeping Chef in line, grammatically correct and caffeinated! Thank you to Thomas Roger for the French humour and occasional glass to keep us sane. Thank you to Boris Messmer for the insight into all things Claridge's and for taking such great care of me. Thank you to Oli and Denis in the bar, for the recipes and libations. And thank you to the entire Foyer restaurant staff for keeping me forever enraptured with this dining room.

Now onto the business of publishing this book...

Thank you to Stephanie Jackson for being a 'yes' woman. The loose leash you gave us allowed for this book to happen as it did. Thank you for believing. Thank you to Polly Poulter for a steady hand and great patience. You made an almost impossible deadline, well, possible.

Thank you to our copy editor Jo Murray: I never met you but thank God you exist!

Thank you to Jonathan Christie for taking on the challenge of designing a book for Claridge's. Not easy, and you excelled.

Thank you to Ellen Bashford for your PR magic. And to Kim Witherspoon and Felicity Rubinstein for their overall shepherding (and agent-ing) in making this project happen.

Thank you to my family: in particular Mom, Dad and Paul. It's a daughter's dream to call her mother to say she's writing Claridge's book. So this one is for you, mom.

Martyn Nail would like to thank:
As I write this, I'm thinking of the hard work, dedication, commitment, loyalty and endless friendships of all the people I've had the honour of working with these past 35 years...

Me writing these acknowledgements would most definitely not have happened without Meredith Erickson, the co-author of this book, but first a guest in our Foyer...that was where this story began, with Meredith asking for the chicken pie recipe – well, actually, a copy of the Claridge's cookbook, which of course didn't exist. Meredith, you are now a great personal friend who I have the upmost respect and admiration for, your knowledge and attention to detail are an inspiration, and you are definitely one to watch.

Kendra McKnight – recipe queen, or is that wizard? John Carey for those amazing photos and endless hours of work. The Octopus team: Stephanie, Polly, Jonathan, Ellen and Felicity for all your help and expertise in bringing this idea to fruition.

Our suppliers – without whom our day would be finished before it got started – who work tirelessly to bring us the very best every day, come rain or shine, and especially when we need 3 more, 5 less, bigger, smaller...We rely on you to look after our producers, using both their and your knowledge and expertise to deliver quality consistently to our back door, all while ensuring the product is raised sustainably for the wellbeing of us all. They are: Henrietta Lovell from Rare Tea; Gordon, Chris and Alex Hogg at Finclass; Darren and Dominic Sadd, of Sadd Butchers in Shrewsbury; Michael Kukan, Peter Tonka and Darren Beany of Hepburns; Ray Steadman of Chamberlain & Thelwell; Dai Francis at Severn & Wye Smoked Salmon; Ben and Nick Assirati of Portland Shellfish; Charlie and James Mash of Mash Purveyors; Angelo Ferreira, Tania Gomes, Silvia Silva and Tony Loi from Golden Fruit; Laura King and her team in King's Fine Foods, for everything; Jonty and Jason Hirst of Evogro; Yun Hider of Mountain Food, for your endless knowledge and help; Patrik and Maria, the Buttervikings – Noma's loss, our gain, due to you moving to the UK and bringing us your lovely butter; Andrew Henderson of Nemi Dairy; Judith, Nick and Eli Gifford at Tea Together; Ruby Bawa at Foodspeed; Classic Fine Foods and last, but not least, Ritter Courivaud for their support with specialist kitchen and pastry products; Ioannis Papapostolou who takes care of ordering as well as taking care of the Sous Chefs and I, thank heavens you're a fast and good tipper.

To the current army of soldiers, Adam Peirson for his endless energy and professional dedication with the kitchen team, Kimberly Lin – our wonderful pastry chef – and her talented team for looking after our guests without hesitation, and, not to forget, every department in the hotel that weaves and upholds this tight net of standards and supports the work of each and every one of us daily: you deliver our vision of respect and quality endlessly.

Russell Platt and the F&B team, Paula Fitzherbert and Orla Hickey for your tireless support, the Communications team and, of course, Paul Jackson, Claridge's General Manager.

Paddy McKillen, our owner, who has supported this project.

All the people I've met along the way who have helped me, told me off(!), taught and inspired me. John Williams, Marjan Lesnik, René Redzepi, Matt Orlando and their amazing team, Jude Rozario, Ewan Simpson, Andrew Jones, Curt Reeve, Nick Patterson, Ross Sneddon, and to all the wonderful people I've crossed paths with, both in and out of Claridge's.

The Royal Academy of Culinary Arts, for their continuous support with apprentices and Chefs adopt-a-school.

To the ones we've loved and lost, for the everlasting qualities you've given us and the legacy you leave: Anne McGrath, Jack and Norma Melchor, dear Martin Mash and John King.

A very special thanks to my family: my Mum, Dad, Peter, Louise, Oliver and Grace.

And finally, auntie Sue and uncle Alun. Who assist us in many very helpful ways.

Glossary

UK	US
Baking beans	Pie weights
Baking paper	Parchment paper
Beef rump	Sirloin steak
beef tournedo	Tenderloin steak, filet mignon
Beetroot	Beet
Bicarbonate of soda	Baking soda
Biscuits	Cookies
Broad bean	Fava bean
Caster sugar	Superfine sugar
Cavalo nero	Black or Tuscan kale
Cèpes mushrooms	Porcini mushrooms
Cider vinegar	Apple cider vinegar
Clingfilm	Plastic wrap
Clotted cream	Use crème fraîche
Cornflour	Cornstarch
Courgette	Zucchini
Damson	Can use Mirabelle plums or regular plums (the latter are sweeter)
Dark chocolate	Semisweet chocolate; if 62 percent cocoa or more, use bittersweet chocolate
Desiccated coconut	Unsweetened dried coconut
Dessertspoon	A spoon for eating that holds about 2 teaspoons
Double cream	Heavy cream
Dover sole	Sole; can use flounder
Elevenses	Midmorning snack
Finger	Thin slice or strip
Flaked nut	Slivered or sliced nut such as slivered almonds
Glacé cherry	Candied cherry
Golden syrup	Substitute with light corn syrup
Greaseproof paper	Wax paper
Grill	Broil or broiler
Ground almonds	Almond meal
Icing sugar	Confectioners' sugar; powdered sugar
Jelly	Gelatin, as in the wobbly dessert, but sometimes the spreadable jelly
Jersey Royal potato	Use new potato
Jug	Pitcher; liquid measuring cup
Kitchen paper	Paper towels
Langoustine	Dublin Bay prawn or Norway lobster
Leaf gelatine	Gelatin sheet
Maris Piper potato	Use Yukon Gold potato
Minced	Ground when referring to meat
Mixed peel	Candied peel
Mixed spice	Blend of spices similar to allspice
Muscovado sugar	Can use regular light or dark brown sugar
Muslin cloth	Cheesecloth
Natural yogurt	Plain yogurt
Palette knife	Flexible spatula
Pastry case	Pastry shell or crust
Piping bag	Pastry bag
Plain flour	All-purpose flour
Prawn	Shrimp
Pudding basin	A deep, round heatproof bowl with a rim that kitchen twine can be tied around for securing cheesecloth to steam a pudding
Rapeseed oil	Canola oil
Rocket	Arugula
Semi-skimmed milk	Low-fat milk
Skewer	Use a toothpick
Sieve	Strainer; sifter
Sirloin beef	Tenderloin steak
Sponge finger	Ladyfinger
Spring onion	Scallion
Spring roll pastry sheet	Spring roll wrapper or egg roll wrapper
Streaky bacon rasher	Use regular bacon slice/strip
Stick blender	Immersion blender
Strong flour	Bread flour
Sultanas	Golden raisins
Swede	Rutabaga
Sweet shortcrust pastry	Flaky pastry
Swiss roll	Jellyroll
Tea towel	Dish towel
Tomato purée	Tomato paste
Top and trim	Trim (both ends)
Treacle	Use molasses
Vanilla pod	Vanilla bean
Vegetable suet	Can use vegetable shortening; to use, freeze for 30 minutes, grate, then freeze again for 10–15 minutes before using

Dedication

**To the entire Claridge's kitchen team past
and present: thank you for everything you do.
You are unsung heroes and without you this
book wouldn't be possible.**

An Hachette UK Company
www.hachette.co.uk

First published in Great Britain in 2017 by Mitchell Beazley,
a division of Octopus Publishing Group Ltd
Carmelite House, 50 Victoria Embankment
London EC4Y 0DZ
www.octopusbooks.co.uk

Design and Layout Copyright © Octopus Publishing Ltd 2017
Text and Illustrations Copyright © Claridge's and Meredith Erickson 2017

Distributed in the US by Hachette Book Group
1290 Avenue of the Americas , 4th and 5th Floors
New York, NY 10104

Distributed in Canada by Canadian Manda Group
664 Annette St., Toronto, Ontario,
Canada M6S 2C8

ISBN 978-1-78472-329-3

A CIP catalogue record for this book is available from the British Library.

Printed and bound in China

10 9 8 7 6 5 4

Publishing Director: Stephanie Jackson
Creative Director: Jonathan Christie
Editor: Pollyanna Poulter
Copy Editor: Jo Murray
Senior Production Manager: Peter Hunt
Production Controller: Sarah Kulasek-Boyd
Photographer: John Carey
Illustrator: Clym Evernden